A Global History of War

A Global History of War

From Assyria to the Twenty-First Century

Gérard Chaliand

*Translated by Michèle Mangin-Woods
and David Woods*

Foreword by R. Bin Wong

UNIVERSITY OF CALIFORNIA PRESS

University of California Press, one of the most
distinguished university presses in the United States,
enriches lives around the world by advancing scholarship
in the humanities, social sciences, and natural sciences. Its
activities are supported by the UC Press Foundation and
by philanthropic contributions from individuals and
institutions. For more information, visit www.ucpress.edu.

University of California Press
Oakland, California

Library of Congress Cataloging-in-Publication Data

Chaliand, Gérard, 1934–
    [Guerres et civilisations. English]
    A global history of war: From Assyria to the
twenty-first century / Gerard Chaliand ; translated by
Michele Mangin-Woods and David Woods ; foreword by
R. Bin Wong.
        pages   cm.
    Includes bibliographical references and index.
    ISBN 978-0-520-28360-2 (cloth : alk. paper)—
    ISBN 978-0-520-28361-9 (pbk. : alk. paper)—
    ISBN 978-0-520-95943-9 (e-book)
    1. Strategy—History.   2. War—History.   3. War and
civilization.   I. Mangin-Woods, Michele, 1942–
translator.   II. Woods, David, 1947– translator.   III. Title.
    U162.C424513   2014
    355.0209—dc23   2014010257

Manufactured in the United States of America

23 22 21 20 19 18 17 16 15 14
10 9 8 7 6 5 4 3 2 1

In keeping with a commitment to support
environmentally responsible and sustainable printing
practices, UC Press has printed this book on Natures
Natural, a fiber that contains 30% post-consumer waste
and meets the minimum requirements of ANSI/NISO
Z39.48–1992 (R 1997) (*Permanence of Paper*).

Contents

Maps

Foreword

R. BIN WONG

Military history has long been a popular subject for general readers, at least the male gender among us. Most everyone regrettably recognizes that war has shaped the fates of peoples and places in the dimly distant past and is violently visible in our global present. For all its manifest importance, scholars have, however, produced very little research intended to anchor our appreciation of contemporary military issues by considering the causes and consequences of war historically. Not surprisingly, much of what has been written about war historically concerns European examples, whether ancient, medieval, or modern, including wars both among Europeans and those they exported to others. But war has been a recurring feature of histories both within and beyond the boundaries of Europe. The turn toward world history has affected social studies teaching at all levels, inspired new training fields within the discipline of history, and guided approaches to new subjects of research. We might have expected that these developments would also have included among these achievements greater attention to the roles of war in human history. In fact, little has been done. World history has been a capacious framework for examining different clusters of connections and comparisons of cultural, economic, political, and social activities across long distances, but the topic of war and civilization fails to fit comfortably into the taxonomy of subjects that defines world or global history.

Moving away from a European focus on war and civilization demands a willingness and ability to consider different places as one moves through time, which is foreign to the usual aspiration of world history studies for consistent spatial coverage. What principles of historical practice can guide such an intellectual journey, and why would such a journey be worth making? What makes such an exploration feasible is the identification of some basic elements to the geostrategies of war: the demands placed upon leaders bent upon pursuing such activities and the impacts of wars upon people. If one further decides to investigate locations according to the importance of a place's war-making more generally, a scholar could lead us through a variety of subjects rarely juxtaposed in a single study. The payoff from these historical travels would include a far sharper understanding of how and why contemporary conditions of war and their outcomes include dilemmas that individual states and their competitors have faced since the early days of warfare, as well as present-day problems and possibilities unimaginable in the past.

Even if such an expedition across time and space to chart war-making and its human consequences can be traced on an intellectual map, is there an adventuresome explorer to lead us? Enter Gérard Chaliand, a renowned expert on international relations and violent conflict, who has investigated armed conflict both in the field and through study. Dr. Chaliand has a skill set that spans the strengths typically found among professors, policy analysts, and journalists. I am tempted to wonder if only a European could achieve the requisite mix of capacities and commitments to understand and communicate a Eurasian-based knowledge of war and civilization over more than two and a half millennia. In this book, readers are offered a remarkable synthesis of information about the long history of Eurasian war-making, which accompanied the emergence of civilizations and has marked the human condition ever since. This is a different kind of world history, covering moments over a two-and-a-half-millennia span and offering a distinct perspective on fundamental features of our global present.

Preface

The outline of this book began to emerge shortly after the publication of my *Anthologie mondiale de la stratégie: Des origines au nucléaire* (Paris: R. Laffont, 1990), translated as *The Art of War in World History* (Berkeley: University of California Press, 1994). From that date forward, the elaboration of the history of war has been one of my principal objectives. Because Western military histories remain particularly self-centered, I didn't wish to revisit in condensed form the military histories of Europe and the West. Numerous works in German, English, and French have dealt with the history of European conflicts in Greece, Rome, the Middle Ages, the Renaissance, and more recent periods.

I therefore focused primarily on non-European societies. Orientalist studies of Islam, India, China, and the Middle East have rarely explored the military and strategic cultures that allowed those civilizations to flourish. Rather, they have largely focused on the languages, religions, and institutions of the Eastern world. In the nineteenth and twentieth centuries, Europe conquered and colonized these regions, extinguishing the little remaining interest in the martial traditions of the vanquished. Conversely, the recent increase in interest in the sixth-century B.C.E. author Sun Zi was initially owing to study of the writings of Mao Zedong in an effort to understand his military success in 1949.

Even the great nineteenth- and early twentieth-century military historian Hans Delbrück paid relatively little attention to non-European events, dismissing the Mongols, who created the largest contiguous empire ever known, in three lines in the seven volumes of his *Geschichte der Kriegskunst* (*History of the Art of War*), on the grounds that they never developed "strategic thinking."* However, success in war does not derive only from abstract strategic theory. Rather, successful strategic theory evolves from lessons learned during the actual experience of war. The greatest school of war has always been battle. In the gap in strategic writings between the works of Flavius Vegetius (fourth century C.E.) and Machiavelli (sixteenth century C.E.), wars were fought for twelve centuries in western Europe with little formal strategy.

During this long period, formal strategic theories continued to be elaborated in the Eastern Roman Empire, that is, Byzantium, as exemplified by the *Stratēgikon*, a book attributed to the emperor Maurice (sixth century C.E.) and the *Taktika*, attributed to the emperor Leo VI, the Wise (tenth century C.E.). Similarly, the military history of the Ottoman Empire has been sadly neglected, despite the fact that the Ottomans terrified Europe in the sixteenth century and remained a formidable force until the final quarter of the seventeenth century.

My book *Miroirs d'un désastre: Chronique de la conquête espagnole de l'Amérique* (Paris: Plon, 1990), translated as *Mirrors of a Disaster: The Spanish Conquest of America* (New Brunswick, NJ: Transaction Publishers, 2005), was one of the first to give Hernán Cortés his rightful place in history as a military strategist. Until then, the fall of Tenochtitlán (now Mexico City) had never been identified as a "decisive battle." Yet, although it was fought without large armies, it was indeed decisive and its historical consequences were profound.

The current book aims at describing the main strategic cultures that dominated the Eurasian continent over the course of its history, beginning with the first true military empire, Assyria, from the ninth to the seventh centuries B.C.E.

I analyze the military traditions of the Byzantine Empire, which enabled it to survive for a thousand years after the fall of Rome in the fifth century. Its domination of Asia Minor and the Balkans for seven centuries was an extraordinary accomplishment. Moreover, the Byzantine Empire played a critical role in the founding councils that defined Christian theology in religiously turbulent times and served as a mili-

---

* Hans Delbrück, *Geschichte der Kriegskunst im Rahmen der politischen Geschichte*, 7 vols. (Berlin: G. Stilke, 1900–1936). Translated by Walter J. Renfroe Jr. as *History of the Art of War within the Framework of Political History* (4 vols.; Westport, CT: Greenwood Press, 1975–85).

tary bulwark against Islam, particularly at the beginning of the eighth century.

The forces underlying the sudden Arab expansion in the seventh and eighth centuries remain poorly understood by the general public. Indeed, nomadic cultures, including Indo-Europeans, Turks, Arabs, and Mongols, exerted military domination over Eurasia until the introduction of the cannon in the fifteenth century. In *Nomadic Empires: From Mongolia to the Danube* (New Brunswick, N.J.: Transaction Publishers, 2004), I reviewed their critical role in defining Eurasian history for more than two millennia.

The sedentary heirs of the nomads, those whom I call the sons of the steppes—Seljuks, Mamluks, Mughals, and descendants of Tamerlane—built great and occasionally long-lasting empires while largely maintaining the military style of warfare of the steppe. The Ottomans and Mughals adapted the cannon and thus overcame their enemies. In fact, it is important to stress that a real restructuration of Asia and Slavic Europe occurred after the Mongol surge. The "post-Mongol" empires include the Ming in China, the Ottomans, the Safavids in Persia, and the Mughals in India. As for Russia, Muscovy tore itself progressively away from the Tatar yoke beginning in the middle of the sixteenth century. Under Ivan the Terrible, the Russians took revenge on the Mongols: for the first time in history, Eurasian conquest went from West to East.

After the Mongols, the next clash of civilizations was the encounter of a handful of Spaniards, led by their brilliant commander Cortés, and the Aztec Empire. Cortés's triumph foreshadows the nineteenth-century clash of civilizations in the European imperial invasions that overwhelmed Africa and Asia.

The British geopolitician H.J. McKinder argues that the principal opposition in history was between maritime and terrestrial powers. However, throughout time, a much vaster conflict played out between the unsettled nomadic populations of the Asian steppe and the sedentary populations of China, India, Iran, and Russia.

From the beginning of history until the dawn of the fifteenth century, about 4,500 years, world military history has largely played out on the Eurasian landscape, bounded in the north of Central Asia by taiga. In this area, we can sketch out long-term strategies that existed long before modern nation-states. Chapter 11 of this book goes on to describe some of the salient aspects of the military history of China, sketching the advances, retreats, and concepts of military strategy of the mandarin class, which considered itself superior to the army castes of the time.

Western Europe was affected by nomadic incursions until the tenth century. The Hungarians were the last wave of nomads to enter and settle in western Europe. Following a line that goes approximately from Danzig to Trieste and through Vienna, western Europe had the good fortune, from the end of the tenth century on, to avoid invasion. This relative stability set the early stage for the Renaissance, the Reformation, and, finally, the Age of Enlightenment. No such stability existed in Russia, which was conquered and occupied by the Mongols from the thirteenth to the fifteenth centuries, or in the Balkans, which fell under Ottoman domination from the fourteenth to the nineteenth centuries. Starting in the eighteenth century, when Europe became militarily superior to its rivals, colonial conquests became emblematic of asymmetrical wars, which reemerged in the twentieth century. The guerrilla phenomenon, so important in the twentieth century, and its more recent corollary, terrorism, have become increasingly relevant at a time when the United States has unrivaled military superiority and is without opposition, except on the scale of irregular conflicts.

I want to thank my translators, Michèle Mangin-Woods and David Woods, and my copyeditor, Peter Dreyer, for his remarkable work and careful reading of the manuscript.

Introduction

Chapter 1 of this book reviews the different types of war from its origins to the present day. The different forms of war are briefly described: ritual war, wars of conquest, intracommunal conflicts, wars waged against "foreign" peoples considered ripe for conquest, such as the wars between nomads and sedentary populations, and colonial wars such as those of the Americas. And finally, it addresses the cruelest wars: civil wars, whether religious or otherwise.

Chapter 2 describes the first military empire, that of the Assyrians, who subjugated the entire Fertile Crescent and Egypt, that is, the quasi-totality of the Ancient Orient. The extent of the Assyrian Empire would not be surpassed until that of the Achaemenides of Persia (sixth to fourth centuries B.C.E.).

Chapter 3 describes the Byzantine Roman Empire, which endured from the fourth century C.E. until 1453, becoming the longest-lasting empire the world has ever known. Its longevity was due to both the geographical location of its capital and subtle strategy that combined a sophisticated military tradition with skilled diplomacy.

Chapter 4 describes the rapid expansion of Islam, founded on faith in the message of the Prophet Muhammad. Islamic expansion was facilitated by the mutually destructive twenty-year war between the adjacent Byzantine and the Sassanid (Persian) Empires. Shortly after the death of the Prophet, a few key battles led to the Muslim conquest of the majority of the Byzantine Empire (North Africa, Egypt, and Syria-Palestine), while Sassanid Persia was overrun and converted, like the majority of the conquered peoples, to Islam. In one century, the Arabs came to dominate a vast territory from Spain to the frontier of India, and would later continue their advance in Central Asia.

Chapter 5 focuses on the critical conflicts between the nomadic and sedentary peoples of Central Asia. Unlike the conflicts between maritime and continental powers, which are a recent, post-sixteenth-century phenomenon, the conflicts between nomads and sedentary populations profoundly shaped Eurasian history for more than two millennia as wave after wave of nomads (Indo-European, Turkic-speaking, and Mongol) conquered and occupied China, Persia, North India, Russia, and Central Europe.

Chapter 6 discusses the Mamluks, descendants of nomadic warrior-slaves from Central Asia who expanded their power from the thirteenth to sixteenth centuries to control Egypt and Syria.

Chapter 7 describes the expansion of the Mongols, commanded by an illiterate military genius, Genghis Khan, who built the largest empire that the world has ever known. It describes the religious transformation of the Mongols as well as the Pax Mongolica and the long-lasting consequences of Mongol conquest. To a great extent, Asian history after the Mongols reflects the evolution of "post-Mongol empires."

Chapter 8 describes the conquests of Tamerlane, a descendant of the nomads, and is followed by descriptions of other empires of nomadic origin, including the Ottomans and the Moghuls of India.

Chapters 9–14 describe the counteroffensives against the nomadic empires that enabled the sedentary peoples of China (under the Ming dynasty) to end Mongol domination, and that permitted the Russians under Ivan the Terrible to expel the Mongols, with the help of artillery, and begin the Russian expansion through Siberia to the Pacific. These chapters describe key events in world history up to the twentieth century, including

- The long-lasting Ottoman conquest of the Balkans, the Danube basin, and the regions surrounding the Black Sea
- The fall of the Chinese Ming dynasty at the hands of the Manchu Qing dynasty (1644–1911), which was of nomadic origin
- The Muslim domination of the quasi-totality of India
- The expulsion of the Mongols from Russia back to their Central Asia homelands

The final chapters describe more recent events. In the fifteenth and sixteenth centuries, Europe began its vast colonial expansion, which was a cultural shock to the peoples of Asia and Africa. By the second half of the eighteenth century, the Industrial Revolution had begun in Europe and democracy spread, thanks to the ideas of the Enlightenment that took root in western Europe and North America. From 1792 to 1945, Europeans experienced "total wars" and urban insurrections. In the colonies, there were guerrilla wars, irregular or asymmetric wars, and counterinsurrections from the nineteenth century until the 1970s. Mao Zedong transformed guerrilla warfare into revolutionary war, designed to weaken regular armies, with the goal of taking power by mobilizing and controlling the masses. These innovations were validated by the Communist capture of Beijing (1949) and the victory of the Vietnamese Communists at Dien Bien Phu (1954).

In conclusion, chapter 19 describes the complexity of contemporary warfare, where political considerations have largely eliminated the possibility of decisive victories by Western armies in irregular wars where the adversary generally has popular support and geopolitical sanctuaries. Western public opinion will no longer accept significant casualties in what are perceived as inessential wars.

CHAPTER I

Overview

War and History

THE GEOSTRATEGY OF WAR

Can we characterize the strategies that defined war on the Eurasian continent from the steppes of North Asia to the Mediterranean in the south over the long period from the fifth century B.C.E. to the fifteenth century C.E.?

China

From the fourth century B.C.E. until the eighteenth century C.E., China was always coveted by the nomads on its northern border. Chinese civilization, which developed around the Yellow River during the third millennium B.C.E., was already the object of northern nomadic attacks even before Chinese unification (221 B.C.E.). Under the Han dynasty (206 B.C.E. to 219 C.E.), the focus of Chinese culture was north-central China, with the Yangtze Valley as its southern border. Progressively, China extended south under the Tang dynasty (618–907), but it was only under the Song dynasty (960–1279) that the Yangtze Valley came to dominate China both demographically and economically. China's southern frontier region was one of expansion, where Chinese colonizers found fertile lands, inhabited by sedentary populations less advanced than themselves. In the north, however, although the steppe could be farmed, nomadic warriors stood ready to attack. As a result, China's northern frontier was generally a line of defense, as illustrated by the beginning of the Great Wall shortly after unification, which was not completed until the Ming dynasty (1368–1644). Before the nomad Manchu Qing dynasty (1644–1911), Chinese territorial expansion to the north and northwest occurred under the Han and the Tang dynasties. Their goal was to control the northwestern oases of the Silk Road and establish a buffer zone between China and the northern nomads.

Until the Tang period, soldiers retained high prestige in Chinese society. Subsequently, however, the Confucian scholar became the favored role model, particularly after the tenth century, when mandarin competitions were instituted to select bureaucrats according to merit. Soon thereafter, the mandarins, rather than battle-hardened generals, were in control of Chinese military strategy.

From the fourth century on, northern China was constantly harassed and often occupied by nomads. Indeed, the occupation of northern China by nomadic peoples is a recurrent feature of Chinese history. All of China was, in fact, occupied twice by nomad dynasties, both coming from the north: the Mongol Yuan (1279–1368) and the Manchu Qing (1644–1911). The nomad invasions involved relatively small armies, however, which became sinicized within a few generations and were demographically diluted by the immense Chinese population—culture and demography have been China's great assets throughout its history. Nonetheless, the sinicization of the occupiers did not change the geostrategy of the Chinese Empire or diminish its vulnerability in the north.

In order to rule northern China, the nomads needed to control the Ordos Desert, encircled by the rectangular bend of the Yellow River, which flows for more than four hundred miles into the Mongolian steppe. When well led and facing weak Chinese dynasties, nomads effectively dominated the Ordos for fifteen hundred of the two and a half thousand years of Chinese imperial history. Often the nomads would raid settled regions, and occasionally they would conquer northern China and capture its capital cities, Xian, Chang An, or Lo-Yang. However, whenever a great dynasty arose in China, it would take the offensive again with the goal of controlling the oases in the north and west along the Silk Road as far as the Tien Chan Mountains and Dzungaria (northern Xinjiang). This happened under the Han (202 B.C.E. to 220 C.E.), the Tang (618–902), and at the beginning of the Ming (1368–1644) dynasties. The Chinese attacked in early spring, when the nomads' horses were still poorly nourished.

The Ming Empire underwent two distinct periods. The first, offensive, aimed at restoring Chinese imperial greatness. During this period, the Chinese imperial fleet reached as far as East Africa, at a time when the Portuguese had barely reached the southern coast of Morocco. However, beginning in the latter half of the Ming era, in the late fifteenth century, the empire isolated itself behind the Great Wall, and China's coasts were abandoned to Japanese pirates.

After its conquest by the nomad Manchus in 1644, China returned to an expansionist policy. Under the sinicized Kangxi Emperor (1661–1722), the Manchus expanded to the north, crushing the troublesome nomads of Dzungaria. By the end of the eighteenth century the nomad peril had vanished. However, in the nineteenth century, the advance of Russia and the rise of European imperialism would present a far more serious threat to China.

Iran

Persia was another favorite target of the Central Asian nomads. In that respect, Persia and China faced similar challenges. The nomadic populations of Central Asia were concentrated around the northern part of the Oxus River—known today as the Amu Dar'ya, which flows fifteen hundred miles northwest from Afghanistan and Tajikistan to the Aral Sea. The first nomads to occupy this area were the Scythians. Herodotus relates that in the fifth century B.C.E., the Persian Great King Darius organized a campaign against them, which failed: the Scythians' scorched-earth tactics weakened the army of the Achaemenid Empire, forcing Darius to retreat.

Indo-European nomads occupied the northern part of the Oxus from the seventh century B.C.E. to the third century C.E. and spread as far as the Ukrainian steppes. By the sixth century, the Central Asian steppes fell under the domination of Turkic tribes. By the tenth century, in *Book of Kings* (*Shahnameh*), the Persian poet Firdawsī identifies the Touran, that is to say, the turcophones, as Persia's greatest enemies. Meanwhile, in the west, after the fall of the Achaemenid dynasty (550 to 330 B.C.E.), Persia successively confronted the Roman Empire and the Byzantine Empire. Finally, the Arabs put an end to the Persian Sassanid dynasty in 642 C.E.

Afghanistan to the east was never powerful enough really to dominate Persia. It was from the north that Persia was most vulnerable to invasions. The most serious threat came from the Turks beginning in the tenth century. Like the Chinese, the Persians had a civilizing influence on the turcophone nomads. From the eleventh to the end of the twelfth century, Persia was ruled by the Seljuk Turks, whose great vizier Nizam Al-Mulk (1018–92) was, however, a Persian.

Although Persia never had a population as huge as China's, it also culturally assimilated its conquerors. For example, the Arab Abbasid dynasty, which arose in Baghdad after the decline of the Arab Umayyad dynasty centered in Damascus, was gradually influenced by Persian culture. Shiism, which was adopted by the Safavid dynasty at the beginning of the sixteenth century, led Persia further to differentiate itself from the Sunni Arabs and Ottoman Turks.

The French historian René Grousset called Persia the "real middle kingdom." Every powerful dynasty that ruled Persia—Achaemenids, Sassanids (224–642 C.E.), Abbasids (750–945), and Safavids (1502–1722)—dominated Central Asia from Samarkand to the Indus. For almost a thousand years before the nineteenth century, Persian was thus the lingua franca of an area extending from Samarkand and Bukhara to Delhi and Agra. Persian influences are also seen in Central Asian architecture, with its emphasis on elegant gardens, and in cooking techniques that are widely shared from Central Asia to the Punjab.

India

The Indian subcontinent is geographically protected by oceans on two sides and by the Himalayas. Until the early modern European incursions, India was always invaded from the northwest. The history of the Indus Valley's Harappan civilization goes back to the third millennium B.C.E., as witnessed by the remains of the city of Mohenjo-Daro, in today's Pakistan. The Aryan invasion (1800–1500 B.C.E.) marked the beginning of a long succession of invasions, including that of the Hephthalite (or White) Huns in the fourth century B.C.E. This was followed by the great indigenous Indian dynasty of the Maurya (325 to 180 B.C.E.), which produced the remarkable emperor Aśoka the Great (273 to 232 B.C.E.). In his youth, Aśoka was a brilliant military commander, but he later became a devout Buddhist and promulgated laws banning hunting and ending forced labor. The Maurya Empire reached its greatest extent during this period, covering the entire Indian subcontinent and extending to the eastern part of present-day Afghanistan. Later, India would be ruled by another great indigenous state, the Gupta Empire (320 to 550 C.E.).

However, India prior to the modern era knew only one period when it was ruled from a single capital city, that of the Maurya Empire under Aśoka. Throughout its history, Indian unity has been less political than cultural. During most of its history, India was divided in multiple kingdoms, except when it fell under a foreign domination, as during the rule of Sultan Alauddin Khilji (1296–1316), the Mughal Empire under Aurangzeb (1659–1717), and finally under the British.

As early as the tenth century, northern India and, progressively, all of India except the Tamil extreme south fell under Muslim domination. In 1526, Babur, a turcophone fleeing Samarkand following an attack by Uzbeks, set out to conquer India using his artillery. After crossing the northwestern mountains and deserts, he waged battle on the plain of Delhi like the conquerors before him and won because he had cannons. He was victorious at Panipat despite his smaller army. It is interesting to note that the Delhi plain played the same historical role in India as Adrianople in the history of the Byzantine Empire: it was a place where geography and history met.

Unlike that of China, the political influence of India never extended much beyond its borders. However, the cultural influences of both China and India were widespread. East Asia became sinicized, reflecting the Chinese occupation of Korea until the fourth century, and of Vietnam until the tenth century, as well as the indirect influence of China on Japan through Korea, from the fourth century until the fall of the Tang dynasty (907). Similarly, Buddhism, born in India but gradually expelled by it, exerted a considerable influence on Southeast and East Asia beginning in the second century. Thus, India influenced Ceylon (Sri Lanka), Burma, Cambodia, Laos, Thailand, and Indonesia, which would later become Muslim, thanks to the peaceful proselytizing of Muslim merchants.

The Buddhist influence also reached Afghanistan (Gandhara), China, Korea, and Japan, and, in the seventh century, Tibet. The Mongol Yuan dynasty (1260–1370) converted to Buddhism, and Buddhism spread to Mongolia in the fourteenth century. Indian influences are also reflected in the magnificent temple architecture of Pagan in Burma, Borobudur in Java, and Angkor in Cambodia. India was twice subjugated by Muslims and then by Europeans. However, rural India entrenched itself in traditional Hinduism. The Islamic influence was felt most strongly in the north—in eastern Bengal and the northwest.

All nomadic invasions of India, like those of the White Huns and those led by sons of the steppe like the Ghaznavids and Babur, had to cross the same northwestern mountain passes, including the Khyber, and the deserts of Baluchistan before reaching the edge of the Indo-Gangetic plain. It is no surprise that the most warlike populations of the subcontinent, Sikhs, Punjabis, Marathis, and Rajasthanis, are concentrated in the northwest of the country, where conquerors came in droves. Bengal, on the other hand, which was better protected geographically, is known as a province of artists and poets. It was conquered from the sea by the British in the second part of the eighteenth century.

Asia Minor and Egypt

The border between Anatolia and Iran has changed little throughout two millennia, except when a single empire dominated the whole of Asia Minor from Central Asia to northern India. The border that separated the Roman Empire and the Parthians, the Byzantine Empire and the Sassanids, and the Ottomans and the Safavids resembles the border that today separates Turkey and Iran. Armenia has long been a buffer state that hangs in the balance between rival powers seeking alliance or allegiance. Because the power that controlled Anatolia was blocked in the east by the Persians, geostrategic logic forced it to advance toward the Balkans. The strategic key to this expansion is Edirne, previously called Adrianople. The other possible area for expansion is the Syrian-Palestinian corridor to the south. If the circumstances were favorable and the Anatolian empire were powerful, it would dominate the totality of these eastern Mediterranean territories, as in the case of the Byzantine Empire and the Ottoman Empire.

Egypt, "the gift of the Nile," needs to maintain control of the Upper Nile until the fourth cataract. During the colonial period, the British had wisely linked the fate of Sudan to that of Egypt, and accepting their separation after decolonization was an error on the part of the "free officers" Muhammad Naguib and Gamal Abdel Nasser. In 1953, in his manifesto *Falsafat al-thawra* (Philosophy of the Revolution), Nasser sketched a very ambitious plan of pan-Arab geopolitics. In practice, his short-lived alliances with Syria and Yemen were poorly conceived, and in the case of Yemen led to a disastrous conflict. It would have been better to have merged with Sudan and underpopulated Libya, whose oil reserves would have been very useful to Egypt.

Egypt is bordered in the west, east, and south by deserts. Thus, during the Old Kingdom and most of the Middle Kingdom—a period of some fifteen hundred years—Egypt was protected by its geography and the absence of powerful neighbors. The threat came from the northwest, where the Sinai Desert serves as a buffer, but was not sufficient to stop the Hyksos invasion. When possible, Egypt has always tried to secure control of the Syrian-Palestinian corridor, ideally as far as the Euphrates. The battles of Megiddo and Kadesh, the most ancient documented battles in history, were fought to control this corridor. Kadesh, fought between the Hittites and the Egyptians, led to a compromise. As for the small states in the Fertile Crescent, they were safe only when a strong power did not rule Asia Minor or Egypt.

The emergence of superior European armament and technology upset the traditional Eurasian balance of power during the nineteenth and twentieth centuries. Great Britain, an insular power, repeatedly opposed whatever continental power was dominant in Europe (Spain, France twice, and then Germany) by allying itself with other states concerned about the threat of hegemony. Today, the United States, protected by two oceans, faces no serious rivals. However, it was made brutally aware of its vulnerability on September 11, 2001.

WAR AND WEAPONRY IN HISTORY

Sedentarism, the transition from nomadic life to the first urban centers, began some four millennia B.C.E. in Mesopotamia, Egypt, the Indus Valley, and China in the vicinity of the Yellow River. Very early on, Mesopotamia and Egypt became centers of civilization. We know little about the wars of high antiquity, aside from the vestigial archaeological artifacts. The first documented battle in history is that of Megiddo, which occurred in Palestine in 1469 B.C.E.

The weapons of Mesopotamian and Egyptian antiquity were made of bronze. It was only in the second millennium B.C.E. that iron weapons were introduced, with their increased efficiency and durability. Shields and armor made of leather or metal offered little protection. The pike, of variable length, was the classic weapon of antiquity. Swords of varying length were also used, the shortest being the Roman glaive.

The dominant projectile weapon, from China to Europe and throughout Eurasia, was the bow and arrow, though slings and spear-throwers were also used. Nomadic societies developed advanced laminated bows made of multiple woods, with a double curve that provided greater range and more power. The nomads generally used two bows: a short one when mounted, and a long one when on the ground.

Starting in the second millennium B.C.E., the chariot was a symbol of power and the supreme weapon of the sovereign and his nobles. It was used by the Egyptians, the Homeric Greeks, and, in the ancient Orient, by the Chinese. The chariot was often the determining factor in battle. With two wheels, pulled by two horses, it usually carried three warriors: a driver, an archer, and, in the back, the "third one" of Assyrian texts, whose role was to protect the other two with a large shield. Chariots and cavalry were primarily used to break through enemy lines. Behind the chariots came foot soldiers in greater numbers, including both heavy and light infantry. The infantry were grouped according to their weapons, with warriors with bows and slings in one group, and those with pikes and swords in another. Armor usually included a helmet, breastplate, and leggings.

In spite of the terror inspired by chariots, the charioteers were vulnerable if opposing archers could maintain formation and sustain fire over the final one hundred meters of the chariot's charge. In ancient battles, the last one hundred meters were almost always decisive. Cavalry, which appeared at the end of the second millennium B.C.E., reduced the time necessary for the final charge, and became the core of Eurasian nomadic armies from Ukraine to Manchuria. The nomadic mounted archer was a constant feature of war for over two and a half millennia. Stirrups, which added balance and power, originated in Central Asia around the fifth century B.C.E. and were adopted by the Byzantine Empire long before they came into use in Europe. The Maurya Empire (325 to 180 B.C.E.) used elephants in their cavalry, as did Carthage. Elephants could be terrifying when they charged in an orderly manner, but they could also be difficult to control and cause panic in their own army.

Siegecraft, or poliorcetics, was an ancient art mastered by the Assyrians as early as the eighth century B.C.E. From antiquity to the twentieth century, the most famous sieges lasted between six and twelve months, although the siege of Masada is believed to have lasted three years. Tyre was besieged by Alexander the Great for seven months in 332 B.C.E., Sebastopol was besieged for eleven months by the British and French in 1854, and Leningrad was besieged for more than a year by the Germans in 1941–42. However, most sieges were of shorter duration.

The Phoenicians were the first to adopt galleys in warfare at sea. Battles usually involved hand-to-hand combat after the galleys had joined, although ships also attempted to sink their adversaries by ramming their hulls. Galleys were careful to stay as close as possible to the coast. Improvement in their speed and power enabled galleys to rule the Mediterranean for two and a half millennia before they were supplanted by more advanced ships.

On land, opposing forces were arranged in lines or, more often, in columns of various depths, and more rarely in square formations. Each of these formations had its advantages or disadvantages.

- The line, which was effective against envelopment, lacked depth and mobility.
- The column, beginning with the phalanx, played an important role for centuries, but was vulnerable on its flanks.
- The square formation, powerfully defensive and sometimes impregnable, was often static. However, Swiss squares had enough cohesion to be mobile, thus transforming the wall into a battering ram.

Tactical maneuvers, essential in battle, include a few common motifs. The flank attack was designed to destabilize the enemy. The encircling movement was often used by nomadic cavalry, and could include a double attack on both flanks, as well as from the rear. During the Middle Ages, Europeans favored frontal assaults, aimed at breaking through the enemy center and dividing the enemy. These attacks could be waged by foot soldiers organized into columns (phalanxes) or by cavalry. In Europe, Greek and Roman infantry dominated from the fifth century B.C.E. until 378 C.E., when the legions of the Roman emperor Valens were routed by German cavalry.

Nomadic societies had similar strategies regardless of their ethnic origin: harrying the enemy from a distance; using combined mounted archers to destabilize the adversary before attacking him with a decisive frontal assault; envelopment from the sides; and simulating retreat to disperse the enemy and draw them into an ambush. In Central Asia, mounted nomads successfully employed this style of fighting until the sixteenth century.

The role of logistics—managing the army's transportation and the maintenance and deployment of food supplies and weaponry—has always been a key one in warfare. In sum, the adequacy of logistics defines the rhythm and range of military operations. Without it, there can be no campaign. The larger the army, the greater the demand it places on logistics.

It is estimated that each Roman legionnaire carried two weeks' supply of wheat, and that the supply column added four weeks' wheat per soldier, giving the troops six weeks of autonomy. Nomadic mounted archers had greater autonomy. Their well-integrated logistics gave them a vastly larger range of deployment because of their superior operational speed. Indeed, it is uncertain whether the advance of the German panzers on the Russian Front in World War II was faster than the advance of the Mongols over the same region centuries before. Each Mongol soldier had three to four spare horses and was accustomed to living on minimal supplies since childhood. The Mongols preferred winter campaigns, when frozen rivers could be crossed easily.

Strategy deals with ways and means to impose one's will on the adversary. For military historians, it is of little interest to speculate about whether war is characteristic of all so-called primitive societies. What is clear is that since the birth of the city-state, war, both offensive and defensive, has been a constant feature of civilizations.

In antiquity, victory in war meant being able to plunder assets and acquire slaves and land. At different times, and in various societies, war could take ritual forms. For example, it might be a contest between two champions, or sets of champions, representing rival groups. For example, Herodotus (book 1.82) describes the battle between three hundred Lacedaemonian and three hundred Argive champions, which ended with only three fighters remaining alive. Among the Aztecs, who built an empire through conquest, the goal of war was less to destroy the enemy than to capture prisoners to be sacrificed to the sun god. Western feudal battles were also meant to capture knights, whose freedom would be obtained through ransom. In the Renaissance, condottieri (mercenary warlords) were often content with the capture of the adversary, who could be ransomed, and the preservation of their own troops.

Strategies also changed over time. In the fourteenth century, after cavalry had dominated warfare for millennia, it was challenged by the Swiss square infantry formation, whose efficiency depended on its cohesiveness. Each square was formed in a canton, where everyone knew and relied on everyone else, so that neighbor fought alongside neighbor. What made these squares so terrifying to their opponents was that, unlike other troops of that time, the Swiss were not interested in ransom. Not a single prisoner, whatever his rank, was spared. Later, the Swedish king Gustavus Adolphus (1594–1632) introduced another innovation: instead of a slow buildup to battle, he sought a rapid and direct assault, supported by mobile artillery, which proved highly successful.

With the French Revolution, a new way of making war appeared, based, not on mercenary troops, but on the *levée en masse*, or mass conscription of citizens, so that the entire society was involved. With

Napoleon Bonaparte, battles aimed at the annihilation of the enemy armed forces. Armies throughout Europe were gradually nationalized in the nineteenth century, and military service became obligatory. There was considerable progress of fire power due to industrialization. With the increasing harshness of national antagonisms and the demonization of the enemy, as in the religious conflicts of the sixteenth century, the wars of the twentieth century became total wars.

The development of propaganda during World War I, brought forth by democratization, aimed at consolidating public opinion. However, success in prolonged conflicts depended more and more on industrial capacity. In the Spanish Civil War, Guernica anticipated the conflating of military and civilian targets: the civilian population became as much a target as the soldiers. War became yet more total in World War II, as exemplified by the bombing of civilians in Coventry, Dresden, Tokyo, Hiroshima, and Nagasaki. Terrorizing civilian populations in order to destroy their morale in fact revived a tradition long forgotten in Europe.

Europeans emerged from World War I with a sense of disgust at the high price of victory, and painful frustration among the losers, giving rise to widespread pacifism. It is impossible to analyze war from a historical perspective based on today's political sensibilities. Executions, for instance, were public spectacles in many places in Europe before World War I and drew large crowds (as was still the case until recently under dictatorships in Saddam Hussein's Iraq and Mao's China). In western Europe, the military underwent significant changes during World War I: the officer caste was selected more democratically, and foot soldiers sometimes refused to accept the fate of sheep sent to slaughter. Thereafter, war ceased to be perceived as glorious: its price was too painfully heavy. Human life came to be seen as too precious to waste in combat. Elsewhere, outside Europe, poorer countries with demographically younger populations, sometimes with no experience of the two world wars, have not developed similar sensitivity. Their citizens are often dissatisfied with the status quo and have a different attitude toward combat.

The concept of the "decisive" battle, according to which the collapse of the enemy forces is sought, lasted only about a century and a half, from Bonaparte to 1945. Military historians of the second half of the nineteenth century and the first half of the twentieth cite an earlier period when supposedly decisive battles occurred. By the criterion of Anglo-American "grand strategy," only a battle whose politico-military or historical outcome is definitive should be called decisive. In this sense, the conquest of Constantinople (1453) by the Turks and the Arab victories over the Byzantines at Yarmouk (636) and over the Persians at Qadisiya (637), giving them the possession of Syria and of Iraq, were truly decisive. The same could be said of the fall of Tenochtitlán (Mexico City) into the hands of the Spaniards in 1521.

With all the difficulty and complexity involved, it is important to map out different types of wars, starting with acknowledgment that the concept of war and its nature has changed throughout history. If we exclude wars in primitive societies, determined by demography and the struggle to survive, wars can be divided into several different types:

Ritualized wars. They often occur inside a given society or in neighboring societies and are not waged to the death. Generally, they are characteristic of archaic or traditional societies.

Wars with limited objectives. They usually take place in a world where the code of behavior, the values, and rules of combat are implicitly accepted by both antagonists. Dynastic quarrels, for instance, do not seek to overthrow the established order, but have much more modest aims.

Classical wars of conquest. These have predatory objectives and seek to crush the enemy. No compromise is allowed before complete surrender. They can end with the annihilation or subjugation of the adversary.

Mass war. The French Revolution marks its beginning, and it reached its apogee in World War II. Adversaries seek the annihilation of enemy forces through battles, and the collapse of the civilian population through massive use of terror (bombardments, summary executions, mass deportations, and genocide).

Total war. Throughout history, the cruelest wars have been civil wars. The wars of religion, from the end of the sixteenth century to the first part of the seventeenth, are classic examples. Civil wars are ruthless and cause the most casualties. For example, the Thirty Years' War, the French religious wars, and the Civil War in the United States each caused more losses than the Franco-Prussian war (1870). Heavy losses were also seen during the civil war in Russia (1918–20), the Spanish Civil War (1936–39), and in the religious conflicts in India at the time of Partition (1947–48). If strategy consists of evaluating the benefits in relation to the costs, civil wars are the most irrational, since their costs generally exceed their benefits.

Ethnic wars waged against a people considered radically foreign are another type of implacable war. In this category, we can put the conflicts between nomadic and sedentary peoples, such as the invasions of the Mongols in thirteenth-century Central Asia. Colonial conquests in America and Africa are also classical examples of this category. On the Eastern Front in World War II, Hitler's troops exterminated Jews and Gypsies.

In short, the most radical conflict is the conflict between brothers, or where the enemy is considered subhuman. There is a vast difference between wars with limited objectives and total war in the industrial age, which derives from the concept of the nation-state, and between ritualized wars and the devastating clash between radically different societies or the demented fury of religious wars. The type of soldier—mercenary, draftee, or volunteer—almost always matches the type of war.

Since the end of World War II, when nuclear weapons were first unleashed, the doctrine of mutually assured destruction has prevented conflicts between major powers. However, smaller wars persisted during the Cold War, some of them classic conflicts, such as the Indo-Pakistani war and the Israeli-Arab wars, but mostly irregular wars, guerrilla conflicts, and more recently, in a militarily modest way, terrorism.

The Egyptians

The first attempt to extend the reach of the city-state, created by the Sumerians, was by Sargon of Akkad (2325 B.C.E.), who created an empire that extended beyond Mesopotamia, which included Syria. His grandson Naram-Sin (2250 B.C.E.) was the most important sovereign of the Akkad dynasty, which collapsed around 2200 B.C.E. Our knowledge about the military campaigns of the Akkad dynasty is limited to the little information on a few stelae.

Pharaonic Egypt, which appeared around 2900 B.C.E., did not dominate any foreign country, with the exception of Lower Nubia, during the Old Kingdom (2100 B.C.E.) or the Middle Kingdom (1650 B.C.E.). Egypt was well isolated from potential enemies by its surrounding deserts. The main objective of pharaonic power was control of the Nile River as far as the second cataract. The Nile naturally floods regularly, with fertile alluvia that are ideal for farming in the Nile Delta. In contrast, Mesopotamia needed large irrigation systems organized by the state to permit farming. And, unlike in Egypt, there were no natural boundaries to protect Mesopotamia. It derived protection from its armies. Thus, given those conditions, the populations of modern-day

Egypt and Iraq differed, and they continue to be different from a military perspective.

At the beginning of the second millennium B.C.E. until around 1600 B.C.E., Babylon, particularly under Hammurabi (around 1700 B.C.E.), came to dominate the fertile land between the Tigris and Euphrates rivers. The incursions of the Kassites from the Zagros Mountains began around 1750 B.C.E. They were followed by the Hittite capture of Babylon (1585 B.C.E.), which put an end to the Babylonian Empire. Egypt became a military state after some fifteen hundred years of peace uninterrupted by external aggression. The invasion of the Hyksos with their chariots around 1800 B.C.E. put an end to the Middle Kingdom, but after the Egyptians expelled the occupiers, the New Kingdom was created around 1567 B.C.E. Finally, the increasing threats from the northeast led the pharaohs to create a regular army and move the capital south to Thebes, less vulnerable than Memphis to invasions from the north. The impact of war chariots was felt not only in Egypt, but also in the Indus Valley. Unlike the Hyksos, who spoke a Semitic language, the conquerors of North India were Indo-European. In distant China, where chariots may have appeared around 1200 B.C.E., the Shang dynasty invested the Yellow River Valley (1766 B.C.E.), but was overthrown by a southern dynasty, the Zhou, around 1046 B.C.E.

Here is what we know about the first battle ever documented in history: that of Megiddo, where the Egyptian pharaoh confronted the king of Kadesh and his Canaanite army. Using an offensive strategy and defensive tactics, the king of Kadesh marched south from the Orontes River to prevent Pharaoh Thutmose III from marching north. In the spring of 1468 B.C.E., Thutmose moved against the forces of Kadesh, which were camped near Megiddo. It was a remarkable strategic position. Nine days after his departure, Thutmose reached Gaza, having covered around fifteen miles a day. He advanced toward the city of Yehem, where he took counsel. He could choose among three different routes:

- The most direct route through the gorges of the Wadi Ara
- The road to the north leading to the north of Megiddo
- The road to the south, leading to Taanacia, south of Megiddo

Thutmose explained to his captains that information from his scouts suggested that the king of Kadesh was seeking battle at Megiddo. The captains objected to the shortest route, with its steep banks and vulnerability to ambush: if the vanguard was attacked, the rear guard could not intervene. The pharaoh nevertheless decided to take the shortest and most difficult route (calling to mind the first chapter of Edward Luttwak's book *Strategy: The Logic of War and Peace*).* Indeed, the enemy was expecting the Egyptians to advance by the southern or northern route, but not to take the most direct and dangerous approach. The pharaoh started on the shortest road, but accepted the advice of his captains to wait for the rear guard and only to attack when all the Egyptian troops had regrouped. Thutmose accordingly set up camp south of Megiddo, on the banks of the river Qina, and attacked the next morning.

The strategic importance of Megiddo was that it commanded the exit from Wadi Ara, the narrow gorge through the Carmel Mountains that links the coastal plain of Palestine to the Jezreel Valley. This gorge was the famous Via Maris, which served as a communication passage between Egypt, Mesopotamia, Syria, and Anatolia. Whoever controlled Megiddo controlled this route, and consequently, an important part of the Fertile Crescent. There were important battles in Megiddo in 1917 and 1948 and many times before that.

At dawn, Thutmose III started the assault. The Canaanites were routed and took shelter in Megiddo. Instead of pursuing, the Egyptian army pillaged the Canaanite camp. It would take a seven-month siege to capture Megiddo.

The second battle of Megiddo, in 1295 B.C.E., in which the Egyptians fought the Hittite Empire, with its capital in central Anatolia, is rightly famous. When Ramses II become pharaoh—he ruled for thirty-seven years—there were threats on the northeastern frontier. The Hittite king Mouwatalli had formed alliances with tribes in Asia Minor and northern Syria and challenged the Egyptians on land and sea. A clash was unavoidable and both sides were prepared. Here is how Ramses II is celebrated in the long poem commemorating the battle of Kadesh on the Orontes River (in present-day Syria):

> Great are his victories over foreign lands, no one knows when he will start the fight.
> He is a strong wall of protection for his soldiers and their shield on battle days. He is an unequaled archer, stronger than a hundred thousand enemies. When he advances his divine visage strikes fear and inspires a multitude

---

* Edward Luttwak, *Strategy: The Logic of War and Peace* (Cambridge, MA: Belknap Press of Harvard University Press, 1987).

because his spirit is strong. Strong is his heart at the hour of battle as a flame springing to life. Strong is his courage, like a bull before a fight. He knows all things from all countries. A million men could not withstand him and hundreds of thousands faint at his sight. He is the lord of fear whose war cries carry to the ends of the earth.*

In Year 1 of his reign, on the ninth day in the second month of the dry season (late May), Ramses began marching north with twenty thousand men. The four divisions, Amon, Re, Ptah, and Seth, each with five thousand warriors, advanced toward Kadesh. The Hittites were awaiting them northwest of the city. Two of Mouwatalli's spies, pretending to be deserters, told the Egyptians that the Hittite army was still far away in the north, near Aleppo.

Ramses, deceived, set up camp on the north bank of the Orontes, with the divisions of Amon and Re. Those of Ptah and Seth were two hours' march away. Suddenly, two Hittite prisoners who had been captured by Egyptian scouts were brought before him. Questioned, they revealed the truth. However, even before Ramses could react, the Hittites had overrun the Re division, attacked Amon, and entered Ramses's camp.

Then, says the chronicle:

His majesty arises and gallops to the center of the enemy forces from Hatti. He advances alone, no one accompanies him. Looking behind, he sees that he is surrounded by two thousand five hundred chariots. His escape is blocked by the warriors of the hateful Hatti. However, Ramses asks help from the God Amon. Can a father forget his son? Have I not always marched and halted to your orders and never disobeyed your rules? How great is the lord of Egypt: too great to allow foreigners to sully the borders of his lands.

All of Egypt gives you divine offerings and ships bring you foreign tribute. I call upon you, O my father Amon. I am surrounded by innumerable enemies. All of the foreign lands are allied against me. I am all alone and nobody hears when I call. But you, Amon, are worth more than thousands of men. I send this prayer to the ends of the earth and my voice already carries to Hermonthis.

Amon hears me and gives me his hand. I am joyous. He says . . . "Beloved Ramses I am with you. I am your father and my hand is in your hand . . . I, master of victory, who loves courage."

I now realize that my heart is strong and my spirit joyous enough to achieve what I undertake. Suddenly, I see that the two thousand five hundred

---

* Attributed to the scribe Pentaque by Claire Lalouette, *Histoire d'un empire* (Paris, 1992). And see also Miriam Lichtheim, *Ancient Egyptian Literature,* vol. 2: *The New Kingdom* (Berkeley: University of California Press, 2006), 57–71.

chariots are overturned before my horses. None had the strength to fight. They lost heart at the terror that I inspired. Their arms became too weak to bend a bow or lift a spear. They fell down before me, and I killed whom I wanted. None of the fallen will rise again.

They say: "It's not a man, it's Soutekh of great courage, it's Baal himself! This is no man, but Baal himself. Flee before him to save your lives and feel the wind on your skin. See: anyone who approaches him becomes weak and is struck down with paralysis. You cannot lift a bow or a spear when it comes at a gallop."

Thus does the poem celebrate Ramses II's victory at Kadesh. However, in reality, Kadesh was not taken. Although the battle went in Egypt's favor, the Hittites were far from vanquished. The victory was only a truce. Mouwatalli, blocked at Kadesh, resumed the offensive, but without conclusive results. Around 1280 B.C.E., fifteen years after the battle of Kadesh, the Egyptians and the Hittites came to terms with the fact that neither could crush the other. A truce was announced and a treaty signed. The Hittite king died in 1288 B.C.E. Ramses took advantage of Hittite dynastic quarrels and dominated the Near East as far as the Orontes River, reigning until 1233 B.C.E.

The treaty was originally written in Akkadian, the diplomatic language of the time. Although the original has been lost, versions in Egyptian and Hittite remain. The Egyptian version is inscribed on the walls of the Great Temple of Karnak. The Hittite version was among the imperial archives excavated at Hattusa, the Hittite capital in central Anatolia, at the beginning of the twentieth century. Based on the figures cited at the time, the Egyptians were said to have fifty chariots and the Hittites two thousand five hundred. Thus, the Egyptian celebration of Ramses II's victory was attributed to the mythical powers of the pharaoh, reflecting the magical thinking and exaggeration typical of the chronicles of the wars of antiquity. The battle of Kadesh was also recorded at the Ramesseum in Thebes, as well as at Luxor and Abu-Simbel. The Hittites lured the Egyptians north and surprised them with a flank attack, which nearly proved fatal. However, the Egyptians were able to launch a desperate counterattack when the Hittites began pillaging the Egyptian camp instead of pursuing the fleeing Egyptian forces. Egyptian Canaanite reserves routed the Hittite army as they were pillaging, and the remainder of the Hittite army retreated behind the walls of Kadesh. Thus, the outcome remained indecisive, with both armies sustaining heavy causalities. Nevertheless, the battle of Kadesh represents the height of Egyptian power, which slowly declined during the eighteenth dynasty after the reign of Ramses III (1197 to 1165 B.C.E.).

The Assyrian Empire

There were two separate Assyrian imperial periods. The first Assyrian Empire (thirteenth century B.C.E.) pushed back the Hittites and conquered the kingdom of Mittani in northern Syria and southeastern Anatolia. The more important second Assyrian Empire (ninth to seventh centuries B.C.E.) emerged as the first truly military empire in the world. From conquest to conquest, it expanded to extend from western Persia to the Caucasus and included all of Mesopotamia. The Assyrians occupied the Fertile Crescent and Egypt as far south as Thebes. Civil wars, strains on logistics, and a proliferation of enemies brought the Assyrian Empire to an end in 612 B.C.E.

The Greeks and the Romans

The Greek phalanx composed entirely of free infantrymen appeared in the sixth century B.C.E. and introduced a new style of combat. With the exception of Macedonia, most Greek terrain was unfavorable to cavalry. The phalanx was eight or ten men deep. Each soldier carried a shield (used for defense and to push the phalanx forward) and a sarissa, a pike up to seven meters in length, which enabled the men in the first four ranks to reach the enemy. The goal of the phalanx was to break through the enemy's line, and the phalanx's success depended upon its coordination and cohesion.

Greece was more geographically vulnerable than Egypt. However, Greece was not as vulnerable as Mesopotamia, whose peoples had no choice but to conquer or be conquered. The mountainous geography, fertile valleys, and long coastline made it possible for Greek shepherds and sailors to defend their homeland and for the Athenians to create a thalassocracy, or maritime empire.

It was in Sparta that Greek society became most militarized. The distinction between free warriors and slaves was strongly emphasized. Boys began to train for war at the age of seven, while girls practiced physical culture. Girls stayed with their families, but boys lived communally. The training continued until the age of eighteen, when formal military training began. By the age of twenty, a Spartan soldier had to be ready for anything, because soldiers were Sparta's only defense.

Sparta was the greatest military power in the Peloponnesus. Other Greek cities, notably Athens, emphasized their naval power, which reached from Asia Minor and the Crimea in the northeast to Sicily and beyond in the southwest.

Infantrymen in the phalanx carried a shield, the *hoplon*, which gave rise to their name of hoplites. The hoplite helmet protected the nose, face, and neck, while a cuirass (breastplate) and armor protected the legs and arms. The goal of the phalanx, with hoplites massed up to a dozen rows deep, shields locked, and pikes protruding, was to break through and divide the enemy lines with the force provided by the push of soldiers in the rear.

In addition to the pike, the hoplites used a short sword for hand-to-hand combat. The strength of the phalanx derived from its cohesion. Family members, friends, and neighbors fought side by side, sometimes next to famous citizens, such as Aeschylus, who fought at Marathon. Indeed, the armor and tactics of the hoplites required physical interdependence. Each hoplite protected his own right flank with his shield held next to the hoplite on his right, but his left flank was protected by the man on his left. The frontward movement of the tight formation required that each hoplite hold his position while pushing with his shield on the back of the hoplite in front. This increased the impact force of the phalanx, provided that it could maintain its ranks. The fact that all hoplites, even the most illustrious citizens, were similarly armed, without special distinctions, reinforced the idea that they were battling together, among equals, for the city-state.

The phalanx was faced with two somewhat contradictory constraints: increasing the depth of its ranks gave increased force to the charge, while increasing the width of the phalanx would enable it to overrun the flanks of the enemy formation. Usually, the deeper phalanx prevailed, at the risk of seeing its flanks overrun. In contrast, spreading the phalanx was dangerous, because the shallower formation risked collapse in its center. In part, strategy and tactics depended on the shape of the phalanx used. The Theban general Epaminondas defeated the Spartans at Leuctra (371 B.C.E.) and Mantinea (362 B.C.E.) by opposing the traditional dominance of the right flank and increasing the depth of his left flank to fifty rows. Generally, the phalanx had a tendency to veer to the right in battle, because warriors sought the protection of the shield of the soldier on the right. Usually, the right flank of each phalanx would dominate the left flank of its adversary. The battle was then decided by the two right flanks. With Epaminondas, the Spartan right flank faced a strengthened left flank, while the Theban right flank broke through the left flank of the Spartans. Moreover, Epaminondas coordinated the cavalry and phalanx to provide mutual support. Techniques for coordinating phalanx and cavalry were further developed by Philip II of Macedon and his son, Alexander the Great.

The phalanx was limited by the necessity of fighting on a favorable terrain, and each side would carefully select a position prior to battle. Thus, the well-positioned Athenian phalanx defeated the Persian army at Marathon (490 B.C.E.) by breaking through the Persian lines, while the poorly commanded Persian army remained unable to utilize either its archers or its cavalry effectively.

The phalanx at the time, without the support of the cavalry or missile throwers, was vulnerable on its flanks to cavalry and on the front to archers. The only protection was to charge from a short distance in the hope of breaking through enemy lines and spreading panic in their ranks. The phalanx, composed of citizens, was the usual formation in Greece, but light infantry and cavalry progressively gained more importance as harrying forces to protect the phalanx. The Peloponnesian War, with its long campaigns and its strategy aimed at limiting frontal clashes, saw the further development of the light infantry. Besides, the use of mercenary troops led to the introduction of foot soldiers who were less heavily armed and more mobile than the hoplites: the peltasts. The peltasts could manage difficult terrain and had enough protection to come to the rescue, when numerous enough, of the hoplites.

After defeating Persian armies on land (Marathon, Plataea) and at sea (Salamis), the Greek city-states were defeated by Philip II of Macedon, who was able to create an army superior to those of his rivals. Athens and Thebes were crushed at Chaeronea (338), where Philip's son Alexander commanded the left flank of the cavalry, which proved the decisive factor in victory. The Macedonian phalanx was a tactical unit similar to the Greek, but improved: its rows were deeper and closer and its pikes were longer, allowing the first six or seven rows to reach the adversary during battle. The Macedonian phalanx comprised fifteen hundred men, sixteen rows deep, creating sufficient force to break through enemy lines. Light infantry such as peltasts, archers, and slingers supported this heavy infantry.

The cohesion of the Macedonian army came not only from its organization and discipline but also from its regional (one might today say patriotic) identity, with cavalry from tribal areas. The phalanx included two types of hoplites: a larger group of phalangites armed with sarissas and a smaller, more mobile group of hypaspists, armed with shorter pikes.

The cavalry had no stirrups. They were armed with long sarissas, which they used in the initial charge, and with swords. Later, an even larger phalanx was developed, composed of 4,096 combatants, subdivided into units called the *chiliarchia* (1,024 hoplites), *syntagma* (256 hoplites), *taxichia* (128 hoplites), and *tetrarchia* (64 hoplites). The Macedonian army included four phalanxes, or about 16,000 hoplites, to which were added other corps comprising over 8,000 men, including 1,024 cavalry and 2,048 peltasts.

The cavalry played an important role, and Alexander, in his battles with Darius, used it to his advantage. The principal corps of the cavalry was composed of Macedonian aristocrats, called the king's companions, or *hetairoi*, armed with pikes and swords, who participated in the frontal charge, harrying, pursuit, and reconnaissance. Macedonian superiority derived from the disciplined integration of the various tactical elements and their combination and flexibility under the brilliant command of Alexander. The cavalry was capable of supporting the infantry during its charge, but it could also break through enemy lines, while the phalanx, in a defensive posture, could repel the frontal assault of the enemy. The successes of Granicus (334), Issus (334), and Gaugamela (331) in destroying the vast and powerful Achaemenid Empire were owing to the tactical use of the combined Macedonian forces.

The Romans would overcome this Macedonian phalanx and progressively establish their hegemony over the Mediterranean basin. The process started with the defeat of Carthage, which under Hannibal threatened the existence of Rome (battle of Cannae, 216 B.C.E.). The historian Polybius tells us that after a victorious siege, the Roman custom was to destroy the city and kill all of the inhabitants. Pillage could start only after the physical liquidation of the vanquished. In this respect, the Romans did not differ much from other conquerors better known for their brutality.

The Roman infantry was organized into legions consisting of 4,500 to 5,000 men. Each soldier was armed with a *gladius*, or short sword, roughly twenty-four inches long and two inches wide, a weapon highly suitable for close combat, and two *pila*, or javelins, a heavy one and a light one, thrown during the last few yards of the charge.

The legion consisted of ten cohorts (450 to 570 men) each divided into "maniples" (150 to 180 men) and later "centuries" (around 100 men). A consular army usually consisted of four legions. This formation

TABLE I THE EVOLUTION OF THE PHALANX

Unit	Composition	Shape	Width (M)	Depth (M)
Lacedaemonian phalanx, fifth century B.C.E.	2,048 heavily armed infantry	8 rows of 256 lines	520	16
Macedonian phalanx, fourth century B.C.E.	4,096 heavily armed infantry	16 rows of 256 lines	520	35
Family legion, fourth century B.C.E.	3,000 heavily armed infantry, 600 velites (light infantry), 300 cavalry	25 rows of 256 lines	850–900	100–150
Roman legion, third century B.C.E.	4,200 heavily armed infantry, 600 velites (light infantry), 120 cavalry	25 maniples of 10 rows by 12 lines each, and 3 similar maniples on each diagonal	1,100–1,500	100–150
Marius legion (Rome), first century C.E.	6,000 heavily armed infantry, 600 velites (light infantry), 120 cavalry	10 heavy cohorts of 450–570 men with maniples of 150–80 men divided into *centuriae* of roughly 100 men. Plus one cohort of velites.	1,600–2,300	100–300

SOURCE: Éric Muraise, *Introduction à l'histoire militaire* (Paris: Charles-Lavauzelle, 1964).

of infantrymen included light infantry, or *velites;* the *hastati,* young men who formed the first line; more experienced soldiers, or *principes,* in the second line, the legion's center of gravity; and, finally, veterans in the third line, or *triarii.* The legion had more flexibility and adaptability than the phalanx, but was also essentially trained for offense. Its organization, cohesiveness, and discipline made it a formidable force, which was rarely defeated. Each century was led by a centurion. The centurions played a fundamental role throughout the history of Rome, and were the backbone of the Roman legion.

Slightly before the end of the first century B.C.E., some changes were introduced. Marius opened the army to the most disadvantaged popular classes and established a new system of organization. On the battleground, the cohort consisted of five men in the first line with a depth of eight to ten rows, with enough space between two legionaries to allow flexibility as well as strength. During the attack, often waged on the flanks, the two first rows threw their javelins just before closing with the enemy, sword in hand. The next rows threw their javelins and then relieved the previous rows in close combat. Then two other rows would throw javelins again before close combat, and so on, until the enemy line was broken by wave after wave of fresh troops.

The legion was superior to the phalanx in its flexibility, adaptability, and efficiency. However, the Romans never achieved the balanced combination of forces that Alexander had managed. Rome's victories were won by its infantry; but they also suffered reverses, as in the battle of Carrhae in Mesopotamia in 53 B.C.E., where Parthian (Persian) cavalry inflicted a catastrophic defeat on an army of Roman legionaries. At the height of Augustus's reign (27 B.C.E.–14 C.E.), the Roman army included 125,000 Roman soldiers, with an equal number of mercenary troops who were not Roman citizens. Around 63 C.E., with the conquest of England and the subjugation of Armenia, the empire approached its maximum size. Soon afterward, Rome conquered Mesopotamia and Dacia too, but it did not hold them long.

The Romans were masters of siegecraft, as shown in Caesar's siege of Alesia. The legions, when they moved, built a fortified camp each night, and thus were rarely surprised. In the Punic Wars, the fleet played an important role; the power struggle between Antony and Octavian played out at sea in the battle of Actium (31 B.C.E.).

By the third century C.E., the function of the legions on the *limes,* or frontier, which had previously threatened neighboring lands, had become primarily defensive, and the empire was split into its western and eastern halves. Constantine the Great (306–37 C.E.), who emerged victorious in a series of civil wars to become sole ruler of both west and east by 324, reorganized garrisons and regrouped and reinforced the cavalry. However, the Western Roman Empire under the emperor Valens met with disaster at Adrianople (396 C.E.), where the Roman infantry was overcome by Goth cavalry. The Germanic push at the beginning of the fifth century would become an irresistible rush within the next few decades, which ended with the destruction of the Western Empire (476 C.E.). The Byzantine Eastern Roman Empire would last until 1453.

The Byzantine Empire, considered in isolation, is an exceptional model of survival in a difficult geographic situation. It survived, showing exceptional durability, based on an ability to adapt, refined strategic thinking, and subtle, flexible diplomacy. On many occasions, the Byzantine Empire recovered from apparently desperate situations. It played a fundamental role in the history of Christianity, particularly during the critical doctrinal disputes from the fourth to the eighth centuries. The importance of the Byzantine Empire has been deemphasized in Eurocentric versions of history, due in part to the rivalry between Rome and Constantinople at various times. The rising power of Roman Christianity from the eleventh century on (following the schism in 1054) brought forth the Fourth Crusade, which Venice managed to turn against its rival, Constantinople, in 1204. Although the Byzantine Empire was restored half a century later, it lost its ability to face the mounting regional perils. It collapsed in 1453, a thousand years after the fall of Rome.

WESTERN EUROPE

Europe between the fifth and eighth centuries is largely remembered from a military/strategic perspective for the Frankish victory under Charles Martel in the battle of Tours (Poitiers) in France in 732 C.E. that stopped the advance of the Arabs. However, from an Arab perspective, Tours was of minor importance in comparison with the many defeats inflicted on the Muslims by the Byzantines. The major event during this period—which will be dealt with hereafter—was the stunning military expansion of Islam in less than a century.

After the introduction of the stirrup—in the fifth century in Central Asia and China, in the sixth century in Byzantium and Persia, and in the eighth century in western Europe—cavalry became the most important military force. In the battle of Adrianople, it was clear that dominance on the battlefield had shifted: cavalry triumphed over the infantry, reversing the order that had characterized Greek and Roman dominance.

By crowning Charlemagne, Charles Martel's grandson, as Holy Roman emperor in 800 C.E., Pope Leo III challenged the Byzantine emperor in Constantinople, who viewed himself the heir to ancient Rome. The Carolingian cavalry's strategic culture was inherited from both the Germanic tradition and that of the Roman legion, which alike favored frontal assaults. This culture, born in the feudal age, lasted until the fourteenth and fifteenth centuries. Some military historians, like Victor Davis Hanson,* characterize the Western strategic tradition as systematically seeking a frontal assault, expressing a style of combat born in societies where soldiers were citizens. Though many examples support this thesis, there are also many contradictory examples, particularly in the sixteenth and eighteenth centuries. In contrast, the British military historian B.H. Liddell Hart argued that successful military strategies are invariably indirect, even in the West.†

Western Europe faced Saracen incursions on land and Viking incursions at sea. It also confronted nomadic peoples driven from the steppes by the Mongols. Fighting mostly on horseback, using laminated bows, nomads like the Hungarians (Magyars) devastated Italy, Burgundy, Germany, and the countries of the Danube until they were defeated by the German emperor Otto I at Lechfeld in 955. The Hungarians converted to Christianity at the end of the tenth century, and by the fourteenth and fifteenth centuries had become a bulwark against the Turks, before their defeat at Mohács in 1526 at the hands of the Ottomans. The Vikings descended the Russian rivers and settled Ukraine, trading with both Byzantines and Arabs. In the west, they settled in France, England, Iceland, and Greenland, and their descendants the Normans conquered England (1066) and then Sicily. The Saracens were eventually confined to Spain south of Asturias. The reconquest of the rest of Spain did not begin until the eleventh and twelfth centuries.

In the eleventh century, western European populations were increasing, and the economy was growing. Europe felt capable of going on a crusade. Until then, the Carolingians' gains in the east had been modest,

---

  * V.D. Hanson, *Carnage and Culture: Landmark Battles in the Rise of Western Power* (New York: Doubleday, 2001).
  † B.H. Liddell Hart, *The Strategy of Indirect Approach* (1941; new ed., London: Faber & Faber, 1946); reprinted as *Strategy: The Indirect Approach* (New York: Praeger, 1954).

much less than what Christendom had lost in Spain and North Africa, once the homeland of Saint Augustine and Tertullian, founding fathers of the Latin Church. Militarily speaking, the Crusades offered some new lessons to the Europeans. When they reached Anatolia, the Franks clashed with Seljuk Turks and consequently with mounted archers. The Seljuk strategy consisted of hitting the enemy with a shower of arrows shot from the first row of horsemen, which then moved away to make room for the second row and so on, in order to inflict severe losses to their adversary before storming their defenses. The Turkish horsemen, with their lighter arms and armor, were faster than the Franks. Charging, as was the Franks' custom, proved frustrating, since the mounted archers would merely retreat and then return to start harassing them again. The Seljuks also used the classic tactic of nomad warriors, which consisted of feigning a retreat to draw their opponents into a scattered attack and then setting an ambush. Finally, the mounted archers used the technique of envelopment from the sides or rear. In particular, the Seljuks would often attack marching troops from the rear before they could organize themselves. All of these tactics were used in Asia Minor during the Second Crusade (1147), and against the troops of the emperor Frederick Barbarossa in Anatolia during the Third Crusade (1190).

The Seljuk mounted archers would engage in a direct frontal assault only when the enemy had been weakened and disorganized by volleys of arrows. With their greater mobility, the mounted archers could easily retreat if enemy resistance proved too strong. Later, the Franks would be faced with the Fatimids of Egypt, who proved to be even more dangerous than the Seljuks.

Arab tactics were different from those of the Turks and did not include mounted archers, but rather heavy cavalry that would engage in initial frontal assaults with lance and sword, like the Franks. The Kurdish commander Saladin led a successful counteroffensive, but final victory over the Christians at Acre in 1193 would come at the hands of the Mamluks, who combined the harassment of mounted archers with the power of heavy cavalry. During the two centuries of their presence in the Levant, the Franks adapted to the style of combat of their Seljuk, Mamluk, or Arab adversaries, with frontal assaults whenever possible.

Over time in the Levant, Frankish rule was accompanied by the construction of crusader castles. The crusaders had learned from the military architecture of the Byzantines and Armenians, which was well adapted to castle construction in mountainous regions. The influence of crusader architecture remains particularly noticeable in Italy.

The success of the early Crusades was greatly facilitated by divisions among the Muslims. Later, when the Muslims were unified under Saladin as sultan of Egypt and Syria, the situation changed. The battle of Hittin (1187) marks a turning point, when Jerusalem was taken back by the Muslims, although Saladin remained unable to capture the Franks' fortresses. Later, the Mamluks would finish the reconquest at the end of the thirteenth century. The crusaders' defeat was less a consequence of their style of combat than of the size of their armies. Despite the addition of the Knights Templar and Knights Hospitaller, they lacked manpower. The major political result of the Crusades was the irreparable weakening of the Byzantine Empire following the misguided sacking of Constantinople by the Fourth Crusade in 1204.

In Europe, the Hundred Years' War between England and France, from the fourteenth to the fifteenth century, was marked by three battles: Crécy (1346), Poitiers (1356), and Agincourt (1415). Their outcomes reflected the gradual change in performance of archers and heavy cavalry, which was organized for frontal charges and limited in mobility by the weight of armor. The crossbow became more important because of the ability of its bolts to penetrate armor, but remained slow to reload. At Crécy, the six-foot long bow could launch arrows almost five hundred feet, with skilled archers capable of firing eight to ten arrows per minute. Uneven terrain, which impeded the charge of the more numerous French knights, also contributed to the victory of the English at Crécy.

However, the real return to infantry was due to the Swiss. The English won battles with a combination of archers and cavalry, but the Swiss won with their infantry alone. In the battle of Morgarten (1315), Swiss soldiers in square formations defeated the Austrian cavalry. The Austrians, who came to repress restive cantons clamoring for freedom, were routed in a gorge. Later, at Laupen, near Berne (1339), and Sempach (1386), the Swiss square would again triumph over the Austrians and their allies. The Swiss soldiers standing shoulder to shoulder came, not only from the same canton, but from the same valley. Their cohesiveness and patriotism, born of the recently proclaimed freedom in the first three cantons, partly explains Swiss superiority. The Swiss tactic, based on the use of the pike, could be either offensive or defensive, since the Swiss squares could resist on four sides. The Swiss troops were ruthless and ready to die when necessary.

Swiss pikes were over five meters long, making it difficult to reach behind the hedge of pikes created by the first several rows of soldiers. The usual formation consisted of 250 men organized in squares consisting of 16 × 16 rows. Each square also included a small corps of crossbowmen. For almost a century and a half, this Swiss formation was the most successful in Europe.

Firearms appeared progressively over more than a century before they became decisive in the eighteenth century. Long before, from the seventh century until the thirteenth, "Greek fire" had been the secret weapon of the Byzantine Empire, especially in naval battles. The iron bombard firing stone cannonballs appeared in 1325. Its reach was well over two hundred yards. The harquebus appeared on the battlefield in 1425. Mobile bronze cannons that shot iron cannonballs were introduced in 1444 and helped expel the English from France less than ten years later. A giant cannon cast by a renegade Hungarian would help the Ottomans take Constantinople in 1453.

The iron cannon was inexpensive, and bronze cannons, heavier and much more costly, were less widely used on the battlefield. Bronze cannons could weigh as much as three thousand kilos, making them difficult to transport, but their greater firepower was often worth the cost. The crossbow remained in use until the beginning of the sixteenth century, when it was gradually replaced by the harquebus, which had greater firepower, but a shorter range, and was slower to reload. Firearms progressively improved. Gunpowder was also used outside of Europe, although little is known about its deployment in combat.

In 1494, Charles VIII of France surprised Italy with mobile cannons shipped by sea to the port of La Spezia. The use of an armored siege train to take Naples revolutionized the art of war. Cannons proved decisive there, as in the fall of Constantinople forty years earlier.

In the fifteenth century, among tactical innovations, Jan Žižka, who led a peasant rebellion in Bohemia, was one of the first to mount cannons on wheels. He also reemployed the Gothic *Wagenburg*, or wagon fortress, a mobile stronghold consisting of wagons covered with steel plates and linked together in a circle with chains. Between 1420 and 1434, at the head of the Hussites, Žižka made remarkable use of the *Wagenburg* strategy. As soon as an attack was repelled by it, the Hussite cavalry and pikemen would counterattack to seal the enemy's defeat.

At the battle of Marignano (1515), French cannons would put an end to the dominance of Swiss infantry. However, the French were soon outdone by the Spanish, who became the elite troops of Europe. The sixteenth-century battlefield was still dominated by the pike and heavy cavalry. It remained so until the era of Gonzalo de Córdoba and the Spanish *tercio*, a huge formation of up to three thousand infantry, with pikemen in the center and crossbowmen and musketeers on the sides. The Spanish troops were very disciplined and pugnacious and dominated the European battlefield from 1520 to 1620.

Weapons changed slowly. The musket, introduced in Europe around 1520, was a heavy weapon and slow to reload. By the middle of the sixteenth century, a harquebus could still only shoot twice a minute and had an effective range of not much more than a hundred yards. The troops were suspicious of change and slow to adapt to muskets, in part because of the time necessary to reload. Battles were thus often decided by forcefully led cavalry charges.

The Reformation convulsed Europe and unleashed a series of conflicts, culminating in the Thirty Years' War. Important military innovations were made in the forces of Maurice of Nassau, stadtholder of the United Provinces of the Netherlands, during the Dutch rebellion against Catholic Spain, and in those of the Swedish king Gustavus Adolphus (1594–1632). The religious quarrels raging in Europe gave rise to unusual alliances, such as that of France under François I with the Ottomans, formed to weaken the Hapsburgs. A final (Hungarian) attempt at a crusade ended in defeat in the battle of Varna in Bulgaria in 1444. Leaving aside the Catholic coalition that defeated the Ottoman fleet at Lepanto in 1571, there was no longer a confessional basis in Europe for an anti-Muslim alliance.

The revolt of the Netherlands against Catholic Spain lasted over eighty years. Inspired by the discipline of the Roman legions, Maurice of Nassau formed a remarkable army. He standardized artillery and his principal weapon, the howitzer, came to be adopted by many other European countries. Hitherto, siegecraft had lagged behind the art of fortification. Remarkable engineers, such as Niccolò Tartaglia (1500–1557), Edward de Bar-le-Duc, and later the Netherlander Simon Stevin (1548–1620), in the service of Maurice of Nassau, conceived lower and thicker fortifications, while eliminating blind corners. These innovations returned advantage to the defense.

Maurice of Nassau reduced the depth of his infantry formations. The rows were reduced to five instead of fifty, so that more soldiers could participate simultaneously in battle. He introduced a linear formation of fifty pikemen over the five rows, with forty musketeers on the sides arranged in short columns. In total, units contained five hundred men, like a Roman cohort, as described by the humanist Justus Lipsius (1547–1606) in his book *Politicorum sive Civilis doctrinae* (Politics or Civil Doctrine).

These innovations aimed at improving firepower and mobility, to which were added the essential ingredients of the Dutch Protestant army, unusual for the time: discipline, strict drilling, high morale, and regular pay. In contrast, Spanish troops pillaged when they were not paid. During the French wars of religion, the Huguenot commander François de La Noue, called Bras-de-Fer (Iron Arm), who fought in France and Holland, wrote essays on military strategy that influenced Gustavus Adolphus and Cromwell, among others, which are unjustly ignored.*

Until the seventeenth century, galleys dominated the Mediterranean. In the sixteenth century, a well-packed galley could transport four hundred men. The Venetian galley or galleass, was twice as large, and it played an important role at Lepanto. The Turkish galliot (half-galley) was fast and could carry a hundred men with light cannons. Until the sixteenth century, naval battles resembled land battles and were mostly decided by hand-to-hand combat. In the sixteenth century, ocean-going galleons appeared, with heavier cannons for long-distance battle. The era of hand-to-hand naval combat came to an end. The cannon became the foundation of European naval domination. The Portuguese, after rounding the Cape of Good Hope, were able to impose themselves in the Indian Ocean. Their bases at Ormuz (1507), in the Gulf, and at Diu (1509) would enable them to occupy Indonesian and Chinese ports (1557). Meanwhile, the Spanish advanced toward the Philippines and the Americas, beginning in 1492, in voyages that would combine discovery, trade, and war.

The year 1562 marked the beginning of the French religious wars. Six years later, Dutch Protestants revolted against the Catholic domination of Spain. The Reformation sparked a series of conflicts, which soon ravaged all of Europe. Soon after the French and Dutch civil wars, the Thirty Years' War (1618–48) began. These religious conflicts would last eighty years in all and end with Cromwell's Civil War in England.

The Protestants took advantage of advances in the art of fortification and siegecraft. The Huguenot style of fortification was based on a palisade backed by trenches and artillery. The Protestants repelled cavalry charges with soldiers armed with harquebuses called "lost children," since they were undefended by pikemen and were sometimes sacrificed when they failed to halt cavalry charges with sustained fire. After the

---

* See François de La Noue, *Discours politiques et militaires* (1589; Geneva: Droz, 1967). Protestant military thinking was also influenced by Agrippa d'Aubigné's *Histoire universelle* (1616–18) and Henri, duc de Rohan's *Le parfait capitaine* (1631).

end of the sixteenth century, the musket became widespread, despite the fact that it sometimes required more than two minutes to load. By 1650, the range of a wheellock musket was well over two hundred yards, but rain and humidity often made it very difficult to set off the charge. At this time, artillery still played only a peripheral role in many battles.

By the second half of the sixteenth century, cavalry began to use fire-arms. The German introduction of the pistol, fired at short range, was a revolution that spread quickly. It evolved into the caracole, where horse-men armed with two pistols apiece would advance in ranks, turn their horses first to one side and then to the other to discharge their pistols from just out of the range of the enemy pikemen, and then retire to the back of the cavalry formation, up to twelve ranks deep, to reload. Well-coordinated cavalry could deliver a virtually continuous stream of fire.

The French Huguenots sent reinforcements to the Dutch Protestants. François de La Noue would distinguish himself there as a general. The Dutch War of Independence (1568–1648) was not only religious; the Reformation greatly increased the political and economic role of the merchant classes, who would come to play an increasingly important role in seventeenth-century Holland, despite the continued influence of the landed gentry. There were few decisive battles in this war. Dutch dikes, swamps, canals, and estuaries were less conducive to decisive victories than open fields of battle. Military operations were delayed by long sieges and prolonged naval battles. Spain's delays in paying its troops led to a mutiny and the sacking of Antwerp, the largest Netherlandish city of the time, in 1576, a calamity known as the Spanish Fury.

Hostilities of another kind were also faced by Spain, whose galleons were often attacked by pirates supported by the English crown. In 1587, Philip II readied a fleet at Cadiz to invade England. The English priva-teer Sir Francis Drake managed to destroy a portion of the Great Armada, delaying its sailing until the following year. Consisting of 130 ships, including eight galleys, with 7,000 sailors and 17,000 Spanish soldiers, the Armada was an army transported by sea. It was opposed by experienced English captains such as Drake, John Hawkins, and Martin Frobisher, who commanded over a hundred smaller but more maneu-verable ships. The English were victorious, but their victory did not change the balance of power on the continent, which remained largely in favor of Spain.

However, the defeat of the Spanish Armada reduced Spanish pressure on the Netherlands at a time when the House of Orange had an invalu-able leader in Maurice of Nassau. He paid his troops punctually but demanded strict discipline and rigorous training. On the battlefield, his troops proved tactically superior to the Spanish and developed improved siegecraft that enabled them to take previously impregnable fortresses.

Nassau won the battle of Nieuwpoort (1600) with innovative tactics and siegecraft, which may have been of greater importance than the outcome of the battle itself. The rebels recaptured their cities, and the war ended with a truce. The seven Protestant United Provinces became independent, while the southern Netherlands, present-day Belgium, remained Catholic.

Europe was at peace for nine years before the Thirty Years' War, the most murderous war in its history until the twentieth century. The Hapsburgs, backed by the power of Spain and Portugal, sought to crush the German Protestants. The Hapsburg Holy Roman emperor Charles V was king of Spain and was married to Isabella of Portugal. However, Catholic France didn't wish to see the Hapsburgs' power increase and joined with Protestant Sweden to oppose them. Bohemia, Denmark, England, and the United Provinces also sided against the empire. The musket, introduced in the sixteenth century, had improved: it was still slow to shoot, requiring a hundred movements to reload, but had become efficient at distances of over two hundred yards. It could be discharged twice a minute and was heavy enough to require a supporting post.

The Swedish king Gustavus Adolphus, a major figure in the Thirty Years' War, reorganized his army through a series of reforms to improve mobility. Cavalry was strictly reserved for charging enemy lines. The cavalry would fire their pistols and then charge with their sabers. The infantry carried improved muskets, which were capable of firing once a minute, using bullets wrapped in paper, and light enough not to require a mount. Musketeers also had sabers. Pikemen carried shorter and lighter pikes. Gustavus Adolphus's troops, with a large proportion of Swedes and Finns among them, were highly disciplined: pillage and rape were punished by hanging.

For almost a century, the depth of the infantry had been determined by the time needed by musketeers to reload their weapons. Maurice of Nassau reduced the rows to ten after rigorous drills. Gustavus Adolphus, thanks to improved musket design, was able to further reduce them to six rows, thus increasing the mobility of infantry brigades of about fifteen hundred men, half pikemen and the other half musketeers.

The cannon made slow progress until the seventeenth century. In 1624, Gustavus Adolphus introduced a new type of cannon weighing two hundred pounds that could be transported by a single horse and four men. The imperial armies used cannons that weighed half a ton.

Each group of five hundred men in the Swedish army had a cannon, which gave great mobility to Swedish firepower. For the first time, artillery became an integral component of battle and a potent offensive weapon. Finally, the king, at the head of his cavalry, was a commander who knew how to galvanize his troops. His only handicap was the size of his army, which never amounted to more than twenty-five thousand soldiers, and was often much smaller. This didn't stop the Swedish king from winning important battles (e.g., at Breitenfeld in 1631).

Meanwhile, Germany underwent terrible suffering, with pillage, executions, and epidemics that killed one-third or more of the German and Bohemian populations.

France, which sided against the Hapsburgs, won the battle at Rocroi (1643) thanks to Richelieu's disciplined army, inspired by the Swedish model. This victory signaled the end of the supremacy of Spanish infantry and the beginning of French continental hegemony under generals such as Turenne. At sea, the Dutch admiral Cornelis Tromp had crushed the Spanish fleet four years earlier.

It was only in the second half of the sixteenth century that European sovereigns, particularly in France, took effective control of their kingdoms' resources. Once Western sovereigns could raise taxes, they were able to establish permanent armies that could be used to defend the country against foreign enemies and as a coercive force of repression domestically. French influence increased as the power of Spain and the Hapsburgs declined. Richelieu raised taxes to support France's military power, first defined by Michel Le Tellier, and then his son, François Michel Le Tellier, marquis de Louvois, under Louis XIV. The French army, which was placed under the direct control of government ministers, was the largest ever known at the time.

During the Thirty Years' War, most troops were mercenaries. Standing armies increased in the seventeenth century under Louis XIV and his minister, Louvois. Armies became permanent institutions. European armies had generally comprised fewer than fifty thousand men, but Louis XIV's troops numbered as many as four hundred thousand. After adopting the Swedish model of regiments six rows deep with pikemen in the middle and musketeers on the flanks, Louvois reorganized the rest of the army, including heavy and light cavalry, fortifications (under the military engineer Vauban), and logistics. Vauban's theories dominated the technique of fortification and siege in the seventeenth century.

He built thirty fortresses to protect the borders of France and remodeled hundreds more. His siege technique was based on a system of parallels. The first trench was dug about five hundred meters from the walls of the fortress, at the distance reachable by a cannonball of the time. The trench was parallel to the fortress walls. Cannons were installed in the trenches. Under protective fire, sappers dug perpendicular trenches in a zigzag design to limit the efficiency of enemy firepower. During this work, sappers were protected by sandbags. At three hundred meters from the fort, a second trench was excavated, using the same precautions. Then, still protected by cannon fire, the sappers again dug trenches in a zigzag pattern, as previously. At this time, the reserve infantry occupied the second trench, in order to counterattack the besieged if they attempted to escape. Finally, the most perilous trench was constructed, next to the moat, from where artillery volleys could be fired at the castle wall at point-blank range to open gaps and allow the final assault.

These innovations were used all throughout the following century, when sieges were frequent. In spite of Colbert's opposition, Louvois also built a navy, which became the most powerful in the world from 1685 to 1690. The English and the Dutch, even with their admirals Tromp and Michiel de Ruyter, were outclassed. However, the importance of naval power was not appreciated by Louis XIV, notwithstanding the advice of Admiral de Tourville, and the French navy declined.

The seventeenth century, after Gustavus Adolphus, heralded great army captains such as Condé, Turenne, and Raimondo Montecuccoli, who defeated the Turks at the battle of Saint Gotthard (1644). This century also saw European power begin to exceed that of other continents. European strategic thinking, anemic and long dormant, reemerged. Machiavelli, who linked the business of war and government for the first time, was the only exceptional European military theorist since Vegetius.

England had not participated in the Thirty Years' War, but didn't escape the consequences. The English Civil Wars opposed the king and the aristocracy to Parliament and led to the rise of Oliver Cromwell (1642). Cromwell organized a small, highly disciplined and motivated cavalry. Soon, he was authorized to raise an army of volunteers organized according to the principles of Gustavus Adolphus, emphasizing the importance of mobile artillery, cavalry for the final charge, and infantry in six rows. In the course of the second Civil War, Cromwell won the battle of Dunbar (1650). The following year was a further disaster for the royalists. A militant religious ideology contributed to Cromwell's success. He ruled as a dictator for seven years. Protestantism triumphed in England, limiting the divine right of the kings and empowering Parliament.

Shallow ranks, introduced by Gustavus Adolphus, became the rule in the next century. These enabled continuous fire by having each row fire in succession while previous ranks reloaded. In the eighteenth century, the troops were arranged in six rows and fired from the last row to the first, shooting when necessary over the heads of soldiers who reloaded their weapons on their knees. Thus the fire was continuous. As the speed of the shooting increased, the depth of the formations decreased. In the eighteenth century, they were reduced to three or four rows. However, the change from the line to the column was slow, and battles remained static.

There were many technical innovations. The bayonet made its appearance (1703) and was attached to the musket, further reducing the role of the pikemen. The flintlock rifle was introduced around 1760–70. It could be fired twice a minute and was accurate at three hundred meters. Artillery underwent even more spectacular advances. The Swedish cannon of 1620 that could be fired once a minute was followed by Florent-Jean de Vallière's French cannon of 1732 that could be fired three times a minute, with a range of six hundred meters. The remarkable cannon subsequently developed by Jean-Baptiste Vaquette de Gribeauval (1715–89) could be fired four times a minute, at a range of some two miles, with frightful accuracy up to almost 1,650 yards. This was the artillery used during the battles of the Revolution and, with minor improvements, during the French First Empire.

The European powers had long confronted each other in a relatively small geographic area, covering about one-third of Europe, but the stage of conflicts enlarged starting in the sixteenth century. The field of battle reached its maximal extent between the middle of the nineteenth and twentieth century, when it not only included Africa north of the Sahara, but extended worldwide. The Spanish had already invaded Cuba and San Domingo, and from there proceeded to conquer Mexico and Guatemala. Then, from Central America, they conquered Peru, Colombia, Chile, and La Plata. Christianity followed military conquests. In the meantime, the Portuguese circumnavigated Africa and had occupied Brazil.

In the same century, the Russians, recently freed from the Mongols and helped by the Cossacks, advanced across the steppes as far as the Sea of Okhotsk. This first European push in the sixteenth century, by sea routes in the west and by land in the east, was followed by a second push in the seventeenth and eighteenth centuries. The Dutch colonized Indonesia, and the English India. The Ottomans constantly retreated in the face of the Russians and the Hapsburgs in the eighteenth century. The French and the English colonized North America. A third surge took place in the nineteenth century, after the Napoleonic Wars. Progressively, until the last quarter of the nineteenth century, the largest part of the Afro-Asian world was colonized by Europeans: India, Indochina, Australia, New Zealand, Algeria, Tunisia, Egypt, and all of Africa south of the Sahara, with the exception of Abyssinia and Liberia. In the eighteenth century, the Russian Empire had retaken lands conquered by the Ottomans and the Tatars' conquests north of the Black Sea (the Crimea). Russia then took the Caucasus from Qajar Persia, conquered the Central Asian Muslim states (Kazaks, Uzbeks, Turkmen, Tadjiks), and drove the Manchus from the Ussuri River and the north of Manchuria. In the beginning of the twentieth century, Europeans occupied Morocco and Libya. At the end of World War I, Great Britain and France divided the formerly Ottoman Near East into "mandates." In geopolitical terms, the centuries from 1492 (the European discovery of America) to 1945 marked the globalization of conflicts and the hegemony of Europe and its cultural heir, America.

The maritime dimension of the globe became all-important by the end of the fifteenth century, when the nomads lost their military superiority. Naval battles became more frequent in the eighteenth century. Mercenary troops remained important from the fifteenth to eighteenth centuries: Swiss, Scots, Germans, Croats, and Hungarians enlisted and fought indifferently for whoever paid them. The generals themselves, until the eighteenth century, often served rival sovereigns. They could fight in turn for the Hapsburgs, then for the Russian tsar or the Swedish king. France's great Condé joined Spain during the Fronde, and Prince Eugène of Savoy served the Hapsburgs. As for the soldiers, they often came from the lower class and were treated by their officers with severity and disdain.

Until the innovation, improvement, and spread of firepower under Frederick II of Prussia, the superiority of an army did not primarily reside in its armament. The decisive factors in the battle plan of the commander were the organization, drilling, cohesiveness, and morale of the troops. Even the number of troops was not always decisive, as we can see in the battle of Cannae and in many of Napoleon's victories.

When Frederick II, later known as Frederick the Great, ascended the Prussian throne in 1740, he inherited from his father an excellent army numbering eighty thousand men, out of a population of two and a half million. Forty years later, the Prussian army would number a quarter of a million men, out of a population of five million. (For comparison, Louis XIV's France, with a population of twenty million, had an army of four hundred thousand, which was three or four times bigger than any previous army in Europe.) Prussia became a formidable military power.

In the first phase of reorganization, Frederick II improved the offensive capacity of his army: mobility, and rapid firing, as a result of strict drilling skills, allowed the soldiers to maneuver with unequaled cohesion. When necessary, Frederick used diagonal lines of troops, like Epaminondas. Usually, he pressed the attack thanks to great speed, using an infantry organized in three lines, flanked by cavalry and supported by horse-drawn artillery. He later came to realize the decisive role of firepower in attack and considerably reinforced his artillery.

Frederick II also introduced innovations in logistics. He organized supplies in mobile units that would travel with the armies. Frederick operated within a radius of thirty-eight miles, with four days' supplies always available. With the creation of divisions, logistics became yet more complicated. From then on, there would be a line of operation and a line of communication protected by positions and detachments at intervals between the base of operations and the supply depot from where the division advanced.

Thanks to his talent, innovations, and the excellence of his troops, Frederick II won exceptional tactical victories, such as at Leuthen in Silesia in 1757, where his army of thirty-six thousand defeated the Austrian army commanded by Prince Charles Alexander of Lorraine, which was twice its size.

Frederick II of Prussia was the great military figure of the eighteenth century. Firepower already played an important role in battles, but Jacques de Guibert (1715–89) signaled another type of war in his *Traité général de la tactique* (General Treatise on Tactics). The second part of the eighteenth century brought a change in strategy.

Artillery had improved its mobility and was standardized by Gribeauval. The division system and, soon, the column were instituted. The deep formation was preferred to the narrow one, the goal being the charge and not the defensive line. Light infantry, composed of small battalions of *voltigeurs* (skirmishers), moving as needed, broke with the rigid order of the armies of the first part of the eighteenth century. It revolutionized war with new ideas born of the Revolution: those of the sovereign nation and mass conscription in the most populous country in Europe.

With conscription, Gribeauval's division system, and artillery, France already had an exceptional army when an outstanding general emerged: Bonaparte. After trying a voluntary army, then unequal conscription, the Republic chose uniform mandatory service in August 1793. By the end of 1794, 700,000 men were in arms. Napoleon's draft amounted to 10 percent of a population of 26 million. However, by 1812, more than half of the Grande Armée would be foreign-born.

After the French Revolution, wars ceased to be battles between dynasties, and became battles between nations. Thus began, for a century and a half, the era of what Clausewitz called "absolute wars." Political and social upheavals in France produced significant changes in military organization starting in 1793. The army was based on the nation-state and became the expression of the mobilized nation. War changed in nature: It was carried to greater excess (Carnot).

Napoleon inherited the revolutionary conditions of the most populous country on the continent, excluding Russia. He organized the army, as the British historian Michael Howard notes, based on unlimited decentralization under one supreme commander, a model that would be adopted in all European armies during the next century and a half.

With Napoleon almost four centuries of a Western strategy that had often been based on delaying tactics came to an end. He systematically sought to deliver a decisive blow and annihilate the enemy. Napoleon not only won battles after forced marches by concentrating his troops at precise points of weakness, but also pursued enemies in order to rout them completely. His genius lay in his skill at disrupting the enemy's center of gravity, his tactics, and his strategic use of arms.

Napoleon introduced a more mobile and efficient artillery and a lighter, mobile infantry, and simplified logistics on the battlefield by having each soldier carry four days' supplies. The French army's exceptional mobility allowed it to strike the adversary's flanks or front, or both at the same time, with an enveloping maneuver. Operations were simplified, well drilled, and executed under an effectively structured, unified command. Napoleon always attacked while sparing most of the army for a concentrated assault at a critical point in the battle. The cavalry was used both to break the enemy's lines and in pursuit operations after victory to assure the annihilation of the enemy. Finally, cavalry *voltigeurs* were used to surprise the enemy and avoid being surprised. The victorious campaign of Italy was followed by more victories until the campaign of Russia, which was a failure of logistics due to the scorched-earth policy of the retreating Russian army, aided by climate and distance. At sea, the battle of Trafalgar (1805) destroyed the French fleet, signaling the dominance of the British navy.

The French victory over the Prussian army at Jena (1806) kindled a Prussian military reawakening and the development of military strategists including Scharnhorst and Clausewitz. A more meritocratic and efficient patriotic army was needed to face the French, but reforms were deemed dangerous and were unpopular among the European aristocracy. The Prussians reformed by enabling commoners to become career officers, a role hitherto limited to the nobility. After 1813, Prussian patriotism grew and a great coalition of European sovereigns proved capable of defeating Napoleon. However, military art remained influenced by the strategy of Napoleon as reflected in the writings of Clausewitz and Jomini. The Prussians and Russians raised large armies. However, with its naval superiority, Great Britain reduced the number of its troops from 685,000 to 100,000 as early as 1821 and sent half of them to its colonies. During half of the nineteenth century (1830 to 1871), both the French and British armies were primarily occupied with the suppression of domestic upheavals and with colonial expansion.

The nineteenth century was also marked by industrialization and the rise of new powers such as Germany, and, to a lesser extent, Russia and the United States, although the military power of the latter remained far inferior to its industrial capacity. However, the American Civil War was the first modern war from the industrial point of view: railroads played a decisive role, as did naval blockades and firepower.

Whereas the populations of Germany and Great Britain tripled during the nineteenth century, the population of the United States, due to immigration, increased fifteenfold. The population of Europe in the nineteenth century rose from 185 million to 400 million, with only the populations of France and Ireland remaining stagnant. Great Britain, thanks to its maritime superiority, which was unrivaled after 1805, became the world's dominant financial and colonial power. However, by 1890–1900, the industrial power of the United States had even overtaken that of Germany, the greatest industrial power in Europe. Military innovations in the nineteenth century depended on important scientific and industrial innovations:

- The railroad revolutionized logistics, greatly speeding the transport of troops and supplies in comparison with transport by horses or on foot.

- Firepower increased vastly during and after the American Civil War: the rifled cannon enhanced range and accuracy; rifles and cannons became breech-loading, greatly increasing their firing rates; and the introduction of the machine gun and more mobile artillery facilitated well-organized tactical defenses.

- Military communications improved due to the telephone (1876) and the radio, first with Hertz (1885), then with Marconi (1908). The first undersea cable was laid in 1866.

- Naval advances also occurred with the introduction of steel ships, improvements in marine engine design, and larger and more accurate heavy-caliber guns. The "dreadnought" became the new ship of the line.

- Sanitary conditions also improved after the Crimean War (1854–56). Until then, up to 80 percent of combatant deaths were the result of epidemics or wound infections. By the end of the century, these causes would account for 20 percent of fatalities.

The American Civil War (1860–65) heralded the advent of total war, but its lessons went largely unheeded by European chiefs of staff. In both the American North and South, the conflict was at first thought likely to be of short duration. Neither side thought that it would be necessary to mobilize all its human and material resources. The South mobilized one million men, and the more populous North twice as many. The economic resources of the North were infinitely superior to those of the South. The North also benefitted from its maritime superiority, which enabled a blockade of southern ports, and its more advanced railway network, which gave it the capacity to easily move troops by rail. The observation balloon and the telegraph appeared on the battlefield, the breech-loading rifle became more common, and the Gatling machine gun made its appearance. Starting in 1863, the South was split in two, but the fighting continued, relentlessly, until 1865, when the South had been bled dry. The Civil War produced 620,000 casualties, with roughly equal numbers on the two sides. It would be the deadliest war in U.S. history, producing nearly as many casualties as all other American wars—before and since—combined.

Another military innovation was instituted by Prussia in the 1860s. It established a new type of chief of staff, both political and military, whose influence would be decisive until the middle of the twentieth century. The idea was introduced by Scharnhorst and implemented under Helmuth von Moltke, who introduced the study of military theory and tactics, along with permanent rotation of the top chiefs of staff and officers, to facilitate the circulation of stimulating ideas. Admission to war colleges was through competitive examinations. Those who graduated became assistants to the chiefs of staff for two years and were responsible for organizing maneuvers, map exercises, and *Kriegspielen* (war games).

By the eve of the 1870 Franco-Prussian war, most Prussian officers had undergone this training. After 1871, all continental European powers would adopt the model. The long hegemony of the French army, which had lasted since the second half of the seventeenth century, came to an end. Three decades later, Great Britain and the United States would adopt this model too.

However, by the beginning of the twentieth century, technology had wrought more radical changes than were anticipated by even the most astute commanders. Contrary to predictions, the duration of wars would increase. And, in spite of the primacy of attack, defensive strategies would prove decisive. New armaments had made war more static and increased the cost in human and material resources. In short, besides morale, war became more dependent on industrial production. War at sea became increasingly important. And so, in a long war, any coalition supported by the great industrial power of the United States could not lose.

During World War I, together with mass propaganda, a series of new arms appeared: the submarine; the tank, which would play its greatest role in World War II; and the airplane. The Germans laid plans for a two-front war against their continental adversaries as early as 1905. They would strike the French with a pincer maneuver and capture Paris before turning against the Russians, who would take longer to mobilize. This plan was modified and yet failed in World War I, since progress bogged down in the French trenches. But the Russians were defeated (1917). In the Near East, an allied expedition to put the Ottoman Empire out of action ended in failure at Gallipoli (April 1915). Not until 1917 were the Allies able to control the Orient.

The carnage in World War I was terrible: artillery, and, soon, poison gas produced millions of casualties on the two sides on the Western Front alone. General staffs realized that their doctrines had become outdated owing to murderous technological increases in firepower. The machine gun (Maxim, 1884; Hotchkiss, 1897) had, however, already proven its formidable efficiency in the colonial wars of the late nineteenth century and early twentieth centuries, and little seems to have been learned either from the Russo-Japanese war in Manchuria (1904–5).

British and American naval superiority allowed the Americans to intervene on European soil. The French managed to advance in the Balkans. However, early enthusiasm for the war was quickly followed by deep, potentially mutinous, disenchantment. Europe discovered that mobilization would affect all social classes, and that civilians would not be spared the consequences of the war.

By the end of the war in November 1918, France, whose territory included most of the Western Front, had lost 1.7 million young men out of a population of thirty-nine million. The British Empire lost one million men, and Italy lost six hundred thousand. Germany lost two million from its population of almost seventy million.

When World War II erupted in Europe twenty years after the blood bath of World War I, the blitzkrieg, based on combined tank and airplane attacks, made mobility a dominant factor. Prior to World War II, J. F. C. Fuller in Great Britain, Hans von Seeckt in Germany, and General Jean-Baptiste Estienne in France were strong proponents of mechanized force. Marshal of the Royal Air Force Sir Hugh Trenchard had persuaded the British government to endow Great Britain with a very precious instrument, the RAF, which kept the German Luftwaffe in check in 1940. The Manstein plan, executed by Heinz Guderian and his tanks, enabled the Germans to break through French lines in the Ardennes and surround French and British forces. In less than two months, France was forced to sign an armistice.

In World War II, as in the preceding Spanish Civil War, civilian populations became targets. Entire ethnic groups would disappear because of racist Nazi ideology. The morale of civilian populations was targeted in bombings of Coventry, Tokyo, and Dresden (200,000 dead), and with the dropping of the atomic bomb on Hiroshima (70,000 dead) and Nagasaki (130,000 dead).

The success of the blitzkrieg was based on logistics. After Stalingrad, logistical failures compelled Germany to a gradual retreat in good order that would last two years. Great Britain held, and the Soviet Union as of 1941 waged most of the ground war. Japan condemned itself to defeat as early as Pearl Harbor (December 7, 1941) by forcing the United States to enter the War of the Pacific. However, Japan's victories over European powers in Asia (Philippines, Indonesia, Indochina, Singapore, Malaysia) would contribute to new anti-colonialist movements that would soon develop in Asia. The United States, with its industrial might, played a pivotal role on both fronts. Beginning in 1942, the United States alone would defeat the Japanese in the Pacific. The importance of aviation increased greatly with the introduction of aircraft carriers and improved aircraft (B17, B24, and B29). Napalm was used, and missiles appeared (V1 and V2), as well as radar.

The development of nuclear weapons was a qualitative change that revised military strategy. The conflict between the United States and the Soviet Union, between the free world and the Communist states, became the Cold War in 1947. It was punctuated with crises (Berlin, 1948; Cuba, 1962), but direct conflict between the two superpowers was avoided by nuclear dissuasion based on a balance of terror. Any nuclear aggressor would be sure to suffer catastrophic counterstrikes. George Kennan's policy of containment would dominate Western strategic thinking as early as the beginning of the 1950s (the Korean War).

Technological advances were considerable in the second half of the twentieth century, including the hydrogen bomb (1952), intercontinental ballistic missiles launched from land or sea, and nuclear submarines. While these new technologies were developed, guerrilla conflicts occurred, pitting the weak against the strong in battles that used conventional weapons. The Cold War largely played out in conflicts outside developed countries, in what the countries of the Northern Hemisphere then called the Third World, that is, former colonial or semi-colonial states. The unexpected collapse of Communist states in Central Europe and the Balkans, followed by the demise of the Soviet Union in 1991, put an end to forty-five years of hostility. The 1991 Gulf War was made possible by the collapse of the USSR. Saddam Hussein's regime subsequently became a preemptive target for the George W. Bush administration, inaugurating an altered global strategy in the Middle East.

Terrorism, often a substitute for guerrilla warfare, had experienced significant growth since 1968. Shiite Islam emerged in brutal form in Iran in 1979. In the same year, Sunni insurgents, strongly encouraged by the United States, Saudi Arabia, and Pakistan, began to weaken the Soviet hold on Afghanistan. After the Russians left Afghanistan (1989), the same Islamist fundamentalists turned against the United States, and explicitly against "crusaders and the Jews." Al Qaida's attack on the World Trade Center on September 11, 2001, gave rise to the largest counterterrorist operation that the world had ever seen, beginning with attacks on the Afghan sanctuaries where jihadi volunteers from Saudi Arabia, Egypt, Bosnia, Chechnya, Kashmir, and other countries had trained. In the course of the 1990s, U.S. technological progress was particularly important and led to new theories of future warfare, the so-called Revolution in Military Affairs (RMA). Technological developments gave U.S. forces undisputable supremacy. Twice, in Bosnia (1993) and Kosovo (1999), Europeans were forced to call on the United States to settle medium-sized European conflicts.

The war of choice against Iraq, led by U.S. and British forces, was justified by the assumption that Iraq was developing weapons of mass destruction (WMD). It aimed at establishing a bridgehead in the Middle East to remodel the region (Syria-Lebanon and Iran) in the interests of the United States and its regional allies, especially Israel. The American interventions in Iraq and Afghanistan were not a strategic success, and the strategic balance is gradually shifting as a consequence of the increasing economic weight of Asian nations, particularly China.

CHAPTER 2

The First Military Empire

The Assyrians

From the time of the first city-states, at the dawn of history, such as Uruk, Sargon, Akkad, and Babylon, war was one of the most important functions. The first military empire was incontestably that of the Assyrians. Historians of the ancient Near East call it "Neo-Assyrian." Assyria lived through two distinct periods: the first from the fourteenth to the eleventh century B.C.E., when it already evinces martial skills, and the second, Neo-Assyrian period from the ninth to the seventh century B.C.E. During this period, Assyria created an empire through a series of yearly campaigns. It conquered all of Mesopotamia, part of western Iraq, southeastern Anatolia, Syria-Palestine, and finally, Egypt. Assyria ruled the ancient world of its time.

A TRIUMPHAL EXPANSION

At the beginning of its triumphal expansion, Assyria was surrounded by four important states: Babylon in the south, Elam in the southeast, Urartu in the north, and Egypt. In the ninth century, the Assyrian sovereigns imposed their domination on the north of Mesopotamia, the eastern part of present-day Syria, and a southeastern portion of Anatolia. In the course of the ninth–seventh centuries, half a dozen energetic Assyrian sovereigns adopted a deliberate and systematic policy aimed at the building of a "universal empire" that would dominate the known world.

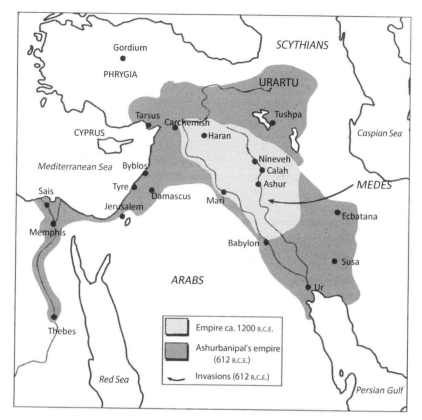

MAP 1. The Assyrian Empire, 1200–612 B.C.E.

Assyria was the first militarized society in the world. Its social structure was based on the same hierarchical organization as its army. Administrative duties were defined in military terms. At the top of this hierarchy was the king. His first responsibility was to wage war for the profit of the god Ashur and the state, with the sovereign himself leading his troops in annual campaigns. The most important dignitaries, all from illustrious families, were the governors of provinces, either in the initial Assyrian state or in the newly conquered regions. Fairly soon, in the middle of the eighth century, the Assyrian sovereigns replaced these illustrious family heirs with eunuchs to reduce conflicts of succession.

The essential goal of ancient warfare was to obtain slaves from those conquered and to exact an annual tribute from the newly occupied regions. In addition, warriors indulged in immediate looting, a quick reward for victorious fights. The winner acquired additional slave man-power and requisitioned the resources of the conquered adversaries.

At the beginning of the Assyrian empire, campaigns traditionally occurred after the harvest, when men became available. However, after the empire's expansion (750–650 B.C.E.), farm work was done by the slaves, and the campaigns occurred year round. The army also con-scripted defeated contingents into the Assyrian military. When Assyria began to establish its hegemony over Syria-Palestine, the Phoenicians were entrusted with building an Assyrian fleet. The state was central-ized, and the sovereigns poured resources into the instrument of their power: the army. The riches acquired by conquest were used mostly to build capitals and monuments to the glory of the victorious sovereign and the god who favored him.

Like others before and after them, if yet more cruel than most, the Assyrians used terror as a calculated weapon in their arsenal. They let it be known during sieges, which were sometimes long and costly, that the consequences of the defeat would be so catastrophic that it would be preferable to surrender. To be a slave was better than being tortured and killed. As an example, the Assyrians would display the mutilated bodies of adversaries, their skin swollen with air, in front of the besieged city's walls. If a city continued to resist, its houses would be destroyed and its fields covered with salt.

As the empire expanded, the deportation of defeated populations to provide labor became systematic.* It is estimated that during the three centuries of its existence, four million people were deported to Assyrian centers, either to populate new cities or to settle populations at the periphery of the empire. This also enabled the empire to recruit the craftsmen that it needed. Thus, a part of the Jewish population of Samaria was deported to the Zagros mountains, east of the core of Assyria.

The power of the empire was reflected in the progressive rebuilding of its capital city. Ashur, the first capital, was abandoned, and Ashurba-nipal II (883–859) built a new and larger capital at Kalhu (Nimrud), surrounded by a wall eight kilometers long. The palace at the top of the citadel measured 200 × 120 meters and took fifteen years to build. Kalhu remained the capital for a century and a half until Sargon II (721–705) built Dur-Sharrukin, a new, larger city, with two citadels.

---

* Bustenay Oded, *Mass Deportations and Deportees in the Neo-Assyrian Empire* (Wiesbaden: L. Reichet, 1979).

Finally, Sennacherib (704–681) renovated the ancient city of Nineveh and made it his capital. Its twelve-kilometer wall surrounded 750 hectares. These sites have not yet been completely excavated, but some of them, like Kalhu, have revealed the wealth of the royal tombs.

Abundant documents, lacking in most previous societies, reveal the power of the Neo-Assyrian empire and chronicle its rulers' military campaigns and building activities. Time is measured relative to important events in a sovereign's reign (e.g., "At the time of my sixth campaign . . ."). The two sovereigns who laid the foundation of the new empire were Ashurbanipal II and Shalmaneser III (859–824). After a series of campaigns, they occupied the region that extends from the Zagros Mountains to the Euphrates, an area frequently invaded by semi-nomadic highlanders. They also dominated the region from the Taurus Mountains to the outskirts of Babylonia. From these territories, it was easy to cross the Euphrates and launch incursions toward the Mediterranean whenever the states in the Syrian-Palestinian corridor were weakened.

Mesopotamia lies between two rivers without natural defenses to either the west or the east. There are only two choices in this region, conquer or be conquered. The Assyrians chose the first alternative. In the north, the Neo-Assyrian empire put an end to Hittite attacks. These are called Neo-Hittites in Middle Eastern historical terminology. In the fourteenth and thirteenth centuries B.C.E., their great dynasties had previously clashed with Egypt. The kingdom of Urartu (Ararat), lying roughly between Lake Van and the present-day city of Yerevan, was another formidable power that the Assyrians conquered.

The Assyrians distinguished between Assyrian territories that were Assyrianized and those under their domination. Those under Assyrian domination were nominally independent states whose sovereigns paid tribute to the Assyrian sovereign and not to the god Ashur, whose cult was not imposed on foreigners. The vassal sovereigns were bound by treaties, and any lapse in tributary payment was punished with maximum force.

In such a centralized structure, dynastic quarrels could become catastrophic. To prevent such occurrences, the powers of provincial governors and generals were gradually reduced. The ninth-century expansion reestablished the past Assyrian grandeur of the second millennium.

The great Neo-Assyrian empire was established within a period of one hundred and thirty years (745–612) and dominated the Near East, including Egypt. Thanks to its remarkable sovereigns, it extended its territorial domination to dimensions never before seen. Tiglath-Pileser III (744–727), Shalmaneser (726–722), Sargon (721–705), Sennacherib (704–681), Esarhaddon (680–669), and Ashurbanipal III (668–627) each played an important role.

As with many other empires, Assyria fell because of its size and internal divisions when faced with a coalition of adversaries seeking to destroy its hegemony. However, before its fall, Assyria reached a military power unsurpassed until the rise of Alexander the Great.

Tiglath-Pileser III restructured and centralized the Neo-Assyrian administration. Around the middle of the eighth century B.C.E., many province governors behaved like small kings who acceded to royal authority. As to external affairs, Tiglath-Pileser attacked Urartu in the north and annexed the tributary states west of the Euphrates, which were previously independent. A great part of Syria and the north of the kingdom of Israel were annexed. Tiglath-Pileser III's last campaign brought him to Babylonia. Expansion continued under Shalmaneser and then Sargon II, who occupied Samaria and deported much of its population, sending Jews to the north and east of Mesopotamia. Other populations replaced them. The kingdom of Judea, on the other hand, remained a tributary state, as did the Phoenician ports, whose trade was important for the Assyrians. Sargon II defeated the Elamites and started a new campaign to subjugate the Babylonians.

The control of Babylonia, so culturally important to Assyria, proved complex. In the south, the swamp region escaped control and served as a haven for the enemy Chaldeans. In the north, power alternated between the Assyrian sovereigns and independent Babylonian states. In order to put an end to the political difficulties with Babylon, Sennacherib succeeded in capturing and sacking the city after a siege of more than a year. Babylon was razed to the ground and its population deported. Rebuilding was forbidden.

His son Esarhaddon decided to rebuild the city. He conquered Egypt as far as Memphis (671). The last of the great Assyrian sovereigns, Ashurbanipal III, had only mediocre heirs. In 612, Nineveh fell under joint attacks by the Medes and the Scythians.

THE ASSYRIAN MILITARY

The most important reform instituted by Tiglath-Pileser III was the creation of a standing army. History shows that military superiority almost always goes to societies that know how to build and maintain a large enough corps of professional soldiers. Only the nomad warriors of Central Asia naturally possessed such an advantage when they were lucky enough to have a great leader. The weakness of feudal armies—whether Frankish or Arab—arose from the undisciplined character of the barons and the seasonal availability of troops. As for mercenaries, they were worth what their officers were worth, and their services were dependent on the regularity of their pay.

War was the basis of power and prosperity in the Assyrian empire. The Assyrians replaced bronze weapons with steel as early as 1000 B.C.E., long before their neighbors. Tiglath-Pileser's professional army was equipped with the best weapons of its time, superior to those of the ancient Hittites. Like all the armies of the time, the Assyrian army had a corps of archers and a considerable number of spearmen, and the discipline of these troops was very strict, unlike that of the later troops of the Achaemenids. The major Assyrian weapon was the chariot, often supported by a small but efficient cavalry.

The Assyrian army in the eighth and seventh centuries B.C.E. was a professional army with excellent equipment, discipline, and a capacity to campaign in any season. It inspired terror in its neighbors and appeared invincible. It was thus able to defeat a series of enemies—Cimmerian nomads, the highlanders of Urartu, and troops from the plains of Babylon and Egypt—with different styles of combat. When conquering a city, the Assyrians were selective. They besieged major centers, such as Babylon and Sidon, but elsewhere they relied on terror. Their siegecraft far surpassed that of the neighboring societies, and was based on the construction of high towers intended to attack the wall directly at the crenellation level of the battlement. In addition, powerful and well-sheltered rams were used to smash open the doors of the enemy stronghold, while archers in the Assyrian siege towers prevented the besieged from intervening. Once again, it was efficiency more than technique that distinguished the Assyrians in battle. Their superior training and organization gave them an advantage.

The Assyrians responded brutally to the threats of the tough highlanders of northern Mesopotamia. Their policy of terror, which paralyzed their adversaries when they became aware of the consequences of defeat, contributed to the relative calm during the centuries of Assyrian hegemony.

Around 640 B.C.E., the Assyrian empire reached its apogee, extending from Persia to Egypt. Ashurbanipal III took Thebes in 663 B.C.E. The Assyrian conquest of Egypt stretched the empire to its limit. All its potential enemies were defeated. Ashurbanipal's long reign lasted until 627 B.C.E. Fifteen years later, Nineveh fell and the empire collapsed.

What are the factors that contributed to its fall besides its sheer size? Assyrian occupations provoked constant unrest and disorder. Babylon and Babylonia were difficult to control and quick to rebel. In 626 B.C.E., a local chief of Assyrian origins declared his independence. Soon afterward, the Medes, who had grown stronger, formed an alliance with Babylon (615).

Ashurbanipal's heirs were not able to appreciate the threat. The Medes, Babylonians, and Scythians formed an alliance and conquered Nineveh (612). Babylon controlled Mesopotamia and Syria-Palestine, while the Medes controlled southeastern Anatolia, western Persia, and the Zagros region. It may be that extreme centralization in the hands of a mediocre ruler is a weakness, whereas it is an asset with an able sovereign. The concept of primogeniture was unknown, and disputes over succession, such as those that erupted between Ashurbanipal and his brother, divided the state and contributed further to the fall of the first military empire.

CHAPTER 3

The Grand Strategy
of the Byzantine Empire

The Byzantine Empire, also known as the Eastern Roman Empire, has received relatively little attention from Western historians, with the exception of a small group of Byzantine specialists. Indeed, the adjective "Byzantine" is often used to refer to matters that are too complex and arcane to merit study. Nevertheless, "Byzantine quarrels" defined Christian theology during the six hundred years that preceded the definitive separation of the Roman Catholic and Greek Orthodox churches in 1054. The Byzantine Empire itself lasted nearly a thousand years after the fall of the Western Roman Empire (476). It survived so long because of an innovative political and military strategy that enabled it to adapt to an often hostile environment, using diplomacy and force to defeat its powerful enemies. No theoretical treatise on the art of war between Vegetius and Machiavelli surpasses the Byzantine masterpiece attributed to the Byzantine emperor Maurice in the late sixth century, the *Stratēgikon.*

To western Europeans, the Byzantine policy of using treaties, concords, and alliances in preference to military force seemed devious. Like the British Empire, the Byzantines sought to pit one enemy against another, looked for alliances that would undermine enemy coalitions, and often sued for peace to avoid war. Above all, Byzantine intelligence kept the emperors well informed about the morale and strategy of their adversaries. However, Byzantine diplomacy would have been much less effective without the formidable Byzantine army, which was capable of

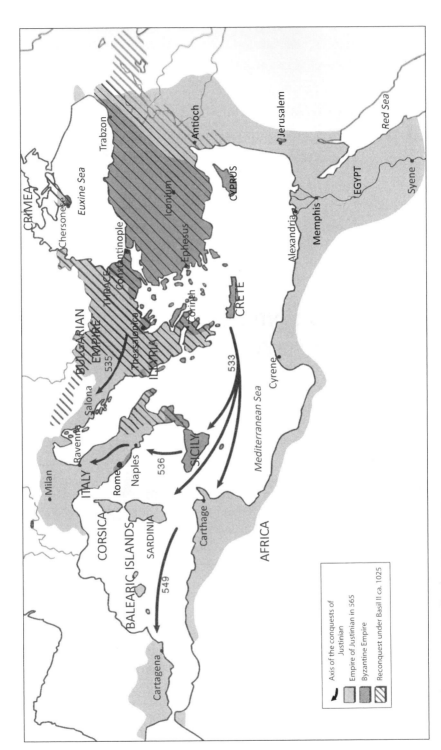

MAP 2. The Eastern Roman Empire, 527–1025 C.E.

Legend:
- Axis of the conquests of Justinian
- Empire of Justinian in 565
- Byzantine Empire
- Reconquest under Basil II ca. 1025

imposing its will if diplomacy failed. Under Justinian I (sixth century) and the Macedonian dynasty (867–1056), the imperial armies were among the best in the world. However, Byzantine emperors never forgot that the goal of war was to produce a stable peace. From Justinian to the Komnenid dynasty (1081–1185), the Byzantine strategy aimed at survival in times of difficulty and maximum security in periods of expansion. Finally, the feeling of being the rightful heirs to the Roman Empire fortified the Byzantines' confidence in the face of constant and simultaneous attacks on all sides. In spite of being badly demographically handicapped by the contraction of its territory, the empire was able to survive until 1453.

THE GEOGRAPHIC ENVIRONMENT

The geographic environment defined Byzantium's political and military conflicts. At its center, Constantinople was the most populous city in the world outside of China, with roughly half a million inhabitants in the sixth century. To the west lay the Balkans, a mountainous zone south of the Danube. North of the Danube, at the end of the steppes, which extend all the way to Mongolia, was Pannonia (present-day Hungary and Transylvania). To the south lay the Anatolian plateau, separated from the Mediterranean Sea by the Taurus Mountains, whose passes, the so-called Cilician Gates, were used by the Byzantines to block Arab advances on Constantinople. East of the Anatolian plateau, beyond the Euphrates, the high Armenian massif played a critical role. It was the origin of great rivers (Euphrates, Tigris, Aras) and a crossroads leading east to Persia, north to Georgia, and south to the desert plains of Syria and northern Mesopotamia. The high Armenian massif was also strategically important, because it commanded critical trade routes: the southern passes of Derbent, toward the Caspian Sea, and the eastern passes to the Caucasus, which opened onto the Aras River. It also gave access to the northern steppes of the Volga and through the Darial Pass, or Bab el-Alan (Alans' Gate), to Tbilisi. In addition, on its borders lay the Bitlis Pass, which opened onto the Syrian plain and Mesopotamia. During different periods of the Byzantine Empire, Armenia played an important role as a buffer state, an ally, or sometimes an enemy power's client state.

Before 636, the Byzantine Empire extended to Syria and Egypt, where major Christian religious centers were located, including Antioch, Alexandria, and Jerusalem. It also included a part of North Africa (Tripolitania,

Tunisia, Cyrenaica) that would later become Muslim in the course of the first Islamic expansion. When the Western Roman Empire disappeared in 476, Constantinople was already the most important city of the Roman Empire and of the Christian world. By 324, Constantine I had constructed fortifications that defended the north, south, and west of the city, while from the east, it was protected by the sea. As Constantinople's population increased, a new wall was erected under Theodosius (408–50), which rose to nine meters and included 96 fortified towers. The Byzantines forbade construction between the old and new walls so that the land there could be cultivated when the city was besieged.

The seven ecumenical councils that defined early Christianity were held in the Byzantine Empire. These councils defined and redefined the fundamental dogmas that formed the basis of a unified Christian theology until the definitive separation of Roman Catholic and Orthodox churches in 1054, with the exception of the split of the Monophysite Coptic and Armenian churches in 451. The first four councils were particularly important.

- The first council, held in Nicaea in 325, condemned Arianism, which held that God the Father, God the Son, and the Holy Spirit constituted a hierarchy, with God prior to and distinct from Jesus. Athanasius of Alexandria and the Cappadocian fathers Basil of Caesarea and Gregory of Nicaea opposed this belief, and the Council of Nicaea asserted that Jesus had been begotten, not created, and was of the same substance as the Father—the so-called Nicene Creed.

- The second council, held in Constantinople in 381, reaffirmed the Nicene Creed.

- The third council, held in Ephesus in 431, condemned Nestorianism, the belief that Jesus had both a distinct human and a divine nature. The council identified Mary as the *Theotokos* (God-bearer) and condemned Pelagianism, which denied original sin.

- The fourth council, held in Chalcedon in 451, condemned the Monophysites, who opposed the concept of the dual, divine and human, nature of Christ (which nevertheless remained a tenet of faith in the Coptic and Armenian churches).

In the fourth century, Theodosius I, the last emperor to rule both eastern and western halves of the Roman Empire, had managed to reconquer part of Armenia, a buffer zone that would often be contested by the Byzantines and the Sassanids. Long before its fall, however, the Western Roman Empire had already lost control of England, western Illyria, large parts of Spain and Gaul, and most of North Africa. In contrast, by virtue of the religious influence of the Orthodox Church, the Byzantine Empire was able to retain many of its Near Eastern possessions, including Antioch and Alexandria. By 478, after the Western Roman Empire had ceased to exist, the Byzantines had lost only Armenia and Georgia to Sassanid Persia.

When the Western Roman Empire was overrun by invasions from Germany and the steppes, the Eastern Empire was most seriously threatened in Dacia (present-day Romania) and Macedonia. Those provinces, then called Illyria, were strategically important. They bordered the Danube, a critical line of defense against the nomadic Goths and Huns. As Western territories were lost during the fourth and fifth centuries, the center of the Roman Empire shifted to the East. Asia Minor became more important as Greek Christianity spread through newly established Christian communities in the region. Indeed, the Eastern Roman Empire, with Constantinople as its capital, would remain a fortress of Christianity until the eleventh century and temporarily prevent the further advance of Islam when the Arabs were repulsed at Constantinople (717–18). Until 1025, the empire remained a formidable military and economic power. The Byzantine gold *nomisma* (or *solidus*) remained the currency of exchange throughout the Mediterranean until it was finally superseded by the Venetian ducat in the fourteenth century.

Soon after the fall of Rome, the Byzantine Empire was threatened on several fronts. The Bulgars, nomadic natives of Central Asia, invaded Illyria (498), while Arab nomads launched incursions into Syria. Both threats were repelled. Taking advantage of the fact that the Byzantine Empire was fighting on two fronts, the Sassanid Empire broke a sixty-year truce and conquered Armenia. However, in 504, the emperor Anastasius succeeded in turning the Arabs against the Persians and reconquered Armenia. The Persian sovereign, himself threatened by the Hephthalite (White) Huns, negotiated a truce. The Byzantine emperor agreed to pay a small tribute to the Sassanids to pacify his eastern front. This success reflected the mixture of Byzantine diplomacy and military strategy, granting provisional concessions in some cases and attacking in others. This combination would help the empire to survive through centuries of conflicts with enemies on both its eastern and western frontiers. As in their alliance with the Arabs, the Byzantines' policy was often designed to divide and conquer. They formed alliances based on mutual strategic interests, bribes, arranged marriages, and the granting of honorific titles with imperial privileges. Of course, the effectiveness of Byzantine diplomacy was due in large part to the strength of the empire's army and navy. By the time Justinian arrived on the throne (527–65), the territory of the Eastern Roman Empire had been almost completely restored. However, it would remain so for only a brief period.

TERRITORIAL RECONQUEST

When Justinian ascended to the throne, the empire was already at war with its major adversary. The Sassanids intended to reconstitute the empire of Alexander the Great, extending from the Hellespont to the confines of India. In the year following Justinian's ascension, his troops lost a major battle to the Persians. He reorganized his military forces by adding new recruits from Armenia and Anatolia to the eastern army under the command of Belisarius, who was to prove to be one of the Byzantine Empire's two peerless generals.

The historian Procopius, who accompanied Belisarius on his campaigns, tells of this triumph. Meanwhile, the western Byzantine army conquered the Crimean coast (the Chersonesus). Over the same period (529–34), a new body of laws was published. The so-called Justinian Code modernized the great Roman juridical tradition; it would inspire the jurists of the University of Bologna many centuries later. The difficult campaign against the Persians ended with the annexation of part of Sassanid Armenia, and the Byzantine forces in Illyria and Thrace defeated the Bulgarians and allied Slavic tribes. A truce was obtained in the east in 532. After Belisarius had crushed an important rebellion, Justinian entrusted him with the task of defeating the Vandals in North Africa. In 553, Belisarius landed not far from Carthage with 15,000 to 18,000 men. It was an opportune time, because the Vandals had embraced the unpopular Arian heresy and were confronting a revolt.

Belisarius's victory was swift. In less than a year, he had conquered Carthage, controlled the North African coast, and subjugated Corsica and Sardinia.* He returned to Constantinople with the captive Vandal king. Justinian was jealous of his success, however, and dispatched a relative as North African consul. The pacification of North Africa

---

* Procopius of Caesarea, *De bello valdalico,* "Ad Decimum et Tricamerum," in id., *De Bello* (The Wars of Justinian), trans. H.B. Dewing, Loeb Classical Library (Cambridge, MA: Harvard University Press, 1914–40).

proved more difficult than the conquest, and Belisarius was needed again.

The reconquest of Italy was much more difficult. When he took Rome in 536, Belisarius had defeated the Ostrogoths, but they still held the countryside and would resist Justinian's armies for another twenty years. After its initial successes, the war of imperial restoration in Italy can be divided into three phases. In the first phase (538–48), the Ostrogoths retook Rome in a long counteroffensive. In the second phase (551), Justinian sent the seventy-year-old Armenian eunuch Narses to lead the Italian campaign, who won a brilliant victory over the Ostrogoths in the battle of Taginae, using a combination of cavalry and infantry. In the third phase, the Franks invaded Italy. As at Taginae, Narses adopted a defensive strategy in his victory at the battle of Casilinum (553), letting the Franks take the initiative before counterattacking with his archers and his reserve troops. He was able to maintain the peace in Italy until 563.

The Sassanids took advantage of the Italian campaign to attack from the east and capture Antioch (540). Belisarius, who had defeated the Huns in Thrace in 559, was recalled to direct the Persian campaign, which continued intermittently from 549 to 562.

By the death of Justinian in 563, the Roman Empire had been largely restored owing to these two exceptional Byzantine generals, Belisarius and Narses. Belisarius was the more brilliant and employed a more offensive strategy. Narses won his three major battles defensively and at limited cost. The Byzantine armies in these campaigns were relatively small. The cavalry was composed of Anatolian and Thracian citizens. The infantry was composed largely of *foederati*, barbarian mercenaries to whom the empire granted land. The armies in the west also included Germans and Huns, while in the east, Armenians formed a large contingent and occupied positions of command. The generals could be either career soldiers like Belisarius or civilians like Narses. The empire was divided into military regions. To reduce the likelihood of a coup d'état, the armies rarely remained under the command of a single leader. Nevertheless, the troops, particularly the *bucellari,* or household troops, remained devoted to their commanders. Under Justinian, the Byzantine cavalry mastered the techniques of their adversaries (Huns, Germans, and Persians) with a combination of light cavalry armed with bows and swords and heavy cavalry armed with spears and swords and wearing laminated or chain-mail armor. After the adoption of the stirrup from the Eurasian nomads of the steppes in the seventh century, the cavalry became more important, and *tagmata,* units of three to four hundred horsemen, were brigaded into regiments of two or three thousand (*moira*).

Belisarius's troops were predominantly cavalry, with the infantry providing support. In contrast, Narses's army was mainly composed of infantry, committed to withstanding an initial enemy charge before the archers and the cavalry on the flanks intervened. These differences were probably owing to the fact that Belisarius was himself a horseman, who often led the final charge against his adversaries. Narses, on the other hand, used the cavalry to support his infantry. The Byzantines continued to adapt their enemies' techniques. From the Avars of the steppes, they adopted the counterattack after harassment, taking care to avoid envelopment. The archers were the essential component of the light infantry. The heavy infantryman was equipped with a large shield, spear, and sword. The swords were longer than the classic Roman sword, and the long spears were probably inspired by the spears of the barbarians. The Byzantine troops were highly disciplined and used multiple formations to their advantage. Byzantine troops increased their mobility to confront the Sassanids, who themselves had adopted the mobility of the Eurasian mounted archers that had harassed the Persian Empire from across the Oxus for many centuries. These influences resulted in the increasing importance of the cavalry under Justinian, even as the infantry often continued to play the major role. The increased importance of archers also reflected the adaptation of nomad techniques. The well-paid cataphracts, or heavy cavalry, were usually held in reserve for the final charge after the light cavalry and archers had weakened the enemy.

Military success under Justinian remained precarious because of the many enemies faced by the empire. Unlike western Europe, the Byzantine Empire was relatively unprotected by geography and was vulnerable to incursions by nomadic cavalry. Its longevity was in part ensured by Constantinople's unique fortifications and location and in part by the strategic and political genius of its elite.

After Justinian, the emperors Tiberius II (578–82) and Maurice (582–602) reorganized the army. Tiberius divided it into three commands, which were made responsible respectively for the defense of the empire's borders in Anatolia and in Thrace, which guarded access to Constantinople, and to control the incursions of nomads in Illyria pushed west by more powerful nomadic populations. Each of these armies consisted of six regiments of three thousand men, or eighteen thousand in all. Each army was led by a *magister militum.*

Here are a few observations about the empire's different adversaries from the *Stratēgikon* attributed to the emperor Maurice:

WITH THE SCYTHIANS, THAT IS TO SAY, THE AVARS, THE TURKS, AND OTHER POPULATIONS WHOSE WAY OF LIFE RESEMBLES THAT OF THE HUNS

The Scythians are all the same in their way of life and organization, which is very primitive and shared by many populations. Among the different populations, only the Turks and the Avars had concerned themselves with military organization, and they were, henceforth, stronger than the other Scythian populations when they came to battle. The Turks are very numerous and independent. They have neither varied talents nor ability in human matters except to conduct themselves bravely against their enemy. The Avars, on the other hand, are devious scoundrels who are very well versed in military matters.

These people have a form of monarchic government and their leaders punish all misconduct brutally. They are ruled not with love but with fear and they bear ordeals and hard work with equanimity. They are superstitious, dirty, treacherous, disloyal, and have an insatiable appetite for wealth. They don't keep their word, do not respect the terms of an agreement, and are not satisfied with gifts. Even before they accept a gift, they are already prepared to betray and violate the agreements they have just entered into. They know perfectly well how to assess a favorable situation and take advantage of it. They prefer to win over the enemy less by force than by treachery, surprise attacks, and attacking supply lines.

They are equipped with mesh armor, sabers, bows, and spears. When they fight, they are doubly armed with a spear slung across their chest, and a bow in hand, and use one or the other accordingly. Not only are they armored, but the horses of the most illustrious warriors have their chests covered with iron or felt. They are particularly adept at shooting the bow while riding.

They are followed by a large pack of horses and mares, which both serve as a source of remounts and give the impression of an immense army. They do not camp behind fortifications like the Persians or the Romans, but, until the day of the battle, they remain with their respective tribes and let their horses graze continually, summer or winter. Then they take the horses they need and hobble them near their tents until the moment when they form their battle lines, which they do while hidden in darkness. They post sentries at some distance, keeping them in contact with one another so that it is not easy to surprise them. Unlike the Romans or the Persians, they do not form their battle lines in three parts, but in several units of different sizes, all close together so as to give the impression of a long, unified front. In addition to their principal troops, they keep a supplementary force that they use to ambush a careless adversary or to reinforce a particularly vulnerable spot. They place their reserve horses immediately behind their principal line and their baggage on the left or the right of the line one or two miles away, under reduced watch. They frequently hold their reserve horses tied together at the rear of the battle line as a means of protection. The depth of their rows depends on the circumstances, with a tendency to make them deep, and their front is dense and regular. They prefer fighting at a distance, ambushes, enveloping maneuvers, simulated retreats, and sudden reversals of direction, as well as corner formations, that is to say, scattered group formations. When they succeed in routing the enemy, unlike the Romans, Persians, and other people, they are not satisfied with pursuing them over a reasonable distance, and pillaging their baggage; they won't stop until they have crushed them totally, and use every possible means to do so. If the pursued enemy takes shelter in a fortress, they try everything to bring about a shortage of food for men and horses. They thus reduce the enemy to their mercy and force them to accept the most favorable conditions for themselves. Their initial demands are rather modest, then, when they have been accepted, they impose much more stringent conditions. . . .

It is advisable to choose unobstructed terrain, and it will be necessary to gather against them a dense and unified massive cavalry force to bring them to close combat. Night attacks are also efficient, with a part of our forces remaining in formation, while the rest are ready for ambushes. They are faced with defections and desertions. They are unreliable, stingy, and, belonging to different tribes, have neither family ties nor unity. If some deserters are welcomed, many more will follow.

When they move toward the battlefield, the first thing to do is to place your scouts at regular intervals. Then take your positions and get ready in case the battle should take a bad turn. Find a good defensive position for emergencies, gather all possible provisions, enough for men and horses for a few days and, above all, have lots of water available. . . .

In the pursuit, the attacking troops should not advance more than three or four arrow shots away from the main line of defense, and the main force should not be included in the charge. . . .

If the battle goes well, don't rush to pursue the enemy, and avoid imprudence. Unlike most others, the men of this nation do not give up after an initial defeat. They will try everything to counterattack until totally exhausted.

WITH LIGHT-HAIRED PEOPLES, SUCH AS THE FRANKS, LOMBARDS, AND OTHERS OF THAT KIND

The men of the light-haired races set great store by freedom. In combat they are daring and fearless. They are so bold and impetuous that they consider any sign of fear or consideration of retreat as dishonorable. They have a quiet disdain for death and they fight ferociously in close combat whether mounted on horse or on foot. If, in a cavalry attack, they find themselves in a difficult situation, they dismount on a prearranged sign and arrange themselves in a line, on foot. Even if they are only a few against numerous horsemen, they do not shy away. They are armed with shields, spears, and short swords carried across their chests. They prefer to fight on foot and like quick charges.

Whether on foot or on horse, they do not come to the battlefield arranged in fixed formations, in regiments or divisions, but according to tribes, the relationship between them, and common interest. It follows that when things turn out badly and friends are killed, they are ready to risk their lives to take revenge. The battlefront is compact and regular. Whether on foot or on horse, their charge is impetuous, as if they were the only people in the world to ignore fear. They do not obey their chiefs well. Anything the least bit complicated is of no interest to them, and they are unconcerned by their security and their own interest. They despise good order, especially when riding. They are greedy and easily corruptible.

They do not endure pain or fatigue well. Even though they are brave and daring, their bodies are soft and oversensitive and do not endure pain calmly. Besides, they are sensitive to heat, cold, rain, and deprivation, particularly the lack of wine and delayed combat. When faced with a cavalry attack, they feel bothered by a rough and wooded terrain. It is easy to set ambushes on their flanks and to the rear of their battle lines, since they are careless about reconnaissance and other security measures. It is easy to have them break ranks by simulating fleeing and then doing a quick about-face. Night attacks by archers are very damaging to them, as they are very messy in their camp's installation. Pretend to conclude agreements with them. Aim at diminishing their audacity and eagerness by shortage of provisions or by taking advantage of the heat or cold at the time.

WITH THE SLAVS, THE ANTES, AND THEIR KIND

The Slavs and the Antes have the same kind of life and the same customs. Both are independent, and refuse to let themselves be enslaved or governed, especially in their own country. They are large, courageous populations who easily endure heat, cold, rain, nudity, and deprivation. . . .

They live in countries of impenetrable forests, rivers, lakes, and swamps, and they have opened passages in all directions to get out of where they live in order to confront potential dangers. They bury their most precious belongings in secret places, keeping only what is necessary in sight. They live like bandits and like to attack their enemies in rough terrain, in gorges or in thick forests.

They are skilled at ambushes, sudden attacks, raids, and use different methods for day or night. Their skill at crossing rivers exceeds everyone else's, and they know how to remain in the water for long periods. Often, when they are surprised in their countries and face a difficult situation, they dive underwater, and there get some long reeds prepared for such an eventuality. They keep them in their mouths, with the end sticking out of the water. Lying on their backs underwater, they remain for hours without being detected. . . .

Because of the absence of government and the lack of unity between them, they have no idea of what constitutes a battle plan. They are not capable either of fighting battles in organized formations or of fighting on open ground. At the moment of the attack, if they find enough courage, they start shouting and rush from a short distance. If, when hearing these shouts, their adversary shows signs of weakening, they then attack violently. Otherwise, they turn tail, not wishing to feel the force of the enemy in close combat. They run into the woods, where they have the advantage, since they are very skilled at fighting in dense forests. Often, too, when they carry booty, they surrender it, pretending panic, to take shelter in the forest. Then, when their pursuers have scattered after looting their booty, they return and inflict great losses. They are ready to use this kind of strategy and many other methods in order to bait their enemy.

They are totally disloyal, and do not respect the treaties to which they consent. They may agree to treaties sometimes to their advantage but most often from fear. If they express different opinions among themselves, they can never agree, for if some of them agree, the others will immediately do the opposite. They are constantly fighting with each other, and nobody wants to surrender.

In combat, they are vulnerable to volleys of arrows, to secondary attacks from different directions, and to hand-to-hand combat against their infantry, especially when it is lightly armed or fighting in open terrain. Our army should thus include cavalry and infantry, mostly lightly armed and with javelin throwers, and it should carry a large quantity of projectiles, not only arrows, but others as well. Get the necessary material to cross rivers, if possible, pontoons. This will allow you to easily cross the many rivers that are not fordable. Build bridges in the Scythian manner, that is, with a few men building the frame, while others lay the boards. You will also need goatskin or leather containers to make rafts enabling your soldiers to cross the rivers and to take the enemy by surprise in summer.

It is, however, preferable to attack in winter, when the bare trees will give few opportunities to hide, and the tracks of fugitives are visible in the snow, the rigorous climate has made their settlements insecure, and it is easy to cross rivers over the ice.*

Under Tiberius II and Maurice, the only remnants of Justinian's conquests were Ravenna and the southern Italian coast. Spain had fallen to the Visigoths. North Africa was still held by the empire, which thus retained control of over two-thirds of the Mediterranean coast. Although North Africa was pacified, Tiberius still had to fight on two fronts: in the east, he faced the Persians; in the west, the Avars, who had conquered lands on the Danube border, where Slavic tribes were also present.

Maurice saw the Sassanids as his major adversary, but he also faced the Avars and Slavs in the Balkans and the Lombards in Italy. He agreed on a truce with Persia and refused to pay tribute to the Avars that had been negotiated by Tiberius. The Avars crossed the Danube. Maurice

---

* An alternative English translation can be found in *Maurice's Strategikon: Handbook of Byzantine Military Strategy*, trans. George T. Dennis (Philadelphia: University of Pennsylvania Press, 1984), 116–22. See also *Three Byzantine Military Treatises*, trans. and ed. George T. Dennis (Washington, DC: Dumbarton Oaks, 2008). Cf. Procopius and other historians of the sixth and seventh centuries, such as Agathias, Menander, and Theophylact.

first defeated the Slavs, and then his troops defeated the Avars at Adrianople (modern Edirne). The following year, the Avars invaded Thrace again. Maurice sued for peace to free his hand in the south. In Italy, he formed an alliance with the Franks to control the Lombards, but was defeated. In the meantime, the Sassanid king Khosrau II was dethroned by a usurper, and offered to cede several territories to Maurice, including a large part of Persian Armenia, in exchange for an alliance to help him regain his throne. The usurper made counteroffers. Maurice, against the advice of his counselors, allied himself with the legitimate king, who regained his throne. Secured on his eastern front, Maurice then again concentrated his troops against the Slavs and the Avars. After crossing the Danube, the campaign was doubly victorious, in defeating first the Slavs and then the Avars (599).

Maurice's policies of austerity, which aimed at replenishing the imperial treasury, were unpopular, and famines occurred in Constantinople. The army overthrew Maurice, who was executed along with his sons, and a general named Phocas proclaimed himself emperor in 602. Maurice was the first emperor to have lost his throne in this way since the foundation of Constantinople, but he would not be the last. Phocas was defeated by the Persians in 607 and overthrown and put to death a few years later, while plague, famine, and unrest continued to ravage Constantinople.

HERACLIUS'S RULE

The history of the Eastern Roman Empire falls into several distinct epochs. From the foundation of Constantinople in 303 to the end of Justinian's reign in 565, the empire not only survived but clung to the idea of recovering the empire's western half, which Justinian attempted to do. The subsequent reigns of Tiberius, Maurice, and Phocas (565–610) saw wars on three fronts: on the eastern front against the Sassanid Empire, in the Balkans against the Slavs and Avars, and in Italy against the Lombards. From 610 to 718, the empire underwent its most dramatic period, fighting for its survival first against the Persians and then against the Arabs. During this period, the Sassanid Empire disappeared, while the Byzantine Empire survived. The greatest existential threat to the empire was the Arab siege of Constantinople (717–18), in which the Arab armies were finally repelled with the help of Greek fire, an incendiary mixture of naphtha and resin that was difficult to extinguish, introduced to the Byzantines by a Syrian Christian, Kallinikos of Heliopolis.

The situation remained volatile until 780, with the empire experiencing external threats as well as internal crises, particularly related to religious doctrine. It is the period from 610 to 780 that we shall now examine.

Heraclius (610–41) became emperor at the age of twenty-six. He had spent most of his youth in Africa, though his family was Armenian, native to Cappadocia. Almost immediately, Heraclius had to face the Persians, who had conquered Mesopotamia and western Syria and taken Antioch, Apamea, and Homs (612). Heraclius abandoned Cilicia, and Persian troops also took Damascus (613) and Jerusalem (614). At the same time that the Persians were occupying the Fertile Crescent, the Avars and the Slavs took advantage of the situation to start a vast offensive, laying siege to Thessalonica (618). A little before, the Visigoths had conquered the few imperial possessions that remained in Spain.

Even worse, Egypt itself was occupied by the Sassanids: Alexandria fell in 619. In fact, it seemed that the empire was about to collapse. Besides Anatolia, only a section of North Africa from the Constantine region to Tunisia remained to it. The war for survival against the Persians had already lasted twenty years, and the Byzantine army had been forced to retreat on all fronts.

Heraclius had no other choice than to retake the initiative. The patriarch of Constantinople granted him financial aid that allowed him to recruit troops, pay back wages, and hire mercenaries. The army was reorganized. The depleted North African army faced the Persians in Egypt. The armies in Illyria and Thrace had suffered greatly in the Slavic attacks. The Armenian armies in the east had also been weakened by Persian offensives. Heraclius joined the Armenian and Thracian armies after neutralizing the Avars with an offer of tribute. Then, Heraclius made a bold decision to invade Persia rather than attempting to reconquer the lost provinces (624). He advanced to the east, reached the capital of Armenia unimpeded, and captured Dvin in a surprise attack. Then he invaded the Persian province of Atropatene. Understanding the danger, the Sassanid monarch Khosrau II recalled his three main generals and dispatched them against Heraclius. Heraclius's army advanced in a forced march and met and defeated the first Persian army before the second arrived, and then crushed the second army before the arrival of the third.

Khosrau II refused all peace offers and copied Heraclius's strategy: he brought the war to the enemy, joining with the Avars in a direct attack on Constantinople (626). Heraclius divided his army into three parts. One went to the Caucasus and made an alliance with the nomad turcophone Khazars, who had just attacked the Sassanids' northern provinces. The second was sent to reinforce the troops defending the capital. The third was used to block the reinforcements sent west by the Persian sovereign. During the siege, the Avars, the Slavs, and the Persians fought together in theory. However, thanks to their naval superiority, the Byzantines prevented the armies, separated by the Bosphorus, from uniting. The Byzantine reinforcements arrived just as the Persian general directing the siege was informed that Khosrau II had killed himself. Nobody knows if the message was a Byzantine ruse. The Persians withdrew and the Avars, short of food, also retreated. Once more, a siege of Constantinople had ended up in failure.

The alliance between the Persians and the Avars came to an end, and the Slavs rebelled against the Avars. Meanwhile, Heraclius secured an alliance with the Khazars, defeated another Persian army, and advanced toward Mesopotamia. At the end of 627, he defeated the Persians at Nineveh. Khosrau II retreated to his capital, Ctesiphon. While he retreated, he was overthrown and executed by his son, who sued for peace (629). Heraclius managed to retake Syria and Egypt after he concluded a treaty with the last Sassanid general. In exchange, the latter requested control of Mesopotamia and support for his attempt to seek the throne.

Heraclius returned triumphant to Constantinople (631) and returned the True Cross to Jerusalem for good measure. Heraclius's victory was complete, thanks to his tenacity, strategic intelligence, and tactical instinct. The main adversary of the empire was vanquished, but other problems remained: the Slavic tribes still occupied the Balkans, the Byzantine economy was in ruins, epidemic plague was raging, and religious tensions had grown with the Egyptians, the Syrians, and the Armenians.

In order to put an end to the squabbles with the monophysites, Heraclius proposed a compromise to the Chalcedonians and the monophysites: monenergism. While accepting the Chalcedonian doctrine that Christ had a dual nature, monoenergism endowed him with a unique energy—a vague term that could be understood as designating a single will, which would satisfy the monophysites.

Patriarch Serge of Constantinople, a Syrian monophysite, backed monoenergism, as did Athanasius, the monophysite patriarch of Antioch. In 631, Heraclius chose a new patriarch for Alexandria who also defended monoenergism. A council of the Armenian Church joined the other churches, and the schism seemed a thing of the past. It was a triumphal moment for the emperor. The Persians were defeated and exhausted. The Avars had just been defeated by the Bulgarians, natives of Central Asia who had arrived north of the Danube. The Slavs occupied the south of the Danube but were disunited. Everything seemed to go well in the years 633–35, in spite of the exhausted public finances and the recurrent plague. Heraclius had done well with the empire.

Suddenly, an unforeseen nomadic tidal wave appeared. Muhammad died in 632, and Abu Bakr, the first caliph of Islam, finished unifying Arabia in 633 and then sent four armies of from five to six thousand men north. The first clash occurred near Gaza between the local Byzantine forces and the Arabs. The Byzantines were defeated. Heraclius dispatched his brother with Anatolian troops. Abu Bakr sent reinforcements, led by the illustrious Khalid Ibn al Walid. The Byzantine troops were again defeated. Meanwhile, the Syrians and the Egyptians showed growing opposition to monoenergism. The patriarch of Constantinople himself seemed to be doubtful about the interpretation of the doctrine, which had been rejected by the pope.

In 626, Heraclius gathered his troops in Syria in front of the river Yarmouk. The Byzantine forces were defeated. Damascus and Antioch collapsed. The following year, the Arab armies won a decisive battle over the Sassanids at Qadisiya and conquered the Persian capital, Ctesiphon. Jerusalem fell in 638.

Heraclius was in poor health. His empire was plagued by theological disputes, and he had to find a compromise with the monophysites to restore unity. The doctrine of a single will, as defined by the pope, was adopted under the name of monothelism. However, the rebellion against this doctrine in Egypt, particularly Alexandria, facilitated Egypt's conquest by the Arabs, which began in 640. Rome also condemned the doctrine of monothelism. Heraclius died in 641, the year before the Arabs decisively defeated the Sassanids at the battle of Nahāvand. Alexandria would fall to the Arabs in 647, after a long siege.

The empire held on to its possessions in North Africa, southern Italy, and Sicily for a few more years after Heraclius died. The Byzantine core around Constantinople, which included Armenia and Anatolia in the east and the Balkans in the west, would persist for another seven centuries. Essentially, the empire was henceforth largely Greek-speaking.

ATTACKS AND COUNTERATTACKS

The decades following the death of Heraclius were dramatic for the Byzantine Empire. The Arab peril was enormous. Prince Reshdouni's Armenia fell under the suzerainty of the Arab general Muawiyah in 652.

The Byzantines briefly regained control of Italy and captured the pope, whom they exiled to the Chersonese. The next pope was more cautious in his condemnations.

In 654, Muawiyah's fleet conquered Rhodes, Crete, and Cyprus, and his ground forces took Trabzon on the Black Sea. The next year he invaded the Cappadocia, but could not take Caesarea. During these campaigns, a dispute arose between Uthman and Ali over the caliphate's succession. Muawiyah's armies were recalled, giving the empire time to reorganize.

Around this time, Heraclius's grandson, the emperor Constans II, introduced the system of military administrative settlement units called *themata*, initially on the eastern frontier, where the empire was most vulnerable. In order to make garrison service in Anatolia more attractive, each soldier received a piece of land to tie him to the area under the *thema* system. The three major Asiatic *themata* were the Anatolikon, Armenikon, and Opsikion. The farmer-soldier enjoyed the products of his land, but was required to mobilize in case of foreign incursions. The property was inherited by the elder son, under the same conditions as for his father. The introduction of the *thema* system created an important distinction in the army between the border troops and the forces of the capital. The *themata* gradually escaped the control of civilian administrators and came to be managed independently by the *strategos* (general) responsible for civilian and military affairs in the region. However, the *strategos* could not collect taxes, which remained the sole responsibility of the financial official assigned to the *thema* area. The *thema* system took 150 years to reach its full efficiency. The *themata* multiplied and were named after the region where they were located or after the region of origin of the troops of which they were composed—for example, Armenikon, located west of Armenia, comprised Armenians.

The empire still controlled the Taurus Mountains and their passes, the Cilician Gates. In 659, Muawiyah, fearing a Byzantine victory, negotiated a truce. Meanwhile, Constans reorganized the army and created new *themata*, including those of Thrace and Isauria, in addition to the first three, Armenikon, Opsikion, and Anatolikon. A special naval force was also created, to be based on the island of Samos.

The Arab civil war ended in 661 with the assassination of Ali. Muawiyah became caliph and created the Umayyad Caliphate, with Damascus as its capital. The Byzantine Empire entered a tumultuous period characterized by military revolts, riots, and coups d'état. The Arab threat spread from land to sea. In 672, three Arab fleets besieged Constantinople, only to be defeated by Greek fire. Theological disputes persisted. In 680, the sixth ecumenical council met in Constantinople and reaffirmed the two-century-old Chalcedonian doctrine of the double nature of Christ.

Arab naval incursions continued. In 677, the emperor Constantine IV defeated the Arabs, but the Slavs besieged Thessalonica. In Syria, the Arabs faced a Christian uprising by the Mardaites. Meanwhile, the Bulgarians conquered regions south of the Danube. The emperor arranged a brief truce with the Bulgarians in order to open a second front against the Arabs.

Arab allies defected, and both Christian Armenia and Georgia sought the support of the Byzantine Empire. Justinian II (669–771), who became sole emperor in 681, attacked on two fronts: in the east against the Arabs and in the West against the Bulgarians. After creating a buffer zone in Thrace to separate the empire from the Bulgarians, he attacked the Arab armies at Sebastopol (689) but suffered a major defeat. Armenia again fell under Arab control. The Arab victories continued and Justinian II was overthrown in 695 and went into exile.

The caliph brought a new fleet from Egypt and Ifriqiya (modern Tunisia and Tripolitania) and a new army from Syria to reinforce his troops who had besieged Constantinople. They were intercepted by the Byzantines in Nicaea and destroyed. At the same time, the Egyptian Christian crews of the Arab relief fleet rebelled and joined the besieged. An epidemic occurred among the Arab army and the empire's Bulgarian allies killed a large number of Muslim soldiers. The Arabs retreated after thirteen months of siege on August 15, 718, the Feast of the Dormition of the Virgin.

The Byzantines reoccupied part of western Armenia and negotiated an alliance with the Khazars. The emperor Leo III, the Isaurian, wedded his son to a Khazar princess. Leo III was also able to push the Arabs back to the Taurus and severely damage their fleet. However, the Arab stranglehold was not yet over: the Arabs would besiege Nicaea in 727.

By 751, the empire had no possessions remaining in Italy north of Calabria. It remained threatened on two fronts: by the Bulgarians in the west, and the Arabs in the east. Internally, it also had to deal with the religious tensions created by iconoclasm. Leo III reorganized and enhanced the *thema* system and restored public finances. His son, Constantine V, was equally remarkable. He won a two-year civil war, defeated the Bulgarians, and, taking advantage of the Umayyad decline, defeated the Arabs in several battles. He was efficient in administration and finance, but his religious policy was unpopular.

Religious quarrels began in 726, when Constantine V, an iconoclast, decreed a ban on the veneration (he said adoration) of images and ordered the destruction of icons depicting Christ and the saints. Iconoclasm had considerable support with the military and also in Asia Minor, but it was very unpopular with the monks and the majority of Constantinople's population. In Ravenna, iconoclasm was rejected violently. Constantine V's successor Leo IV (775–80) was in turn succeeded by his widow, the regent queen Irene of Athens, who was an iconodule—that is, venerated icons. Her iconoclastically inclined son Constantine VI was blinded and imprisoned by her supporters, and Irene made peace with Rome and summoned the sixth ecumenical council in Nicaea (787), which reaffirmed the veneration of images.

Irene was deposed in 802 by her treasurer, two years after Charlemagne was crowned Holy Roman Emperor by the pope. The Byzantine Empire survived Arab victories in Sicily and Crete in the first part of the ninth century. In 838, three Arab armies defeated a large Byzantine force and advanced on Ankara. Unrest, both inside and outside the empire, remained strong. The empress Irene's erstwhile treasurer, who had assumed the throne as Nikephoros I (802–11), fought both the Bulgarians and the Arabs. Crete was lost, and the emperor was killed in a battle with the Bulgarians. The throne then went briefly to his son, Staurakios, then to his son-in-law, Michael I (811–13). The latter was dethroned by a general, who reigned as Leo V (813–20) and revived iconoclasm, reigniting tensions. He was murdered in 820 by supporters of one of his own generals, who thereafter reigned as Michael II (820–29).

The Amorian dynasty founded by Michael II (named for the city of Amorium in Phrygia, where he was born) lasted less than fifty years. Michael was also an iconoclast who upset the Church, as was his son, Theophilius (829–42), who fought the Arabs with mixed success. His widow, Theodora (842–55), an iconodule, then became regent. She restored the veneration of images with the support of Constantinople's population. The greatest success of this period, racked by quarrels about images and by power struggles, was the conversion of the Bulgarians to Christianity. However, the relationship between the pope and the patriarch of Constantinople remained adversarial.

In summary, in the sixth century, the Byzantine Empire attempted to reconstitute the territory of the earlier Roman Empire and almost succeeded. However, over the next two centuries, from the end of the sixth century to the beginning of the eighth, the empire struggled for survival. Although it was threatened on two fronts, divided by power struggles, and riven by controversies over image worship, it nonetheless found the resources to survive and to work for restoration of its former grandeur.

The Byzantines' survival had depended on taking advantage of their enemies' weaknesses, either dynastic quarrels or unstable alliances. The empire would again take the offensive with the Macedonian dynasty (876–1056), which restored much of its ancient glory.

THE ARMY

Despite its internal troubles, the Byzantine Empire gave full support to the army, upon which its survival depended. Military strategy was a subject of study and the reflections of Byzantine historians, from Procopius to Anna Komnēnē (1083–1153), show a deep interest in military affairs. The armies, reorganized by Tiberius and Maurice, allowed Heraclius to defeat the Sassanids. The development of the *themata* created a defensive force tied to their region by the landholdings of the soldiers. The soldiers of the frontier fought brilliantly for many centuries, particularly on the Anatolian border. They served as the model for the Byzantine epic *Digenēs Akritēs*.

In the ninth century, the *thema* system was backed up by four *tagmata,* or regiments, of imperial guards, the Scholai, Exkubitoi, Arithmos, and Hikanatoi, each comprising fifteen hundred horsemen and four thousand infantry. For security reasons, the personal guard of the emperor was made up of foreigners recruited among the Varangians (Vikings). The *themata* had the task of containing the enemy advance, and, if the enemy intervention was significantly large, to hold them for a sufficient time to permit a counterattack with the help of the *tagmata.*

The Byzantine strategy was primarily a defensive one. From Justinian's reign until the end of the ninth century, prudence was the rule. The threats were so frequent and varied that simply avoiding catastrophic defeat was the central goal of military policy. The Byzantine army was numerically inferior to the Arabs' forces. As in most classic strategic treatises, Byzantine manuals stressed the necessity of having a superior force before attacking. They also advised recourse to diplomatic and political ruses to weaken the enemy and recommended the use of stratagems and surprises whenever possible. The Byzantines' advantage was their strategic intelligence, their knowledge of the adversary's methods, and their experience with appropriate countermeasures. Byzantine writers note that although able to call on very large, highly mobile forces of hardened fighters, the Arabs were undisciplined and poorly organized. In defeat, their morale collapsed, and they were known to suffer badly from the cold and rain. Their cavalry was no match for Byzantine cavalry when the forces were of equal size. In fact, Byzantine heavy cavalry, the cataphracts, were the elite force of the time.

The Byzantine military organization put in place by the emperor Maurice in the sixth century remained more or less unchanged until the eleventh century. Indeed, the *Taktika* of Leo VI, the Wise, written in the tenth century, largely reiterates the principles and the methods of organization of Maurice's *Stratēgikon*.

By the tenth century, rather than being called a *tagma*, the basic light infantry unit was termed a *bandon*, which numbered 256 men (16 × 16). Three-quarters of the heavy infantry were pikemen, and the remaining quarter were archers. Light infantry archers carried out reconnaissance and harassed the enemy. A light cavalry unit numbered three hundred men. Three to five *banda* constituted a battalion-sized *moira*, and three *moirai* in turn made up a *tourma*.

It is difficult to evaluate the size of the Byzantine army. It may have consisted of about 120,000 men, although more modest estimates of 40,000 to 60,000 appear in some historical documents. The Byzantine troops were well paid, with the best-paid stationed on the more dangerous eastern front.

The cavalry usually wore armor made up of small plates, as seen in the paintings of the knights of the time, though some wore chain mail. The helmet was often made of metal, but was sometimes constructed of strips of leather and metal. The shape of the shields varied, with the cavalry using round shields and the infantry longer ones. Infantrymen carried spears that were four meters long, as well as swords. The composite bow had been adopted from the steppe nomads by both the infantry and the light cavalry.

In the tenth century, the proportion of cavalry to archers increased to 40 percent to more adequately confront the nomad horsemen of the steppes. Four elite regiments were based in Constantinople to ensure the emperor's security. Each regiment included 3,500 to 4,000 cavalry and 1,500 to 2,000 infantry, forming a *tagma* of 5,000 to 6,000 men. The emperor had about 20,000 elite troops at his disposal in Constantinople. When at war, he probably led half of them. His personal guard, created in the tenth century, consisted of two thousand Varangians—Swedish Vikings from Russia—who were well paid and skilled with the battle-axe. Kekaumenos's *Stratēgikon*, from the middle of the eleventh century, emphasized their valor. Each regiment needed chariots to transport necessary supplies. At night, the chariots formed a circle to protect the men and horses, with an extra fence to increase protection. Priests accompanied the army, and scouts were sent ahead. Prisoners who could be used as slaves were rarely killed, and prisoners of high rank were routinely ransomed.

In the tenth century, each *thema* was under the command of a *strategos* (general), assisted by three civilian administrators, who took care of the finances, including the soldiers' pay and the collection of taxes. The number of *themata* increased over time as the empire expanded from Armenia to southern Italy, the Balkans, and Syria. Under Basil II at the beginning of the eleventh century there were at least forty-six. *Themata* varied in size: the biggest comprised 10,000 men, the less important ones from 2,000 to 4,000.

This suggests that the Byzantine army may have numbered as many as 150,000 men by 1025, if one includes the coastal *themata* of Anatolia, in the Peloponnese, and on Mediterranean islands (Sicily, Samos, etc.). Nevertheless, the military situation degraded rapidly after the death of the emperor Basil II, the Bulgar-Slayer (1025), before again stabilizing under Alexios I Komnenos (1048–1118).

THE BYZANTINE FLEET

The Byzantine fleet played an important role until the twelfth century. The empire's naval power underpinned the victories of Belisarius in Africa and Narses in Africa under Justinian in the sixth century. But Byzantine naval superiority was often contested. The Vandals had a large fleet, and the Arabs built a formidable naval force soon after their victories over the Sassanid and Byzantine Empires. Control of the Mediterranean was disputed.

The Byzantine Empire controlled the Black Sea from Chersonesus (modern Sevastopol) in southern Crimea, so Byzantine naval superiority united the imperial possessions from the Caucasus to North Africa. After the Arab conquests deprived the empire of its colonies in North Africa, Egypt, and Syria-Palestine, however, Constantinople was left with only Sicily, Crete, Cyprus, and Rhodes from which to control the eastern Mediterranean, from southern Italy to the coast of Asia Minor.

The creation of an Umayyad fleet began a new era in Mediterranean maritime history. In the middle of the seventh century, the Arabs proved their naval superiority by defeating the Byzantine fleet. Greek fire, which broke the Arab siege of Constantinople (717–18), was used in naval battles against the Muslims too, however, and also enabled the Byzantines to get rid of Rus (i.e., Viking) pirates. Byzantine naval hegemony had nevertheless ended forever.

A single command for the coastal fleet was instituted in the seventh century. Maritime *themata* were also created: the imperial fleet was reserved for major expeditions, while smaller *thema* fleets supplied by the provinces and manned by local crews defended threatened Byzantine coasts and islands.

Although the Arabs never conquered Asia Minor, they ruled a vast territory from Spain to Central Asia. In 751, an Abbasid Arab force defeated Tang Chinese troops on the Talas River in Transoxiana (present-day Kazakhstan/Kyrgyzstan). Moreover, to the south, Muslims had reached the Indian frontier. By 965, too, the Muslims had conquered all of Sicily. The Latin population of the empire, never a majority, further declined, and Greek speakers became very largely predominant.

After the *themata* in Asia Minor, created to confront the Arab threat, *themata* were created in Thrace and Macedonia to control the Bulgarians. The Byzantines, while surpassed at sea by the Arabs, still maintained regional maritime control over the south of Italy, the Aegean, and the Black Sea. With the loss of Sicily, in the middle of the ninth century, Byzantine naval power ebbed. This was the time of the Arab naval hegemony in the Mediterranean.

The Byzantine navy was reorganized in the ninth and tenth centuries, when the Empire had to confront both the Rus on the Black Sea coast and the Arabs in the Mediterranean. From then on, the Byzantine maritime strategy focused on the Orient and was designed primarily to support the army.

The only surviving naval military treatise from the Byzantine Empire is the *Naumachia,* which recalls the aphorisms of Leon VI in his *Taktika.* Here are some excerpts:

> The Saracens are of Arab origins and formerly inhabited Arabia Felix. After receiving Muhammad's laws, they spread into Syria and Palestine. They conquered Mesopotamia and Egypt during the time when the Roman Empire was fighting the Persians. They blaspheme against Christ whom they do not consider the true God and Savior of the world. . . . They observe their law strictly but are carnal and sexual. They satisfy their senses and dirty their souls. We, who follow a holy and divine law, hate their impiety and fight them to support our faith.
>
> They use camels to carry their baggage rather than oxen, mules, and donkeys. The look and smell of camels scare our horses, which makes them preferable to their Arab masters. The Saracens also scare enemy horses with the noise of kettledrums and cymbals, to which they have accustomed their own animals. They put their camels and other pack animals in the middle of

their army. They attach pennants and flags to them so as to make others believe that they are more numerous. The Saracens are hot-tempered, since they are born in blazing hot regions. Their infantry is composed of Ethiopians, who carry large bows. They place them in front of the cavalry, which makes it difficult to attack. The cavalry leaves the infantry behind when the expedition returns close to their frontiers. The cavalry are equipped with swords, spears, axes, and also with arrows. They wear helmets, cuirasses, short boots, and gauntlets in the Roman fashion. They like to adorn their belts, their swords, and their horses with silver ornaments.

Once scattered, they do not regroup easily. They only think of saving their lives. When they anticipate victory, they are very courageous, but lose their spirit when threatened with defeat. They are convinced that their troubles are sent by God, like everything else. This is why they face misfortune without complaining, and await a more propitious time to do battle. . . . To protect themselves from surprise attack, they fortify their camp and keep good watch all night long.

Their battle formation is a large square, reinforced on every side, and difficult to penetrate. They use this formation when they march or fight. Thus, they imitate the Romans in the form and manner of attacks.

When they are in formation and ready, they do not rush to charge. They withstand the first shock firmly and remain steadfast after the battle is engaged. When they see the enemy weakening they counterattack vigorously. They fight at sea as they do on land: standing near each other, and protected by their shields to block enemy arrows. Once the enemy has used up his arrows and becomes tired, they rush into hand-to-hand combat. This is why one must be very cautious with them.

Their precepts and methods for war are much more valuable than those of other more experienced nations. This was reported by our generals and our pious Father who often battled with them.

They fear the rigors of winter: cold and rain upset them and make them ill. That is why rainy weather is the best time to attack them. It so happens that when the strings of their bows are wet, they slacken and can no longer be used effectively. So it is usually during the heat of summer that they emerge from Tarsus and the other cities of Cilicia to attack.

There is great risk in engaging them, even though they seem weak in numbers. It is better to stay covered in a good post from where they can be spied upon. When they come during the winter to explore the country and gather information, it is possible to attack them by surprise, even if they are a large army.

They neither draft soldiers nor use a lottery. Men come in large numbers from Syria and Palestine to volunteer, the rich for love of country, the poor in hope of amassing booty. Their army also attracts very young men who are not yet of age, and whom women are pleased to arm. . . . When they pass through the gorges of the Taurus [Mountains] . . . or, rather, when they return, tired, encumbered with cattle and other spoils, it is possible to attack their cavalry from higher ground, with good archers and slings. One can also let boulders roll down on them or, as I said before, ambush them.

They never break formation, even when they are attacked on three sides at the same time. They fight together until victory seems at hand or, if losing, they become dispirited and flee. They should be attacked first with arrows. Their mounted archers, Ethiopians and others, whom they place ahead of their cavalry, are naked, easily wounded, and prone to fleeing. They also fear losing their horses, which are their safeguard.*

On land, the Macedonian dynasty rebuilt much of the empire in less than a century by regaining control over Cilicia, Syria, and Crete. The empire also strengthened its fleet to support Byzantine possessions in southern Italy. The fleet was composed of galleys that could transport up to three hundred men. The naval troops, or Karabisianoi, were a standing force from the mid-seventh century on. Religious quarrels about the veneration of images persisted, with the army tending toward iconoclasm, while the navy preferred the veneration of images.

In the tenth century, the Byzantines briefly regained their maritime superiority. In that time their galleys were equipped with spurs to shatter the hulls and break the oars of enemy ships. They also used Greek fire to terrorize enemy crews and set their vessels afire. The recipe for Greek fire was a fiercely kept secret, which remained a monopoly of the Byzantines for many centuries.

Leon VI, in his *Taktika,* advised using the fleet sparingly, because of its cost. Naval battles were to be avoided unless there was an overwhelming advantage. The preferred formation of the Byzantine fleet was a half moon, which allowed the envelopment of the adversary. The fleet was neglected during the Arab wars, but was then refurbished to respond to the growing menace of the Kievan Rus. In the eleventh century, the fleet declined again and was not able to match the more advanced fleets of Venice or Genoa.

THE ADMINISTRATION

Constantine the Great had established a senate in Constantinople. Its authority varied, increasing in the eleventh century when Michael Psellos, a Byzantine monk who also wrote a history of Byzantine emperors, became its president. The army was often more powerful than the Senate, but the emperor was, in theory, all-powerful.

The imperial cabinet, appointed by the emperor, acted as an advisory board and had vastly more power than the Senate. The provincial

* *Naumachia,* attributed to Syrianus Magister.

districts proliferated along with the *themata*. There were fewer than twenty-five at the beginning of the tenth century, but forty-six at the death of Basil II (1025), at the height of the reconquest. The system was abandoned in the fourteenth century with the Ottoman victories, when the empire was reduced to a few possessions in the Balkans. Greek was the official language of the empire, but Latin remained in use by scholars. The Justinian Code was the law of the empire and underwent modifications under Basil I (867–86), the first emperor of the Macedonian dynasty. A forty-volume compilation called the *Epanagōgē* (ca. 886) summarized Byzantine law and specified the powers of the emperor, the patriarch, and the state.

DIPLOMACY

Foreign policy was the emperor's responsibility. However, the military commander in the Crimea was responsible for the foreign policy on the steppes. He informed the emperor of instability in the steppes when new invaders from the east displaced residents westward. This movement continued throughout Byzantine history, driven by the Huns, turcophone populations, and the Mongols.

The empire used diplomacy, money, and military force to assure its survival. Like the Chinese emperor, the Byzantine emperor received diplomats in a formal manner, with ambassadors kowtowing to the emperor. Diplomacy consisted primarily of forming alliances to counter the influence of the empire's principal enemies. Often, the empire would agree to pay tribute and arrange a truce with one enemy in order to confront another. Arranged marriages between Byzantine princesses and foreign nobles were frequent.

After the Avar threat, the empire used diplomacy to pacify other nomadic invaders from the steppes, including the Pechenegs, the Cumans, the Magyars, and the Khazars. The expense of Byzantine diplomacy was relatively unimportant as long as the standard currency of the Mediterranean areas remained the Byzantine *nomisma*, which persisted until the eleventh century.

THE WAR FRONTS OF THE EMPIRE

Before the period of the reconquest that began under Basil I and was completed during the Macedonian dynasty, the Byzantine Empire faced conflict on many fronts.

The Western Provinces

The provinces that Justinian had reconquered had again been lost. The Visigoths were victorious in Spain (624) before being themselves overrun by the Arabs. Italy, north of the Po River, had been occupied by the Lombards, who then progressively conquered the largest part of the peninsula and Corsica. The empire retained Sardinia, southern Italy, and Ravenna. In the eighth century, the empire had been reduced to Calabria and adjacent regions in Italy. At this time, Greek remained the language of Sicily and Calabria. The last emperor of Constantinople to visit Rome was Constans II (663). Thereafter, the empire was unable to hold central Italy, too far from its base and dominated by the Lombards. Ravenna fell in 751.

The quarrel with the pope escalated when the emperor Leo III (714–41) seized papal properties in Sicily, southern Italy, and Illyria and placed them under the authority of the patriarch of Constantinople. Theological quarrels over the *filioque* ("and [from] the Son," a controversial formula in the Creed) between Rome and Constantinople and iconoclasm exacerbated tensions. In 800, the pope crowned Charlemagne as Roman emperor, but Constantinople regarded him as merely a king (*basileus*). Although North Africa was also lost with the successes of the Arab expansion at the end of the seventh century, the empire would retain its base in southern Italy until Constantinople itself fell.

The Balkans

The Balkans represented a constant danger on the western front. The Avar kingdom was very powerful at the beginning of the sixth century, when it conquered the Hungarian plains. However, the Avar khan failed to take Constantinople in 626, and the Avar Empire disintegrated thereafter owing to internal struggles and conflicts with the Bulgarians and the Slavs.

Whenever the Byzantines had to fight the Arabs in the east, the Bulgarians took the opportunity of launching an offensive in the west. The Bulgarians remained the principal source of concern on the western front even after their conversion to Christianity (865). A series of Bulgarian campaigns (680, 687–89, 709, 759–75) were undertaken with mixed success, most under Constantine V. Two different strategies were pursued. In some campaigns, the Byzantines advanced along the Black Sea coast and fought on open terrain. In others, they attempted to surprise the Bulgarians by advancing over the mountain passes.

In 811, a Byzantine campaign ended in disaster when the emperor Nikephoros I himself was killed. The Bulgarian khan subsequently boasted of drinking from a cup made of the emperor's skull, rimmed in gold. In 813, the Bulgarians took Adrianople, but they remained unable to take Constantinople.

By 860, the Bulgarians controlled most formerly Byzantine territories in the Balkans, despite Constantinople's alliance with the Khazars. The Bulgarians' conversion to Christianity was followed by a brief period of peace. However, conflict soon resumed and the emperor Leo VI (896–912) turned to the Hungarians for help. The Bulgarians formed an alliance with the Pechenegs and defeated the Byzantine army near Adrianople (896), threatening the capital anew.

In 904, the Arabs sacked Thessalonica. In 913, the Bulgarians besieged Constantinople. The Byzantines agreed to regard the Bulgarian khan as an emperor, meanwhile concluding a counteralliance with the Pechenegs. Nevertheless, the Bulgarians defeated the Byzantine forces in 917, then again in 920 at the gates of Constantinople, forcing the Byzantine emperor to pay tribute to them (927). The Bulgarian Empire remained dominant for forty years, but was itself surrounded by powerful adversaries: Pechenegs, Magyars, Rus, Serbs, and Croats. Constantinople itself faced a series of Magyar raids (934, 943, 958, 961) from outside the Bulgarian territories.

The emperor Nikephoros Phokas (963–69) refused to pay tribute to the Bulgarians and sought the intervention of the ruler of Kievan Rus, Sviatoslav I, who occupied the Bulgarian capital at Preslav. However, Sviatoslav quickly returned to Kiev to fight the Pechenegs, who were then allied with Constantinople. After defeating the Pechenegs, Sviatoslav turned against the Byzantines and marched on Constantinople (971). The Byzantines were victorious under the emperor John I Tzimiskes (969–976), an Armenian general who had murdered Nikephoros with the complicity of the latter's wife and succeeded him.

In the meantime, the Bulgarian Empire declined. The Bulgarian sovereign was demoted in Byzantine diplomacy from emperor to *magistros*, and the Bulgarian Empire was crushed by the Byzantines at the beginning of the eleventh century.

The Khazars

The Khazars were heirs to the Göktürk khaganate, which ruled the steppe from the borders of Ukraine to the Mongol borders during the sixth century. After it split, around 559, the Göktürks of the western khaganate invaded the Volga steppe, pushing the Avars toward Hungary. In 627, in the Byzantine tradition of forming alliances with the nomadic rulers of the steppe, the emperor Heraclius allied himself with the Göktürks against the Sassanids. Similarly, the Khazars, then settled on the Volga, allied with the Byzantines against the Bulgarians.

In 640–50, the Arabs, at the height of their territorial expansion, attempted to conquer the steppes north of the Caucasus and failed. Khazars and Arabs clashed many times between 730 and 737, and after an Arab victory, a Khazar khan converted to Islam. Many Khazars also converted to Judaism. When the Umayyads were in decline, the Khazars raided Arab territories south of the Caucasus with the Byzantines' blessing. After the Khazars became sedentary, they were in turn attacked by Rus in the north and by the Pechenegs and the Oguz, or Turkmen, in the south, the latter driven west by the Uzbeks. Power relationships in the steppes of Volga and Turkestan remained unstable throughout the ninth century. Whenever possible, the Byzantine Empire formed alliances with the Khazars or the Pechenegs against their more dangerous enemies, the Arabs and Bulgarians.

The Rus Front

Russia is today a country that extends from the Black Sea to the Arctic Ocean, divided from south to north into steppe, forests, and tundra. It did not exist as such in the Middle Ages. Modern Russia was founded in Kiev by the Varangians, Swedish Vikings who had traveled down the Russian rivers. The word "Rus" refers to the Varangians of Kiev. Under pressure from the nomads of the steppe, the Rus took shelter in the northern forests before creating the grand duchy of Muscovy in the thirteenth century. The steppe south of Kiev was controlled by the Mongols for more than two centuries.

The Rus vainly attacked Constantinople in 860. In the tenth century, Russian Slavic power increased, progressively assimilating the Varangians, and Russia destroyed the Khazar khaganate (950). Prince Igor of Kiev led another land and sea expedition against Constantinople (941), but was defeated, and a second invasion also failed (944). A treaty was signed (971) between the Byzantine Empire and Sviatoslav of Kiev, by which he agreed to provide troops to the empire when necessary in exchange for commercial concessions. However, the relationships remained adversarial until Russia converted to the Christian faith (988). From then on, Russia became the Byzantine Empire's main ally.

Armenia

Before ending our survey of the Byzantine Empire, we should examine Armenia. Armenia's history goes back at least to the sixth century B.C.E., and it was fought over by Persia and Rome. It converted to the Christian faith even before Rome, and was not Chalcedonian. For geopolitical reasons, it remained a center of conflict between the Sassanids and the Eastern Roman Empire.

The Umayyad Arab invasions targeted Armenia and enabled it to play a pivotal role in the defense of the Byzantine Empire. Subsequently, Armenia found itself allied either to Constantinople or to the Abbasids. Four of the most remarkable Byzantine emperors were Armenian: Leo V (813–20), Basil I (867–85), Romanus I (920–44), and John I Tzimiskes (969–76), the Armenian general of Mesopotamia, who succeeded Nikephoros (963–69). The empress Theodora, who restored orthodoxy in 844, was also Armenian. An important part of the army, including many of the *themata* of Anatolia, were dominated by Armenian soldiers and generals (Narses, Kourkouas, Ardavast, Bardanes, Bardas, Selerus, Symbatius). Armenia thus became a critical ally of the empire, and its collapse in 1054 presaged the Byzantine Empire's great defeat by the Seljuk Turks in the battle of Manzikert (1071), fought on Armenian territory.

THE RECONQUEST

The Macedonian dynasty was a period of restoration of Byzantine power (867–1058). The *themata*, which numbered four in the sixth century, grew to forty-six by the death of Basil II (1025). A century before, the empire had been defeated by the Abbasids and could barely resist the Bulgarians, whose khan demanded to be treated as an equal of the Eastern Roman emperor. By the time Charlemagne was crowned emperor of the Holy Roman Empire in the west, the situation had changed dramatically. The territory of the Byzantine Empire had doubled and extended east to Armenia and southeast to Syria and Mesopotamia. The empire was surrounded by client states, and the political and religious influence of the Byzantines reached as far to the north as Kiev in the Ukraine.

This period can be divided into two parts: 867–962, when conditions improved significantly, and 863–1025, when the empire's triumph was complete. In fact, by 1025, the empire's traditional rivals had been almost entirely destroyed. The Sassanids had been overrun during the tumultuous Arab expansion, and by the beginning of the eleventh century, the Arabs themselves had been weakened by the Turks. The various nomad invasions—by Avars, Oguz, Pechenegs, Cumans, and so on—had withered. The Bulgarians had been crushed. The Rus had been Christianized and considered themselves faithful allies. The Byzantine reconquest waged against Islam thus appeared successful.

Internally, religious quarrels had diminished and military revolts, famines, and epidemics had become rare. The Byzantine currency, the *nomisma,* was strong. While the Roman Church converted the Scandinavians, Hungarians, Croats, Poles, Czechs, and Balts, the Eastern Orthodox Church did the same for the Bulgarians, the Russians, the Serbs, the Macedonians, and the Romanians.

The Cyrillic alphabet was important for transmitting liturgy to Bulgarians, Serbs, and Russians. At the beginning of the eleventh century, Constantinople had 500,000–800,000 inhabitants, making it the most populous city in the world outside China. Thessalonica, the empire's second city, had more than 100,000 inhabitants. Antioch, its third most populous city, had been retaken. Alexandria, Antioch, Constantinople, and Rome were the four largest cities of the Christian world. The administration was working smoothly under the Macedonian dynasty, which ruled continuously from 867 to 1056, and included the emperors Romanos I, Nikephoros II, and John I Tzimiskes.

The reconquest started by first strengthening the empire's borders. Piracy was eliminated on its coasts, and buffer zones were created following the victories on its eastern borders. The emperors of the first period occupied only a small region in Italy and Greece. A more significant expansion would await Nikephoros II.

In the middle of the eleventh century, the empire had to confront a militarized Armenian sect, the Paulician dualists, who regarded the world as the scene of a cosmic struggle between a beneficent God and an evil demiurge. They occupied the upper Euphrates until 878 with a fortress in Divriği. After their defeat, the Paulicians did not disappear, but moved to Bulgaria and their creed mutated into Bogomilism, which influenced subsequent Christian sects such as the Vaudois and the Cathars in France.

The empire's borders remained vulnerable. Byzantine incursions in Cilicia were inconclusive, and an attempt to capture Tarsus in 882 was a disaster. In addition, unrest in Sicily, southern Italy, and the Balkans required that troops be sent to the west. The annual Arab raids continued into the last part of the ninth century, but the border was moved to the east of the Taurus at the beginning of the tenth century. There the empire gained an important ally: the Armenian princes, a significant regional military power at the beginning of the tenth century, who had previously been allied with the Arabs. The Byzantines ignored the eastern front to confront the Bulgarians in 917. However, ten years later, the emperor Romanos I Lekapenos sent the Armenian general John Kourkouas to capture Dvin and take control of the Bitlis Pass, some 350 kilometers east of the Byzantine border. The Armenian high plateau was progressively subjugated, and Armenian sovereigns such as Gagik I, king of Vaspurakan, and the prince Achot Bagratuni, surrendered around the middle of the tenth century. Arab power collapsed in Armenia and Transcaucasia during this period.

In the last quarter of the tenth century, internal power struggles plagued the Byzantine Empire with three regime changes, two coups d'état, and a rebellion. However, it was also a period of military progress and victories. The capital of the emirate of Malatya in eastern Anatolia, the origin of Arab raids over three centuries, was sacked, and it was subjected to Byzantine rule. The Byzantines also conquered all of Cilicia (962).

WAR ACCORDING TO NIKEPHOROS

The general Nikephoros Phokas inaugurated a glorious reign as the emperor Nikephoros II (963– 69). In order to consolidate his conquests, he created three new *themata*: Cyprus, Tarsus, and Mopsuestia, and expanded those in Cilicia. He was diplomatic enough to resolve old religious quarrels, and he encouraged monophysite Christians to settle in Cilician regions that had been recently abandoned by the Arabs. In Armenia, Nikephoros created additional *themata* under the command of his nephew, Bardas Phokas. In order to confront the famine that ravaged the empire, he passed a law limiting land speculation.

The emperor was an experienced general who had long pondered the various military strategies that could be used for defending the most vulnerable *themata*. How to confront an adversary who was often more numerous and more powerful? Was it best to use skirmishes or frontal assaults? In a treatise on military strategy titled *Peri paradromēs* (On Skirmishing), he described these methods:

LOOKOUT POSTS: HOW FAR APART THEY OUGHT TO BE

Commanders who have assumed responsibility for large border *themata* and who have authority over mountain passes. . . . should place observation posts on them. The posts for the sentries should be about three or four miles apart. When they observe the enemy moving out, they should quickly hurry off to the next station and report what they observed. In turn, those men should race off to the next station. In this way, the information will eventually reach the cavalry posts situated on more level terrain. They will then inform the general of the alien incursion.

The men should spend fifteen days in watching the roads, bringing enough provisions with them for that number of days. Lists of soldiers should be carefully drawn up and the men gotten ready by the officers, so that replacements may be sent to relieve the men at the posts. The full complement of troops as set down in the lists must be sent out on a regular basis, and nobody should be allowed to stay at home by the officers because of shameful gain.

The sentries should be on the lookout for places in which the enemy are likely to make camp. These are usually places in which the ground is level and there is plenty of water. Other men should look for places in which the roadway narrows, and still others where there is a river difficult to cross. If they guard these places carefully, the enemy will not be able to move out secretly. Trustworthy, very experienced men should be sent out to check and see if the sentries are guarding their areas carefully and without slacking. The exact number of sentries as listed should go out, with none missing; they should not leave the posts to which they have been assigned to observe and guard the roads. They should not stay in the same station for a long time, but should change and move to another place. Otherwise, if they are too long in the same place, they will be recognized and might easily be captured by the enemy.

OCCUPY DIFFICULT TERRAIN BEFORE THE ENEMY ATTACKS

Upon learning that the enemy have begun to move, the general should assemble and arm his own troops and proceed to the border areas. The entire infantry force should advance toward the road along which the enemy will soon move out. If he learns that only a small enemy force is riding out, he should make haste to meet them and have the infantry together with the cavalry overwhelm them, if indeed he has been able to assemble and organize the infantry. Since the infantry is more suited for fighting on narrow and difficult ground, it is necessary to make use of it to occupy the mountain heights in advance and to hold on to them. If the terrain permits, infantry units should be stationed on both sides. In sectors that are also suited for cavalry action, have the horsemen join with the infantry. When the enemy hear about our preparations and that we have occupied the passes, they will either slow down their advance or, with God's help, they will be beaten back. If the ground is not suited for launching an attack from both sides, but only from one, then that elevated part ought to be occupied in advance. In places that are not suitable and that do not allow us to launch our attack from a high mountain, but in which the road rises gradually and is rough and narrowed by little streams, the infantry units must still be positioned on higher ground. They should seize the road and block it with soldiers bearing shields and javelins. Behind them should be archers, men who can throw rocks, and more slingers. Get a second line organized to stand behind the first. On both sides of the line guarding the road down the middle, station men with javelins, light-armed troops, and slingers. If they say that there are other roads, of the sort that the border guards call *atrapoi*, off to the right or to the left of the line guarding the public road, not close by but further off, these too should be seized by the infantry and tightly guarded. Otherwise, if the enemy find out that the public road is securely held by a large number of troops, they will advance along one of those off to the side. If this should not be well and securely guarded, the enemy will use that to find a way through and will appear to the sides or the rear of our formation, injecting confusion and fear into the Roman army.

SKIRMISHING TACTICS IN SINGLE RAIDS AND ESTIMATING THE ENEMY'S NUMBER

What we call a single raid is launched from the enemy's territory without infantry. They usually ride along rapidly and keep going the whole night without camping anywhere, but make brief stops to rest their horses only in order to feed them. In general, these single raids start out with a very small but select body of troops. They make an effort to move most rapidly to the territory they want to raid.

When the general, therefore, learns from the road sentries and guards that they have started out, he should move with all haste to the areas on the frontier. He should send ... a very experienced, competent officer ahead, with some selected junior officers and good horses. They should catch up with the enemy, keep a close and experienced eye on them, follow them along, and report back to the general if it is possible, in the place they have reached, to observe the number of soldiers in the party. It is not only by visual observation that one can estimate the numerical strength of the enemy. First, there are the hoof prints of the horses. For when there is a large amount of grass in a deserted area and if it is all trampled down by the horses' feet, experienced scouts can form an approximate estimate from this of the quantity of troops. In like manner, one can examine the ground at river crossings. A more precise estimate can be formed from the enemy's camp after they have vacated it. When the general learns of the approach of an enemy raid and figures out which regions they intend to invade, he should move closer to them. Finding a good location to conceal himself and his men, he should send out mounted scouts in all directions. When he has obtained information about them and they have been observed riding out and scattering all over, then, while they are disorganized, he should march out after them, and he should have no difficulty in defeating them.

PURSUING RAIDING BANDS ON THE MOVE

Upon learning that a raiding band has begun to move, the general should immediately send out another officer with some selected cavalrymen. . . . [who] should be accompanied by one of the men who had been sent . . . to inform the general of the raiding party's movement. . . . The general himself, together with his troops, should march out behind the officer he is sending. . . . This following behind the enemy ought to be carried out with precision and without deviation, adhering to their tracks and line of march. . . .

The general should have figured out the places and villages which the enemy plan to attack. Before dawn, then, he should angle out to either the right or the left of them, whichever appears to him as providing safer ground. Quickening his pace, he should move out from their flank about two miles. As mentioned, this should be done before daybreak, so the enemy will not see the clouds of dust and become aware of the general's presence. On reaching safe ground, the general should conceal his troops. With a few horsemen, let him draw more closely to the enemy. He should mount a high vantage point and hasten to get a good look at them. As they move out for attack and scatter for plunder, the general should remain in that spot until the third or fourth hour of the day. He should study the battle formation of the emir and form a careful estimate of the number of his men. When the troops going out to raid have gotten far enough away from the emir's battle formation so that they cannot retreat to it again, or so they will not even be aware of an attack upon the formation, since each man will be rushing to get to the villages and gather as much booty as possible, then the general should set his own battle line in proper order and launch his attack against that of the emir, now undermanned, and with the aid of God he will be victorious and bring about the complete and utter destruction of the enemy.

LAYING AN AMBUSH FOR THE SO-CALLED SURVEYORS AT THEIR CAMP

When the enemy are ravaging our country without breaking their military formation and not sending their raiding parties out to any great distance, but playing it very safe, the general will have to devise other ways of getting at them. You ought to reconnoiter and form an estimate of the place in which the enemy's camp is presently located and the place in which they are likely to set up camp the next day. If the distance from the present camp is very long, say sixteen miles or further, so that the length of the road is quite likely to wear out both them and their horses, then investigate the ground in the vicinity of the place in which they will probably encamp, find a good place for an ambush, carefully pick out three hundred or fewer combat-ready horsemen and conceal them there. You should set up another ambuscade with all of your people in a suitable location that is protected by some fortifications. If there is also a fortress in the vicinity, this will be a big help and will greatly increase your security. If foot soldiers are needed, have them come from the fortress to assist you in the fighting.

The enemy usually sends an advance party of troops, whom the Romans generally call surveyors [Latin, *mensuratores*], ahead to the site to set up the camp for them. While they are engaged in this, have the soldiers whom you had earlier stationed in the first ambuscade near their camp charge out fiercely with great force, and, with the help of God, you will subdue them. Even if the enemy should pursue them to the place in which you have stationed your strong ambush force, then assail and overpower the pursuers with a noble, brave charge and win a memorable victory.

SEPARATING FROM THE BAGGAGE TRAIN

. . . After the baggage train has separated from you, you should gather provisions for the troops and fodder for the horses, enough for two or three days, and have them transported on fast mules or in saddlebags on the horses. When you intend following a raiding party of the enemy at night, the entire fighting force should have its armor on, and each man should have his proper weapon in hand ready for battle. Be sure, moreover, to have the so-called *saka* following along behind you. Now, if the enemy's route takes them through difficult terrain, then each *thema*, or even *tagma*, if present, ought to march separately. . . . In this manner, then, the rest of the force . . . should follow along one after the other, and they will march smoothly during the night without noise or confusion. Orders should be given . . . to be very cautious, in fact, to be overly cautious and alert, else if the enemy ever perceive that they are being followed by you, they might . . . hide themselves in an ambush and unexpectedly attack you. We remember an ambush of this sort made by the people of Tarsus in the villages further on. The general at that time observed clouds of dust from the troops riding out to plunder. But it was not a real raiding party, only a simulated one composed of a few worthless men. He pressed on to attack them, but . . . quite unawares the general fell right into an ambush. To prevent anything of this sort happening to you, general, you must take every precaution. Have some cavalrymen with swift horses who thoroughly know the region investigate the hollows and other hiding places in the area. About daybreak, divide the army in two if it is large and numbers up to three thousand.

Send the grooms and the men carrying the fodder for the horses away to a strong place. In the event of unexpected ambushes laid by the enemy, the battle formation ought to be set up in the following manner. Let the first have as its commander one of the more outstanding generals and a third of the troops in your army. . . . You follow the first with the main part of the formation, keeping the *saka* following behind you with a few horsemen. If it happens that the enemy lie in wait for you and station large numbers of their fighting men in ambuscades, and attack the division commander following them, the first formation, the one marching ahead of you, will come to his support. Then when battle has been joined with them, the enemy become scattered about in the fighting and break ranks. When you find them dispersed like this, you will overwhelm them. But when the enemy have not prepared themselves for an ambush of this sort, and are anxious only to ride out and ravage the countryside, then before dawn you should conceal the units of your army in places where they will not be visible to the enemy. They should stay in these ambuscades until the third or fourth hour of the day, until the enemy have ridden out to plunder. Once they are a good distance away from the emir's battle formation, in which there are only a few men left, not many at all, then attack it. First send out three formations of equal size to begin the onslaught. You should remain with the other three or four formations following closely along behind the first three. When these three begin the fighting in close, as you see your own men struggling, so you should provide support. First of all, have the formations following along on either side of you advance to join battle with the enemy, attacking, if possible, from the wings and the flank and fight hand to hand. Then, if necessary, you yourself should attack if your troops are not, in fact, proving the stronger. Actually, though, with only a few troops, as we said, left in the emir's battle line, it will not be able to make a stand against your army, which numbers about three thousand. All this we are setting forth as experience teaches. It is up to you to apply it to circumstances and the urgent needs of the time.

HOW TO MOUNT AN AMBUSH WHEN THE ENEMY INVADE IN FORCE

If the entire enemy army, cavalry and infantry, gets together and with great and heavy force breaks out into our country, riding about and plundering, and if it is planning to penetrate more deeply and search around more thoroughly, and if it should happen that the Roman army has been gathering at about the same time, and the enemy are made to hear about its presence, they will exercise great caution with their troops, not allowing any of them to scatter about in the villages without protection. They will then devise ways of setting up ambushes against our own people and will strive to take them by surprise, pursue, and overwhelm them. For your part, you have to display the utmost caution so that you will not be caught by surprise by them, and in turn you must devise countermeasures to defeat them. You will accomplish something noble and memorable. Once they have been hurt by you, in no way will they spend time plundering our lands.

It is your task, therefore, to reconnoiter likely locations in which the invading enemy will ride in search of food and booty. Station mounted ambuscades in those places, all set to charge out against them. Let the number of horsemen assigned to the ambush be over two hundred, and their commander should be brave and have a great deal of experience with ambushes of this sort. The commander of the whole army who has five or six thousand warlike horsemen and the assistance of God will not need anything more. This army should be divided in two. Two thousand should be stationed further ahead in a suitable ambuscade that has a high observation post with a good view, so he can see his men from far off being pursued and pursuing. Behind the two thousand should be the three thousand, and the infantry units with them ought to be posted in a concealed place, which has some natural protection, as an ambush. If there happens to be a fortified town nearby, that will be helpful to him. But even if the general is attacked by a large number of the enemy and the fighting becomes fierce, he should never even think of getting inside the fortified town before he has seen to the safety of his own people. For that would not only be dishonorable and despicable but would lead to damage and the devastation and utter destruction of the country. But if he has fallen into serious trouble, then he and his infantry should fight back strenuously outside in the strong places near the fortress. He should be greatly helped by the terrain, and he also has the support of the foot soldiers in the fortified town.

The commander, then, of the three hundred men who had been dispatched to guard the villages may stand in an observation post and see the enemy riding into the villages. When they dismount and start searching through the houses of the villagers, then he should take a few more than a hundred out of his three hundred men and send them off with orders to attack the enemy vigorously. The men sent on this mission should outnumber the enemy raiding the village. . . . They should fall upon them and, by the favor of Christ, they should kill many and take many prisoners.

Those of the enemy who have been able to get back on their own horses will take to flight. The rest of our men should then carefully pursue them, until they are chased by the units of the enemy posted to protect their comrades. If our man commanding the three hundred notices that those pursuers are not numerous and are carrying out the pursuit in a disorderly and undisciplined manner, he should wait in the hiding places until his own men who are being chased arrive and pass by. Then he should ride out fiercely from the hiding place and, with his troops, charge upon [the enemy], and, by the power and favor of Christ, he will be successful. He will take prisoners, and he will kill and wound many of the enemy.

Should more of the enemy arrive and their numbers keep increasing, and should they carry out their pursuit more vigorously, then he ought to send the prisoners he has taken, along with their horses and weapons, on ahead to the place where the general is stationed. In good order, then, he and his men should withdraw, provoking the enemy to chase them and skillfully drawing them along. None of his people should know the places in which the general is lying in ambush, but only the commander. Should a large number of the enemy attack him, and should their pursuit be disorderly, he should have some of his men, brave, outstanding, and with vigorous horses, wheel about and strike the pursuers. This will allow him to get his own wounded to safety and let the men whose horses have become weary or wounded mount others. Then, giving rein to their horses, they ride faster to put a little more distance between themselves and their pursuers. In this way they obtain a little relief from the constant pressure of the enemy on them. The enemy, for their part, will spur their horses on in pursuit, which will only make them weary and faint. Then, as our people who are being pursued approach the ambuscade, let them pass to the right or the left, so that when the men in ambush charge out at that place, they will not run into them and end up injuring one another. After this the troops being pursued should join with those in the ambush and wheel around. Having the attack against the enemy come from two sides will obviously be to the advantage of our army. Let the site of the ambush be such as to provide a good hiding place for our soldiers.

IF THE ENEMY PERSIST IN THEIR AGGRESSION AGAINST OUR COUNTRY, OUR ARMY SHOULD INVADE THEIRS

When large numbers of the enemy wander about our country ravaging, destroying, and making plans to besiege fortified places, they will indeed be on their guard to avoid being ambushed by the Roman units; in fact, they will be devising plans to ambush us. If a Roman army, large enough and capable of defeating them is not there to confront them, then you, general, must take action such as was taken in the past, described in the [*Taktika*] of the revered and most wise emperor Leo. . . .

Therefore, general, when you are at a loss about how to injure the enemy with stratagems and ambushes, because they are very cautious and guard themselves carefully, or if, on the other hand, it is because your forces are not up to facing them openly in battle, then this is what you ought to do. Either you march quickly against the lands of the enemy, leaving the most responsible of the other generals behind, with enough troops for skirmishing and for the security of the *themata*. Or else, if you carry out the skirmishing, then send your best general, well known and esteemed for his courage and vast experience, with a significant force of cavalry and infantry down to the country of the enemy. He should stay there a while, burning, destroying, and besieging fortified towns. When the enemy hear of this, they will force their leader, even if he is unwilling, to come back to defend their own country.

NIGHT FIGHTING

If the enemy should form another plan that they hope will work to their advantage, once they become aware of your presence, that night they will pitch their tents and set up camp. Then you should attack them at night, making sure to prepare the assault as explained. You should launch your attack from the rear with infantry units. Divide the remaining infantry into six divisions; station three off to the right side of the enemy and three off to the left. If the nature of the ground requires that their camp be set up in an extended way, they should be about a bow shot apart or a little less. Leave open and unguarded the road, and that alone, which provides safe passage for the enemy toward their own land. After they have been vigorously assaulted and they discover the open road, beguiled by the idea of being saved, of fleeing the battle, and of getting back to their own land, they mount their horses and race along that road to escape, each man concerned only about his own safety.

If they have not set up their camp in an extended way but have been compelled by the nature of the ground to make it in a circle, you must form your infantry units in a circle around it and get them ready for battle. Be sure, as we mentioned, to leave only that one road free and open which leads to their own country. After you have drawn up your foot soldiers in this manner, have the units set up camp close to the enemy and light a large number of fires. Over each one of the infantry units, station a brave and competent officer. Each unit should also be accompanied by some horsemen under outstanding officers stationed to the rear, as space allows. You should also order all the infantry troops to obey them. When preparations have been made in this manner, pick out some brave, fleet-footed, light-armed troops and send them ahead. They should silently move up as close as possible to the enemy. Give orders that those stationed in the middle are to lead the attack, then the troops in front. If the ground rises higher on both sides, have the infantry attack the enemy from both directions. As the enemy are struck by stones hurled by hand or slings or arrows from above on both sides, they will quickly fall apart. If the nature of the ground is not such but rises up only on one side, in like manner, it is easier to have them hurl rocks and shoot arrows against them from that direction. If the fighting is on level ground, though, it is necessary to exercise greater care. If the enemy want to mount their horses and charge against our light-armed troops, they will not cause them any serious harm, because the terrain will help them. But, rather, they will inflict great damage upon themselves.

Have all the infantry units descend from both directions and have all the trumpets sounded, and raise a shout and battle cry. Then the general coming up from the rear should join battle with all his strength. If the enemy still hold out and do not dash into flight, then the fast light troops and the ones who had been sent out ahead should be aroused by their officers to go into the tents of the enemy. The rugged terrain will make this easy for them. When, after such a start, they get hold of the enemy's horses, mules, and other belongings and start taking prisoners, they will all rush in to join in the pillaging. They will go through the tents sparing nobody, cutting them down with the sword. Then the enemy will rush to escape. The ones who can do so will mount their horses, and others will be on foot as they try to hide and find safety in the mountains and ravines.*

FROM THE HEIGHT OF THE EMPIRE TO ITS DECLINE

While the Byzantine Empire grew stronger during the Macedonian dynasty, its main adversary, the Abbasid Caliphate, declined. The Arabs' great expansion ended in the middle of the eighth century with the battle of Talas in Transoxiana in 751, when they defeated a Tang army with the help of the Karluk Turks. Between 860 and 870, Turkic slave-soldiers called *ghilman,* whom the Arabs regarded as barbarians, increasingly asserted their power in the Abbasid Caliphate. The Byzantine

* Nikephoros II Phokas, emperor, *Peri paradromēs* (On Skirmishing), trans. Gilbert Dagron as *Le traité sur la guérilla (De velitatione) de l'empereur Nicéphore Phocas,* ed. Dagron and Haralambie Mihăescu (Paris: CNRS, 1986), i, iii, ix, xiii, xvi, xvii, xx, xxiv; in Gérard Chaliand, *Anthologie mondiale de la stratégie: Des origines au nucléaire* (Paris: R. Laffont, 1990).

Empire profited from this situation until the rise of the Seljuk Turks in the eleventh century.

Byzantine conquests continued:

960: Crete reconquered and reconverted to Christianity

962: Beginning of the reconquest of Cilicia; Aleppo retaken

964: Retaking of Adana by John I Tzimiskes

965: Retaking of Tarsus

967: Annexation of the Armenian principality of Taron

969: Retaking of Antioch by the *strategos* Michael Bourtzes

Tzimiskes kept battling until 975 and conquered southern Syria. Baalbek fell, Beirut was retaken, and Damascus consented to pay tribute to the empire. The emperor took the castles of Sayun and Barzuya in Syria's An-Nusayriyah Mountains. The authority of the Baghdad caliph waned. The Abbasids were further weakened by internal quarrels and by the rebellion of the Qarmatians (who originated from Bahrain), who besieged Damascus and Baghdad (927–30), then sacked Mecca. They also had to confront the rise of the Fatimids (Shiites) from North Africa, who occupied Egypt, and the Zanj rebellion of black slaves in the southern marshes of Mesopotamia, which was severely suppressed (869–83).

Byzantine emperors in this era reconquered provinces with large Christian populations such as Bulgaria, Armenia, Cyprus, and Antioch. The client states in the east were Armenia, Georgia, and the Muslim states of the Merwanids (Kurds). The Byzantine decline began insidiously at the death of Basil II and continued until the middle of the eleventh century after the defeat of the Byzantine army at Manzikert at the hands of the Seljuk Turks in 1071.

None of Basil II's heirs were of his stature. A long crisis between the civil administration and the military erupted. Under the military emperors, the empire continued to decline. The currency depreciated. Constantine IX Monomachos (1042–55) was responsible for the most important reforms of the era. The emperor tried to centralize power in Constantinople by reducing the *themata* and abolishing the autonomous fleets. The percentage of mercenaries in the Byzantine armed forces increased. The Normans became more aggressive in southern Italy and the Pechenegs crossed the Danube (1048). In addition, the Oguz crossed the Balkans, fleeing the Cumans. In the east, the Seljuks, who had converted to Islam, became more and more powerful. Monomachos, however, defeated the Normans in Sicily, overran the Pechenegs, and reestablished order on the Danube border. Yet Monomachos's decision to transform the military obligations of the *themata* into a tax was one of the principal causes of the loss of eastern Anatolia. Nearly 50,000 troops from the *themata* of Iberia (on the Armeno-Georgian frontier) and Mesopotamia disappeared from the eastern border. The empire still needed to protect the coast of Asia Minor and the maritime routes to Cyprus, Rhodes, Crete, and southern Italy, but the navy had been downsized. Times had changed since Nikephoros Phokas had told the papal ambassador: "I alone rule the seas."

This decline of the Eastern Roman Empire became clearly noticeable by the middle of the eleventh century. Western Christianity's power was growing both demographically and economically, and the power of Venice had increased. The relationship between the pope and the patriarch of Constantinople deteriorated, leading to mutual excommunications that ended up with a schism (1054), and attempts at reconciliation over the following years failed. In the east, the nomads continued their traditional seasonal attacks, now led by the Turks. The Normans conquered Sicily and most of the Byzantine possessions in southern Italy. In the years 1025–55, Byzantine emperors, including Monomachos, had limited military experience. They reduced the funding and political influence of the army and the navy. Monomachos's reforming of the *themata* inaugurated an irreversible military decline.

At first, there were only sporadic raids by the Seljuks in eastern Anatolia, but Syria and Egypt were the real objectives of the Seljuk sultan Alp Arslan. En route to Aleppo, he learned that a large Byzantine army under the command of the emperor Romanos IV Diogenes was advancing in Armenia. Was the battle of Manzikert really necessary? Perhaps it would have been better to let Alp Arslan march south as he had intended? After refusing a truce, the Byzantine emperor decided to wage battle, against his generals' advice. The Byzantine troops were predominantly mercenaries, including a large contingent of Oguz (Turkmen), who would defect to the enemy. The Byzantine army was positioned in two lines. The second line reserves were commanded by Andronikos Dukas, a nephew of the previous emperor, who had little loyalty to Romanos. In the first line, Romanos was positioned in the center, surrounded by Greek troops and cavalry. The flanks were part mercenary, part Greek. The Byzantines advanced and the Seljuk troops retreated in good order. The Byzantines continued their advance until at the periphery of the Seljuk camp. At this point, the Byzantine emperor became worried about his own camp, which had been left unprotected, and gave the order to retreat. The center of the line obeyed, but the flanks were surprised and hesitated. Alp Arslan seized the moment and charged with his cavalry into the void left by the retreating center. The right flank panicked and collapsed; the left held a little longer. Dukas, who could have intervened, did not move. The center continued to fight until the emperor was made prisoner, an unprecedented catastrophe for the Byzantines. Alp Arslan treated him honorably.

It took ten chaotic years before the empire again found a capable monarch. Alexios I Komnenos (1081–1118), to whom his daughter would later dedicate the *Alexiad*, had to fight on all fronts simultaneously. Part of Anatolia had been lost, the Pechenegs and the Hungarians threatened Byzantine possessions in the Balkans, and the Normans had captured Bari and Durres (in Albania). Alexios implemented administrative and military reforms and led a successful counterattack against the Normans. He allied himself with the Cumans and expelled the Pechenegs (1091). He was also victorious against the Turks. The Turks had rival principalities in Anatolia, only some of which recognized the authority of the Seljuk sultan of Baghdad. Alexios played these rivals against each other.

The rise of the Turks was not initially perceived as a serious threat, but as a nomadic incursion, something to which the empire was well accustomed, and that it could use to advantage against other rivals. None of the Seljuk principalities initially represented a real danger for the empire, and it would take almost a century for this threat to become serious. However, part of the empire's core was no longer under the control of Constantinople. In the twelfth century, the empire began to use mercenaries more and more, since it had lost its principal bases of recruitment, Anatolia and Armenia.

The First Crusade (1096–99) showcased the power of Latin Christianity and put the Byzantine Empire in the ambiguous position of being both an ally and a commercial rival. The Crusades weakened the Seljuks and enabled Alexios to reconquer their capital, Nicaea. The Byzantine Empire rebuilt its fleet and regained control over the coasts of Asia Minor, including Cilicia, where Armenian nobles had taken refuge. Alexios won a significant victory over the Seljuks in 1116 at Philomelion. However, conflicts between the western Europeans and the Byzantines increased. The economy of Constantinople was in decline, and the Byzantines offered important commercial concessions to the Venetians. The reconquest of Cilicia (1104) intensified tensions with the Normans.

Alexios I's reign was one of the empire's final moments of grandeur. Under his son, John II Komnenos (1118–43), the Byzantines allied with the Cumans and won military victories over the Seljuks. However, the empire was forced to grant commercial concessions to Venice, Genoa, and Pisa in exchange for the help of Venice against the Normans. Later, in agreement with Pisa and Genoa, Manuel I Komnenos confiscated Venetian assets in Constantinople, but the Byzantine currency depreciated. A Byzantine army was defeated by the Seljuks at Myriokephalon (1176), only a short distance from Constantinople. The vise was tightening.

Italian merchants enjoyed great economic power in the empire until the emperor Andronikos I Komnenos (1183–85) massacred the Italian merchants of Constantinople (1183). The empire was now reduced to the Greek peninsula, Thrace, and scattered possessions in Asia Minor. In 1204, during the Fourth Crusade, aimed at Jerusalem, the crusaders took advantage of a Byzantine power struggle to capture and sack Constantinople with the help of a Venetian fleet, virtually putting an end to the Byzantine Empire. The Byzantine leadership took refuge in Nicaea, Thessalonica, and Trabzon, each of which hosted a rival pretender to the throne. Constantinople was recovered in 1261 from the subsequent, short-lived Latin Empire, and Michael VIII Palaiologos became emperor of Byzantium. The Palaiologan dynasty would rule in Constantinople until 1453.

The empire survived due to its formidable reputation, but it had no army worthy of the name. A Catalan company that had been hired to recruit mercenaries to fight the Turks mutinied, occupied Byzantine lands in Greece, and blockaded Constantinople (1305–7). The Ottoman Turks, who had fled before the Mongols, captured Bursa (1326), Nicaea (1329), and Nicomedia (1337). At the same time, Stephen Dushan led a Serbian army that threatened Constantinople, which was itself on the verge of a civil war. Confusion was total in Constantinople and lasted half a century (1341–91). During that time, the Ottomans, not as yet considered a deadly threat, crossed the Hellespont, captured Gallipoli (1335) and made Adrianople (Edirne) their capital. Their victories in Maritsa (1371) and Kosovo (1389) gave them Bulgaria and Serbia. The Byzantine Empire outside Constantinople was now limited to Thessalonica and the Peloponnese, with its fortified city of Mystras.

The Byzantine emperors desperately needed help from the Latins and the pope. A contingent of crusaders arrived and was defeated by the Turks at Nicopolis (1396). The first Turkish siege of Constantinople failed (1397). The emergence of the Turco-Mongol Tamerlane brought some respite to the Byzantines. Tamerlane defeated the Ottoman Sultan

Bayezid in 1402 near Ankara, but the Byzantine Empire was too weak to take advantage of this defeat. The vise tightened again. The Ottomans took Thessalonica in 1430. A last crusade arrived to confront the Ottomans and was defeated at Varna in 1444. Mehmed II laid siege to Constantinople with 80,000 Turks, equipped for the first time with large cannons, against only 7,000 Greek and Genoan defenders. On May 29, 1453, the order was given for the final assault and the city fell, along with its last emperor, Constantine XI Palaiologos.

The Empire of Trabzon remained independent, although weak, until its final collapse in 1461.

CHAPTER 4

The Arabs

The first Arab expansion was prodigious. Soon after the death of the Prophet Muhammad (632), the Islamized Arabs conquered the Sassanid Empire and took Syria, Palestine, Egypt, and North Africa from the Eastern Roman Empire. Within a century, the Arabs occupied territories extending from Spain to the borders of India and had defeated Chinese troops of the Tang Empire at Talas (751). This expansion was swift and militarily exceptional. Except in Spain, it was also durable, because it was religious.

THE REASONS FOR ARAB SUCCESS

Islam first unified the Bedouin nomads of the Arabian Peninsula and converted Arab city dwellers and merchants. The Bedouin were loyal to their tribes and often fought skirmishes and small wars motivated by revenge or plunder. The religious fervor aroused by the Prophet unified the various tribes, who set out at his death to conquer the world. However, the conquest began without a clear objective. The Prophet had not designated a successor and his followers chose Abu Bakr, the Prophet's advisor and father-in-law, as caliph (632), and not Ali, the Prophet's cousin and the husband of his daughter Fatima. Abu Bakr, followed by Omar, organized the conquest. It was indeed a propitious period for the expansion of Islam because the two empires bordering the Arabian Peninsula—the Eastern Roman Empire and the Sassanid Persian Empire—had both been

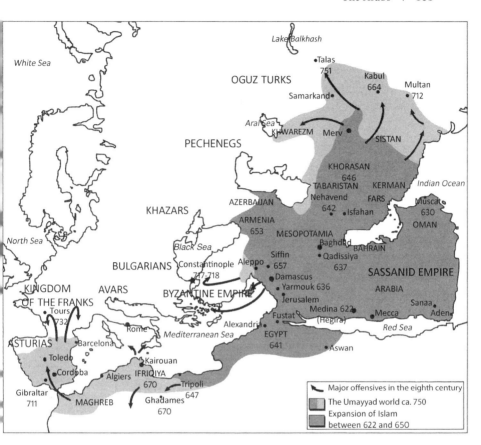

Lake Balkhash
White Sea
OGUZ TURKS
•Talas
751
Kabul
664
Multan
• 712
Samarkand•
Aral Sea
KHWAREZM Merv •
SISTAN
PECHENEGS
KHORASAN
646
TABARISTAN KERMAN *Indian Ocean*
AZERBAIJAN
Nehavend FARS
642 •Isfahan
Muscat•
630
KHAZARS
ARMENIA
653 MESOPOTAMIA
OMAN
North Sea
Black Sea
Baghdad
BAHRAIN
BULGARIANS Constantinople Aleppo
Siffin
• Qadissiya
717-718
• 657
637
SASSANID EMPIRE
Damascus
KINGDOM AVARS
BYZANTINE EMPIRE
• Yarmouk 636
ARABIA
OF THE FRANKS
Jerusalem
Sanaa•
Tours
Medina 622•
Mecca
Aden•
•732
Fustat (Hegira)
Red Sea
ASTURIAS •Barcelona
Rome
Mediterranean Sea
Alexandria•
EGYPT
641
•Aswan
•Toledo
•Kairouan
•Cordoba
Algiers IFRIQIYA
670 Tripoli
Gibraltar
Ghadames 647
711 MAGHREB
670

Major offensives in the eighth century
The Umayyad world ca. 750
Expansion of Islam
between 622 and 650

MAP 3. The expansion of Islam, 622–750 C.E.

weakened by internal struggles for succession and faced significant internal religious, ethnic, and social conflicts.

In the Byzantine Empire, religious quarrels had persisted since the fifth century, with the Coptic monophysites of Egypt and the Arameans of Syria opposing Church orthodoxy. The landowners supported the Eastern Roman Empire, but the empire was unpopular with the people because of the heavy taxes levied to support its military campaigns. The Sassanid Empire was also struggling, with a dominant Zoroastrian faction ruling a population that did not share its faith. Unrest increased further in the Sassanid Empire after the exhausting struggle with Constantinople, which ended in defeat.

The Bedouin tribes were skilled at raiding and skirmishing. In his *Muqaddimah* (1377), the Arab historian Ibn Khaldun sketched a remarkable portrait of the Bedouin: "The nomads have neither walls nor doors. Hence, they must trust to themselves for their protection. They always carry weapons and are constantly alert on every side. They take short naps and do so only when they are in a group or riding their camels or horses. They pay attention to the faintest barking. Fortitude is one of their character traits, and courage is their nature."

The Arab expansion was as unexpected as was the weakened status of the two empires which it faced. The Arabian Peninsula has desert or semi-desert areas to the north, the plains and mountains of the Syrian-Palestinian corridor to the west, and, to the east, Mesopotamia. The Arabs moved easily on camelback through this familiar sea of sand, whereas Byzantine and Sassanid troops traveled by foot or on horse-back and were ill at ease in the desert. Initially, the Arabs would fight their adversary at the borders of deserts into which they could easily retreat.

THE FIRST CONQUEST

On the Sassanid frontier, Abu Bakr, the successor to the Prophet and first caliph, sent an experienced general, Khalid ibn al-Walid, toward the southwest of Iraq. The warriors of the Beni Bakr tribe joined him, and the combined force captured al-Hirah, not far from Basra (633). From this base, the Arabs harassed the Persians. Khalid then took advantage of the paralysis of the Sassanid state to march north, skirting the desert. He crossed the Euphrates in an area populated by nomads. His mission was not the conquest of Iraq, but the eradication of the apostasies of false Iraqi prophets such as Tulieha and Musaylimah.

On the Byzantine frontier, the Arabs were familiar with the Syrian-Palestinian corridor. Ibn Abi Obeida led an Arab army supported by reserves into Palestine. It split into two. One group marched to the coast in Gaza, and the other advanced through the interior, targeting Damas-cus. Gaza was captured, but the Arabs' advance on Damascus was halted by the Byzantines with the aid of a popular revolt in Palestine that occurred behind Ibn Abi Obeida's lines.

Abu Bakr, fearing for Abi Obeida's troops, sent Khalid to Palestine. Khalid crossed the Syrian Desert, crushed the revolt, reunited the two Muslim armies, and then defeated a Byzantine army at Ajnadayn (634). Next, the Arabs headed north and besieged Damascus and Aleppo. Both surrendered quickly, despite the fact that Khalid's combined troops numbered fewer than fifteen thousand.

The Byzantine Emperor Heraclius sent a large army to Yarmouk, not far from the Sea of Galilee. The new caliph, Umar ibn al-Khatab, wanted to replace Khalid with Abi Obeida as supreme commander, but the latter did not join the battle until after it was nearly lost. Despite their numerical advantage, the Byzantine troops were demoralized by the presence of mercenary soldiers in their camps and by internal quarrels among the Byzantine generals. That situation was in clear contrast with the Arab troops' enthusiasm, stoked by religious fervor and the prospect of booty. Fresh troops arrived to reinforce the Arab contingent and allowed them to cut the Byzantine lines of communication.

The battle took place on August 20, 636, at Yarmouk. A sandstorm blew from the desert and blinded the Byzantine troops. They were defeated and their commander in chief was killed. By the fall of 636, the Arabs had conquered Syria and Palestine as far as the Taurus Mountains, with the exception of Jerusalem and Caesarea. A base was established in Jabiyah from where the army could rapidly intervene in case of insurrection.

On the Persian front, the Arabs were encamped some two hundred kilometers from Ctesiphon, the Sassanid capital. Fresh Persian troops were drafted for a counterattack, which pushed the Arabs back toward the desert, and al-Hirah was recaptured. Caliph Umar sent reinforcements under the command of Saad ibn Abi Wagar, a cousin of the Prophet. He left Medina with three thousand men, mostly Yemenis, along with four thousand members of the Beni Temin tribe. A third contingent of Hadramaut troops were added en route. Saad first went 120 kilometers into the desert to avoid attack by the Persian cavalry while he organized his army. We know little about the Arab organization and tactics, but the discipline and cohesion of the troops from the three tribes, which risked disunion and fragmentation, was paramount.*

The Arabs rapidly adopted the classic structure of the regular armies that they confronted: a center, flanks, a rearguard, and later on, a vanguard. Their arms included bows, spears, and swords. Group cohesion was based on tribal ties. Discipline, a problem in all tribal armies, improved greatly because obedience was now understood as a religious obligation.

After the victory at Yarmouk over the Byzantines, half of the western Islamic army was ordered back to Iraq. However, its command had

---

* John Bagot Glubb, *The Great Arab Conquests* (1953; London: Quartet Books, 1980).

been transferred from Khalid to Saad ibn Abu Waraz. The Persian sovereign Yazdigerd III had organized a large army under the command of a skilled general, Rostam Farrokhzād. Rostam advanced to the outskirts of Babylon and, for as long as his army remained intact, blocked the Arabs from crossing the Euphrates. The Arabs sent a delegation to propose that Yazdigerd convert to Islam. He refused and, tired of Arab raiding from across the Euphrates, gave Rostam the order to cross the river and attack. As the two armies approached each other, the Arabs led the Persians to the borders of the desert, where they could easily retreat if they failed to win.

The battle remained undecided for several days. The Arabs were frightened by the Persian elephants, and Rostam was preoccupied with the arrival of extra troops. The Bedouin attacked at night on the fourth day of the battle and succeeded in overrunning the Persian defenses and killing Rostam. At the death of their commander, the Persian army collapsed, with the exception of a small elite contingent, which died fighting.

The battle of al-Qadisiyya (637) was as fatal to the Persian control of Iraq as was the battle of Yarmouk to the Byzantine control of Syria. The Persian army, which had once threatened Constantinople, had been vanquished by Arab tribes. The Prophet Muhammad had conceded "people of the Book status" only to the Christians and the Jews, but it was now extended to Zoroastrians. The booty from the conquered regions was huge, and after 20 percent had been sent to the caliph in Medina, the troops were well rewarded. The conquest of Iraq continued with the capture of Ctesiphon. Meanwhile, the young Sassanid sovereign Yazdigerd raised another army to defend his throne.

THE CONSOLIDATION OF VICTORY

In 638, six years after the death of the Prophet, the newly conquered Muslim territories needed protection against counterattacks from the Eastern Roman Empire and the Sassanids. The conquest of Syria extended Arab rule as far as Mardin and Diyarbakir in eastern Anatolia. The population of these regions was diverse: in the cities the majority were Greek; in the east of Syria and Palestine, a sizable part of the population were Christian Arabs who spoke Aramaic. There were also Jewish and Phoenician minorities. However, the occupation was largely accepted by the population. Each non-Muslim had to pay an annual tax unless he converted. The churches were left intact, but new church construction was forbidden, as was the ringing of church bells. Christian religious processions were also banned. Nevertheless, the population was under the protection of the Muslims, and their existence and possessions remained secure. The administration remained in the hands of Byzantines and Persians, and Christians and Jews were judged under their own laws. Jews and Christians would continue to enjoy considerable religious and social autonomy under the later Ottoman Muslim occupiers.

The Arab victories were the outcome of a strong, unifying Muslim ideology and the weakening of the two great empires. They were also due to the quality of the Bedouin warriors, to their strategy based on mobility, and to their exceptional generals, such as Khalid ibn al-Walid. To that we might add the dissatisfaction of the local populations with Byzantine orthodoxy.

Muslim Arabs remained a minority, however, and to avoid being absorbed by the local population in a few generations, they garrisoned Jabiya in Syria and Kufa and Basra in Iraq as a ruling military caste. Muslims were forbidden to farm. The children of the conquerors, whose mothers were generally locals, were educated in the garrison towns. However, the modest local taxes were insufficient for the ever growing needs of the army. Funding the troops required more conquests.

The conquest of Egypt was led by Amr ibn al-As, the conqueror of Gaza and Jerusalem, who crossed the Sinai with a few thousand men and arrived in Egypt in 639. The following year, he besieged the Byzantine fortress of Babylon, located close to today's Cairo. Babylon surrendered in 641. Then he laid siege to Alexandria, capital of Egypt and headquarters of the Levantine Byzantine fleet. The persecution of the Coptic Church had reduced support for the Byzantine Empire in Egypt. Besides, Alexandria had a very diverse population, including Jews, Greeks, and Italians. Alexandria surrendered (641) and Egypt was occupied. Shortly thereafter (645), Alexandria rebelled, encouraged by the arrival of a Byzantine fleet. The insurrection was repressed. Amr was replaced by another governor, Abdullah ibn Saad (646), who built an Arab fleet that defeated the Byzantines ten years later and ended Byzantine naval dominance in the eastern Mediterranean.

This capture of Alexandria was of considerable importance. It was one of the most important cities in the world after Constantinople, and Egypt was an extremely rich country. It had been the granary of Rome and it played the same role for Constantinople. The conquest of Egypt from the Byzantines was soon followed by a definitive victory over the Sassanids.

Caliph Umar had not intended to conquer Persia. He had given orders to Saad ibn Abu Waraz not to cross the Zagros Mountains. The fertile plains of Iraq were enough and the Zagros constituted an easily defensible border with Persia. However, the Sassanid emperor Yazdigerd did not want a stable border, but to reconquer Iraq. A new Arab army was dispatched, and the battle that took place in Nehavand ended in Persian defeat (642).

Yazdigerd withdrew to Rei, while Rostam's brother raised another army to confront the Arabs. Another defeat for the Persians followed (643). Yazdigerd took shelter in Isfahan, which was captured in turn. By the time Yazdigerd was finally assassinated in 651, the Arabs controlled all of Persia and also occupied Armenia.

THE SUCCESSION AND ITS CONSEQUENCES

Remarkable generals led Caliph Umar's army, but several, including Khalid ibn al-Walid and Saad ibn Abu Waraz, were removed from their command when they became too famous. Umar was assassinated by a Persian slave in 644 and was succeeded by Uthman ibn Affan, who belonged to the Quraysh aristocracy of Mecca, powerful merchants who had originally opposed Muhammad.

When Uthman became caliph, the conquered regions remained at peace, with the exception of Persia. The expansion ended with the conquest of Cyprus (646) and Tripolitania (647). In Egypt, the Arab troops were quartered in their capital at Fustat. Uthman also named a loyal governor, Muawiya, in Damascus. Uthman dismissed the governor of Egypt and replaced him with a family friend. Uthman's nepotism sparked the hostility of the Prophet's young widow, Aisha, and that of her cousin and son-in law, Ali. Uthman was assassinated in 656, and a struggle for succession ensued.

Ali was supported by Aisha, but the Quraysh aristocracy, who wanted to avenge Uthman's death, supported his kinsman, Muawiya. At first, Muawiya, a skilled politician with strong support in Syria, prevailed against Aisha at the battle of the Camel (656). The battle for succession between Ali and Muawiya continued in a battle at Siffin (657), which was halted when Muawiya's troops attached sheets of the Koran to their spears and asked for religious arbitration. The arbitrators ruled in Muawiya's favor, and he became caliph (658).

However, Ali refused to accept the verdict. Ali's Kharijite allies had supported the arbitration and deserted his camp when they learned of his refusal. He massacred them in Nahrawan. A Kharijite assassinated Ali in 661 before he could continue the fight against Muawiya. The Kharijites remain a small minority to this day and still can be found in M'zab, Algeria, and Djerba, Tunisia.

Muawiyah's family, the Umayyads, gave their name to the first great Arab dynasty, which chose Damascus as its capital. However, the schism between Muawiyah and Ali would endure, splitting the Shias who supported Ali, and the Sunnis who supported Muawiyah and consider themselves the rightful heirs of Muhammad.

The Umayyad dynasty continued the expansion of Arab Islam. The new caliph, Muawiya, exercised power from Damascus, but the holy cities of Medina and Mecca retained their religious importance.

The conquests continued on a lesser scale. The Arabs had defeated the Sassanid Empire and the Eastern Roman Empire. Now they attempted to cross the Cilician Gates of the Taurus Mountains onto the Anatolian plain. Numerous raids and forays occurred, but the land was never conquered. In the north, a part of the mountainous Armenia resisted occupation. Most of the Caucasus also resisted, with the exception of today's Azerbaijan.

In 650, the Byzantine Empire still controlled Anatolia as far as the Euphrates, and its Balkan possessions remained intact. The indirect influence of Constantinople on the Umayyad dynasty was considerable, as would be that of the Abbasid caliphate in Baghdad, which split from the Umayyad caliphate a century later.

The Arab conquests continued from Egypt along the North African coast. An Arab garrison had been established in Kairouan (Tunisia) in 670, and Carthage fell in 696. The Berber inhabitants of the mountainous Constantine region (northeastern Algeria) resisted fiercely, however, and the uprising led by the Berber heroine Dihya (al-Kahina) in the Aurès Mountains obliged the Arabs to bring in reinforcements. However, after the pacification of the Berbers and their conversion to Islam, they would be the first troops to cross the straits of Gibraltar into Spain (711).

CHAPTER 5

The Nomads of the Eurasian Steppes

The military importance of the nomadic populations of the Eurasian steppes for the history of the Middle East and Europe has been largely ignored until recently, except for René Grousset's seminal book, *The Empire of the Steppes*.*

I argued many years ago that these nomadic populations had exerted a dominant influence on Eurasian civilization for more than two thousand years, fueled by a chronic geopolitical antagonism between nomadic and sedentary populations. Throughout history, no group had more militarily influence on Eurasia than the waves of nomads, from the Scythians to the Mongols, who swept through the civilizations of antiquity and the Middle Ages. Their impact was felt from China to Europe, and continuously in Persia, India, the Byzantine Empire, and Russia. Nevertheless, the military accomplishments of the peoples of the steppe have been largely ignored or analyzed piecemeal in the context of specific countries.

The nomads of Central Asia belonged to neither a state nor an empire, nor to a single tribe or race. None of the nomadic peoples represented the totality of the steppes. The nomads have often been studied in ethnographic or geographic isolation, based on histories largely writ-

---

* René Grousset, *L'empire des steppes* (1939; 4th ed., Paris: Payot, 1980); trans. as *The Empire of the Steppes: A History of Central Asia* (New Brunswick, NJ: Rutgers University Press, 1991).

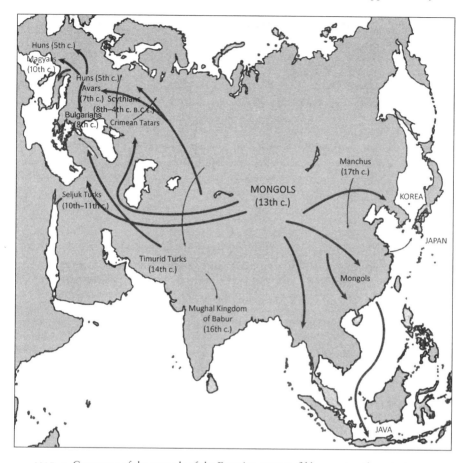

MAP 4. Conquests of the nomads of the Eurasian steppes, fifth–seventeenth centuries.

ten by sedentary authors. Texts were rare among the nomads, with a few nomad inscriptions of the eighth century, the (anonymous thirteenth-century) *Secret History of the Mongols,** and rare archeological material of limited interest. In contrast, the records from Chinese, Persian, Arab, Byzantine, Armenian, and Russian sources are more numerous. Generally, eyewitness accounts paint an unflattering portrait of the nomads. Contemporary historiography has been influenced by these

---

* *The Secret History of the Mongols: The Origin of Chinghis Khan: An Adaptation of the Yuan ch'ao pi shih, Based Primarily on the English Translation by Francis Woodman Cleaves,* ed. Paul Kahn (San Francisco: North Point Press, 1984).

negative accounts from witnesses who were often the victims of nomadic conquest. As a result, modern historians have given scant attention to the important strategic culture of the nomads.

THE PEOPLE OF THE STEPPE

The nomads' pastoral lifestyle remained remarkably stable over thousands of years, but the nomadic populations changed. The nomads are usually classified by linguistic group. Populations of Indo-European language speakers included the Scythians, Sarmatians, Alans, Sakas (Indo-Scythians), and Cimmerians. The speakers of Altaic languages included the Turks, Mongols, Avars, Kazaks, and Uighurs. Gradually, the Indo-European nomads disappeared, with the exception of the Ossetians, and were absorbed or supplanted by larger Altaic populations. The Altaic-speaking groups played a dominant role in the steppe from the fifth century to the thirteenth, when the Mongols created the largest contiguous empire ever known. A few nomadic people also spoke Finno-Ugrian languages, Finnish, Hungarian, Lapp, and Samoyed.

The nomad advances followed a trajectory from east to west. The pastoral nomads occupied the Eurasian steppe, which extends from northern China through Mongolia and Central Asia as far west as the Danube and the Hungarian plain. The Altai Mountains in East Central Asia, which are linked to the mountain range of Tin Shan and the Pamir, and can be crossed through Dzungaria (northern Xinjiang), are the only geographic barrier.

There are three kinds of steppe. In the center, an ocean of grass that smells of wormwood extends from the mouth of the Ordos in China to the Hungarian plain, and includes Mongolia, northern Kazakhstan, the north of the Caucasus, and the southern plains of Russia and Ukraine. To the north are wooded steppes, more humid and with rougher terrain. To the south, there is a semi-desert region, which runs from Lake Balkhash through Kazakhstan to the lower Volga. In Central Asia, the desert is dotted with oases and patches of fertile land amid brutal deserts, such as the Karakum in Turkestan, the Kyzyl Kum in Uzbekistan, and the Gobi in the south of Mongolia.

Nomad populations generally settled in a limited area where tribes and clans controlled their own seasonal pastures, moving in the summer from the plain to the mountains, as do the Kyrgyz today. Tribes often had permanent mountain settlements, where they buried their dead under tumuli. Sometimes nomadic groups settled in conquered cities.

When conflicts arose over resources, the defeated usually migrated westward. The *Völkerwanderungen* were the result.

The nomad economy was pastoral, and sheep were its most important resource. Horses were used for shepherding and for fighting wars. They were robust small horses, able to find their own food even in the most unfavorable conditions. Nomad horsemanship was unsurpassed, and was further improved by the nomads' early invention of the stirrup.

The nomads' food was the meat and milk of their sheep, supplemented with mares' milk. Wool was used for making felt and weaving, which was important for making yurts and boots. War was their other main activity, aided by steppe metallurgy, which was advanced for its time.

The nomads lived in yurts, or circular tents, which were used throughout the steppe. The frame was made of wood slats, usually of willow or juniper, tied with leather straps. Yurts were easy to dismantle and fold. Their insulation depended on the thickness of the felt walls.

The social organization of the steppe people was stable over the centuries. At the top were the kagans or khans, who claimed sacred origins. Below the khans were the aristocrats born to powerful clans. The remaining nomads were free people. The status of women was generally superior to that of women in sedentary populations. Women could fight and shared in religious and political responsibilities. Prisoners were treated as slaves and typically sold.

Turco-Mongol peoples all worshipped the same god, Tengri, while the Indo-European nomads, like the Scythians, had an Iranian type of religion. Shamanism played an important role in all these societies. The nomads at first rejected proselytization by other religions, but later converted. The Uighurs adopted Manichaeism, and many of the Khazars converted to Judaism. Nestorian Christianity also became very influential in Central Asia, but for the most part, Islam was adopted by Turkic populations and Mongols embraced Tantric Buddhism.

Although the list is not exhaustive, these were some of the main nomadic groups of the steppe:

- Indo-European Cimmerians, Scythians, Sarmatians, and Alans occupied the western steppes from the seventh century B.C.E. to the first century C.E. The ancestors of the Bulgarians and Hungarians were to be found there too. From the sixth to the fourth centuries B.C.E., the Massagetae, mentioned by Herodotus, and the Saka inhabited the Asian steppes, as did the Quchan, who cohered until the fourth century C.E.

- Asian nomads along the borders of China from the third century B.C.E. to the fourth century C.E. included the Xianbei, the Tuoba, the Huns, the Rouran, and, from the fourth century C.E. to the seventh, the Avars.

- Turcophone peoples, including the Turks (called Tujue by the Chinese), flourished on the steppe. Turcophone federations in the Middle Ages included the Kyrghyze, the Oguz, the Karluks, the Karakhanids, the Pechenegs, and the Cumans. The Uighurs occupied the Altai and eastern Turkestan in the eighth and ninth centuries, and in the thirteenth and fourteenth centuries, the Mongols created a vast empire covering most of Eurasia.

NOMAD WARFARE

War played a central role in the nomad culture. It was a society where living well also meant dying well, that is, dying heroically in combat. From the youngest age, the nomad preparation for war began with hunting. Most conflicts were short struggles over grazing rights and livestock ownership between neighboring tribes, but they sometimes escalated to total war, with the annihilation of the defeated adversary. More often, the losers would flee and the winners would expand to occupy their lands. A central motif of the history of the steppes is the constant migration of populations from east to west over more than two millennia, from the sixth century B.C.E. to the first half of the sixteenth century C.E. Wars against sedentary populations were typically seasonal incursions whose goal was booty and slaves.

The special feature of nomad war was the great mobility of the mounted archers, who could travel for days without stopping, depending only on extra horses for logistical support. The nomads practiced the technique of harassment, envelopment, and fighting at a distance, where their powerful bows could reach the enemy unopposed. Common tactics were shared by nomad groups throughout history, such as a simulated flight to lure the adversary into an ambush.

"Barbarism" was not incompatible with the development of sophisticated military strategy. For example, the nomads developed innovative defensive techniques, such as the use of chariots that could be transformed into mobile fortresses. More rarely, nomad warriors developed discipline and cohesion that extended beyond their immediate clan and so were able to attack in larger units. And when great leaders emerged, wars could result in massive invasions, as the history of China, India, Persia, Russia, and Europe attests.

Light cavalry formed the backbone of the nomadic armies, but there was also occasionally heavy cavalry armed with spears and wearing suits of armor, whose function was to break through enemy lines. However, unlike European feudal knights, who preferred frontal assaults early in the battle, the heavy nomadic cavalry would only attack late in the battle after the enemy had been weakened by light cavalry archers.

Nomadic armies also included foot soldiers, whose main weapon was a double composite bow of various sizes. The Mongols carried a short bow and a long bow, a sword or saber, a spear, and an axe. Almost all the nomadic armies were equipped with similar weapons and used similar techniques. Their equipment was often adopted by sedentary adversaries, including the Chinese and the Byzantines.

When nomadic armies were well organized and under skilled command, they were fearsome adversaries and won battles against the great empires of their time, including Darius, the Roman legions, the Byzantine Empire, and several Chinese dynasties. The nomads were victorious when they could fight on their own terms and impose their military strategy on their adversaries. Only the best-organized nomad populations, such as the Mongols under Genghis Khan, had sufficient organization to besiege cities and use ships.

The use of the double composite bow to shoot while turned in the saddle, and even while retreating, was learned by nomad archers from childhood. Indeed, Chinese paintings and Persian miniatures show nomad warriors riding small horses and shooting their bows backward from their galloping horses (the "Parthian shot"). Nomad children learned to ride horses as soon as they could walk, and practiced with a bow as soon as they had the strength to bend it. The nomad's skill in the art was evidenced in Genghis Khan's conquests. Mongol logistics were incomparably efficient. Mongols could travel on horseback for very long hours, swapping mounts to maintain their pace, and could survive if necessary by drinking the blood of their horses for nourishment. They were also skilled in psychological war, and their military strategy was dictated by careful reconnaissance. When nomad troops were organized and disciplined under the command of an exceptional leader such as Genghis Khan, they were invincible.

THE CONFLICTS BETWEEN NOMAD AND
SEDENTARY POPULATIONS

For more than two millennia, the Eurasian steppe was the geopolitical axis of conflict in the ancient and medieval world, and was the major source of transformative disruption. Indeed, until the sixteenth century, conflicts between steppe nomads and sedentary populations had far greater influence than the conflict between maritime and continental empires that inspired the British geostrategist Halford Mackinder's theories.

The nomads were shepherds who followed the grass and water and whose pastoral migrations between the high meadows and lower altitudes were dictated by the seasons. In winter the high meadows were bare, and in summer the plains were dry.

"North Asia" designates a region extending from the borders of Manchuria to the plains of Ukraine. The heart of this area is located between Lake Baikal and present-day Mongolia, the original home of the Turco-Mongol peoples. The North Asian climate is harsh: hot in summer and bitter cold in winter.

All sedentary civilizations had to confront nomadic invasions. The Achaemenid king Darius could not crush the Scythians in the sixth century B.C.E. At the battle of Carrhae (53 B.C.E.), Rome suffered disaster at the hands of the Parthians. Northern China was constantly invaded throughout its history and was twice totally occupied by nomads in the thirteenth and fourteenth centuries and again, from the seventeenth century to the beginning of the twentieth. India was invaded by the Huns in the fourth and fifth centuries, like Europe, and later, from the eleventh to the sixteenth century, by waves of Muslims. Persia, together with China, was a frequent victim of nomadic incursions from its northern border. But, like China, it was able to acculturate the nomadic invaders.

Over two thousand years, the nomad incursions to the south were first dominated by Indo-Iranian nomads, and then by Turco-Mongol nomads, who arrived as an irresistible wave from the east. Such was the geopolitics of the steppes until Russia reversed the process in the sixteenth century with the advent of the cannon, pushing the nomadic elements from west to east.

Numerous nomadic tribes from Central Asia also attacked the Byzantine Empire. The Ottomans were themselves a steppe tribe fleeing the Mongol surge of the thirteenth century. Western Europe was twice overrun by Central Asia nomads: by Attila's Huns in the fifth century, and by the Hungarians (Magyars), who later sedentarized and were converted to Christianity in the tenth century.

Western Europe was spared Mongol conquest by Genghis Khan's horde, which halted near present-day Budapest. After the tenth century, western Europe was never again invaded from the steppes, and was thus able to continue its demographic and economic development, while Russia was subjected to two centuries of Mongol occupation and the Balkans underwent four centuries of domination at the hands of the recently sedentarized Ottomans.

In summary, the nomads of North Asia exerted a dominant and lasting influence over Eurasian history, which reached its pinnacle under the Mongols, whose empire ran from China to Europe and included Persia, China, and Russia. Indeed, the Mongol Empire was the largest ever known.

Once they became sedentary, formerly nomadic groupings such as the Seljuks, the Ghaznavids, and the Mamluks also created powerful and sometimes durable empires. Genghis Khan's empire was followed by the nearly equivalent empire of Tamerlane, which was in turn succeeded by post-Mongol empires, including those of the Ottomans, the Safavids, and Mughals, all of which were originally turcophone, even though Persian came to dominate among the Safavids and the Mughals.

Two powers shook off the "Mongol yoke." Ming China freed itself from Mongol occupation in the fourteenth century. Russian Muscovy was freed in the sixteenth, and, under Ivan the Terrible, began a slow advance to the east, which reversed the east-to-west pattern of invasions that had lasted two millennia.

In times of peace, settled communities traded with nomad populations. However, stability was usually fragile, because the two cultures had different goals. The nomads were predatory and looked to take advantage as soon as their military forces had the upper hand. The state wanted stability: it could pay a tribute to the nomads or forge an alliance by marrying local royalty to a nomad chief. Yet peaceful periods were of limited duration. As soon as the nomads gained power, they would demand greater tribute under the threat of attack. Conversely, if the state had the upper hand, it would often launch punitive expeditions against the nomads.

In nomad cultures, populations were small. To defeat their more populous enemies, nomad armies relied on concentrated surprise attacks and the hope of dividing and weakening their adversary. However, the cultural impact of nomadic victories was ephemeral. To consolidate a nomadic victory, the nomads adopted the administrative organization of the conquered population and often their religion. They were then victims of another wave of nomadic invasion. In short, they became urbanized. In the end, sedentary cultures always prevailed.

THE SCYTHIANS

The Scythians are the first nomads who appear in written history. Herodotus relates that the Persian king Darius I's campaign against them had to be abandoned in the face of the Scythians' scorched-earth policy. The Scythians, and the Sarmatians after them, spoke an Iranian language. Archeological remains suggest that the Scythians occupied the steppes of the Don from the seventh to the first centuries B.C.E. However, their military influence spread as far as Mesopotamia, Persia, and Syria. In 612 B.C.E., they were allied with the Medes and the Babylonians in the siege and destruction of Nineveh, which marked the end of the Assyrian empire. In the next century, the Scythians were repelled from eastern Anatolia, but only after they had destroyed the capital of the Urartu kingdom.

The Scythians practiced funeral rites similar to those of subsequent nomad tribes: they buried their dead under tumuli. Important warriors were interred upright on their horses. They were mounted archers, a permanent feature of nomad war cultures. They also practiced the nomadic custom of drinking from the skulls of defeated enemy generals.

Scythian culture reached its pinnacle from the fourth to the first century B.C.E., when the population consisted of two groups, the largest in the Crimea and Ukraine, which they inhabited as far as the Dnieper, and the smaller in present-day Bulgaria. They made exquisite sculptures of animals cast in gold.

The Scythians continued to pillage the Greek cities of Crimea well into the second century B.C.E. until they were repelled eastward with the help of three expeditions launched by King Mithridates of Pontus. The Romans also faced Scythian incursions in the Crimea throughout the first century B.C.E. The nomadic Sarmatians, themselves pursued by the Alans, repelled the Scythians in the east in the second century C.E. Herodotus relates that courage was the highest Scythian virtue: during annual ritual banquets, only Scythians who had killed one or more adversaries were allowed to drink; those not so honored were ridiculed and insulted. Around the third century C.E., the thousand-year history of the Scythians ended, and they were replaced by the Goths.

THE SARMATIANS AND THE ALANS

The military strategy of the Sarmatians and the Alans deviated from steppe tradition: they favored a direct frontal assault, riding their horses with brandished lances. In pictures, they are represented wearing helmets and laminated cuirasses made of flexible leather and riveted metal. The Greek traveler Pausanias, who encountered Sarmatians in the third century B.C.E., reports that their armor was less elegant than that of the Greeks but equally effective. Their horses were also protected with armor.

Around the second century B.C.E., the Sarmatians controlled the steppe north of the Black Sea. They clashed with Roman legions, and Sarmatian contingents were later integrated into the Roman army to fight the Dacians and the Germans. However, later clashes with the Romans occurred when the Sarmatians moved onto the plains north of the Danube. They fought the emperor Trajan and then Marcus Aurelius, who defeated them in 169 C.E., and again in 172–73 C.E., as narrated by the Roman historian Cassius Dio. The Romans imposed a treaty, forcing the Sarmatians to supply five thousand horsemen, whom Marcus Aurelius dispatched to England to defend Hadrian's Wall. However, the Sarmatians and the Alans would soon have to confront an even more formidable adversary: the Huns. The Huns were prototypical steppe warriors and displaced weaker peoples like the Goths and the Gepids. When fleeing the Huns, these other nomads requested the help of Rome, and joined the Roman camps. Was it a ruse or did they truly want Roman protection? Whatever the case, they joined the Roman Empire willingly, but soon rebelled and laid waste to the Balkans. The western Roman emperor Valens fought the Goths near Adrianople in 378 and was killed in a crushing Roman defeat.

THE HUNS

The year 378 is an important date in military history: it marks the end of the preeminence of the infantry that had been at the core of Roman power. Now, cavalry became dominant, particularly the cavalry of the steppes. No other nomads, except the Mongols, provoked such terror as the Huns of the fourth century.

The fourth-century Roman historian Ammianus Marcellinus wrote: "The Huns get as much pleasure from the dangers of war as peaceful people get from their tranquility. They consider that dying at war is a supreme blessing. Those who grow old and die a natural death are treated as cowards and degenerates."

The Huns were a confederation of tribes from North Asia who migrated first toward Ukraine, and then toward the Hungarian plains. They displaced other tribes who, in turn, displaced other nomads before them, including the Sarmatians, the Alans, the Goths, and the Gepids.

The Huns bypassed the Eastern Roman Empire and headed directly toward northern Central Europe. Their advance occurred gradually over many decades. Some Hun contingents were integrated into the Roman Army as *foederati*. Others attacked Roman territories, as in 392, when the Huns and the Visigoths devastated parts of the Balkans.

The Huns were divided into two groups. In Europe, the Black Huns devastated parts of the Balkans and Danube territories before crossing the Rhine. The White, or Hephthalite, Huns ravaged the Khorasan. Sassanid Persia resisted but the White Huns continued to Kabul through Herat and arrived in Punjab around 470.

In 443, Attila killed his brother and became the undisputed chief of the Black Huns. In 448, a Byzantine ambassador, Priscus, visited Attila in his camp and found him both unpretentious and frugal. He calls him a Scythian, the generic term for a nomad warrior.

In 447, the Romans were defeated in Thrace and forced to pay an annual tribute to the Huns and to concede them a buffer zone of several days' march south of the Danube. Later, in 451, Attila confronted the Romans in Gaul along with recently recruited allies including the Ostrogoths, Gepids, Alans, and the Franks of the Rhine. The Roman general, Flavius Aetius, had lived near the Huns during his childhood, however, and knew their style of fighting, their customs, and probably their language.

After Attila captured Metz, Aetius, although a longtime enemy of the Visigoths, sought an alliance with their sovereign, Theodoric I, who ruled from Toulouse. Aetius convinced Theodoric that if the Huns defeated the Romans, they would next turn on the Visigoths.

The adversaries met around Troyes, with the real battle beginning on the second day. Aetius led the left flank while Theodor led the right. Alan mercenaries, whom Theodoric did not trust, were in the center. Facing Aetius and Theodoric, Attila occupied the center, which he thought was the weak point of the enemy's army. Attila's charge broke through the Alans' center, but the Alans retreated, fighting courageously. Then the Roman and Visigoth flanks closed on Attila. Attila, seeing the danger of the pincer maneuver, retreated behind his chariots arranged in a half circle. From there, the Huns' archers successfully repelled their assailants. There were heavy losses on both sides. The Visigoths' king, Theodoric, had been killed. The next day, Aetius wisely did not force Attila into a battle. Nor did Attila take the offensive. Rather, he retreated with his army intact.

In 453, returning across the Danube from battles in Italy, Attila died mysteriously at a marriage feast for a new wife. After his death, his empire disintegrated rapidly. In contrast, the empire of the Hephthalite Huns expanded and endured for another several centuries. The Hephthalite Huns were victorious against the Sassanids and killed the Persian emperor. In India, the Gupta Empire twice repelled the White Huns during the fifth century. However, in the sixth century, dynastic quarrels enabled the White Huns to conquer northern India.

After the dissolution of the Black Huns, Europe faced a series of incursions from other steppe nomads. In 537, the Eastern Roman Empire had expelled the Avars after they had attacked Constantinople. The Avars defeated the Slavs in their path and confronted the Germanic king of Austrasia, Sigebert, in 561, but without success. Soon afterward, the new kagan of the Avars, Bayan, sought an alliance with the Lombards and crushed the Gepids. Then, he installed his horde in Pannonia (Hungary) and expelled the Bulgarians toward Moldavia and Wallachia, from where they would be displaced again by the surge of Magyar nomads. The Bulgarians finally settled on the borders of the Eastern Roman Empire and proved to be a pugnacious adversary, which Constantinople was unable to defeat for more than two centuries (eighth–tenth centuries).

After they were established in Hungary, the Avars attacked and defeated Sigebert's Franks (570). Then they turned against the Eastern Empire and took Belgrade, but were defeated in 587 by the Byzantine general Priscus in Thrace.

The emperor Maurice's *Stratēgikon* describes the strategy of the Avars and how to counter it. The Byzantine general Priscus again defeated the Avars at the battle of Tisza (601) and forced them to retreat from the eastern frontier of the empire. The Avars left two legacies to the Byzantines: stirrups, which were adapted to great advantage by the heavy Byzantine cavalry, the cataphracts, and mounted archers, which became a core component of the Byzantine army.

The Avars attacked northern Italy and then returned with fresh troops and besieged Constantinople unsuccessfully in 619. A few years later, the Avars formed an alliance with the Sassanid king Khosrau II to besiege Constantinople for a third time. The Avars occupied the European side of the Bosphorus, while the Persians camped on the Asian side. During five days, the two armies assaulted the Byzantines before retreating (626). Soon afterward, the Bulgarians, once subjugated by the Avars, became a powerful new enemy that contributed to their demise.

At the end of the eighth century, Charlemagne's Franks first defeated the Saxons, and then attacked the Avars. The war between the Franks and the Avars lasted almost eight years and ended with the defeat of the Avars.

Charlemagne captured the Avar capital in 796 and Avar influence waned. Their decline was accompanied by the rise of the Bulgarians. The Bulgarians could not extend their influence eastward because of the Magyars, and so sought to attack Constantinople. They were defeated by Constantine V in 762. Fifty years later, Nikephoros I captured and looted the Bulgarian capital (811), but was killed in a Bulgarian counterattack. The Bulgarians remained a permanent threat until they were destroyed by Basil II, the last of the great Macedonian emperors.

The last nomadic wave to roil Europe was that of the Magyars, or, Hungarians. The Magyars, who spoke a Finno-Ugrian language, were allied to the Khazars and had migrated west, pursued by the turcophone Pechenegs.

The Magyars joined with the Byzantine Empire to confront the Bulgarians. The Bulgarians formed an alliance with the Pechenegs, who attacked the Magyars in the east. The Magyars fled to Transylvania, then attacked the Moravians (895) and settled in Hungary. From there they advanced toward Italy but were repelled and pursued by the Lombards. They tried to negotiate, but the Lombards rejected their offers. While the Lombard troops were camped on the west bank of the Brenta River (near Venice) and the Hungarians on the east bank, the Hungarians crossed the river and crushed the Lombards in a night attack. It was a traditional steppe tactic, which the Mongols would use three centuries later to attack the Hungarians near Budapest.

In 910, the Magyars defeated a Frankish imperial army near Augsburg with the classic nomad ruse of an ambush that followed a feigned retreat. They went on to devastate Lorraine (919), Italy (924), Burgundy, Provence and Champagne (926), and Berry (927). After a short period of respite, the Hungarians again ravaged Lorraine, Champagne, and Burgundy a generation later.

The Magyars were finally defeated by the Holy Roman emperor Otto I at Lechfeld in 955, and soon afterward, they converted to Christianity.

The Hungarians themselves would later confront the last empire of peoples from the steppe: the Ottomans.

CHINA AND THE NOMADS

For two thousand years, China was confronted with nomad invasions from the northern steppe. In times of weakness, China had to protect itself from the nomad raids, and when China was militarily powerful, it launched counteroffensives to gain control of the crucially important oases along the Silk Road.

The nomad incursions were first recorded around the fourth century B.C.E. Under Wu Ling, king of the northern state of Zhao (325–298 B.C.E.), important military transformations occurred, which are related by the Chinese historian Szu-ma Chien (ca. 145– 87 B.C.E.). In order to confront the Xiongnu nomads, the Chinese army became more mobile. They transformed their chariot force into cavalry, replaced their robes with trousers, more practical for riding, and instituted a corps of mounted archers in the nomad style. These developments were largely ignored outside of northern China. For example, neither Sun Zi's *Art of War* nor Sun Bin's later commentaries mention mounted archers, referring instead to the conventions of war of their time.* They were unaware of the concept of war as practiced during the nomad invasions.

Although Chinese chronicles describe the Xiongnu as Mongolian, they also describe warriors with blond hair and blue eyes, who practiced a religious cult involving a sky god called Tengri, with whom the shamans interceded.

The Yellow River curves in a large loop in the extreme north of China. The area inside that loop is called the Ordos. It is strategically very important for the protection of northern China. Under the Ch'in (Qin) dynasty (221–207 B.C.E.), the Ch'in and the Yen states started building parts of a great wall south of Manchuria, which would one day become the Great Wall of China. This wall was not as efficient as settlements, since empty territories attracted the nomads, who sought control of the Ordos region, from where they could launch predatory raids. The Chinese, aware of the military superiority of the Xiongnu, offered one of their princesses in marriage to the Xiongnu chief Mo Dun. In addition, Mo Dun demanded tribute of silk, grains, and alcohol to forgo

---

* *Sun Zi: The Art of War; Sun Bin: The Art of War* (1995; new ed., Beijing: Foreign Languages Press, 2007).

raids on China. However, once Mo Dun controlled the Ordos, the treaty was soon broken.

Similarly, Mo Dun's successor, who had obtained a yet more favorable treaty, nevertheless decided to invade northern China (158 B.C.E.). Indeed, each new Xiongnu chief would customarily inaugurate his reign with an invasion. The Han negotiated more than ten treaties over fifty years, each ceding more advantages to the Xiongnu.

However, during the second century B.C.E., the Han took the offensive. Campaigns would usually be waged at the end of winter, when grass was scarce and the nomads' herds had been weakened. The Chinese gradually retook control of the Ordos and the oasis in the west as far as the Tien Shan Mountains. Once they controlled the oases, the nomads had to retreat to the northern steppes. At the height of the Han dynasty, the Chinese succeeded in chasing the nomads back to the borders of Ferghana (101 B.C.E.) in Uzbekistan, where the Xiongnu were forced to fight insurrections of people they had previously vanquished. The Han dominated northern Asia as far as Kazakhstan, as did the Tang, the Ming, and finally the Manchu in turn. However, no Chinese policy, not the occupation of oases, the Great Wall, or arranged marriages with Chinese nobility, proved entirely satisfactory. Thus, the history of China is marked by periodic invasions of the nomads.

The Han implanted military colonies and sent more than 100,000 Chinese peasants to the oases they controlled. This policy of demographic occupation was a central aspect of Chinese strategy throughout its history and persists today. Qin Shi Huang Di (247–210 B.C.E.) added fortified walls to connect preexisting fortifications. Wall construction continued throughout Chinese history, with the major part of the Great Wall built during the Ming dynasty (1368–1644). However, even the Great Wall was not able to contain the nomads.

Rather than closing the nomads in, the better strategy for the Chinese was an offensive strategy. By depriving the nomads from their bases on the fringes of the border fortifications, they forced them into the forests, which were less favorable for grazing.

The Han launched four victorious offensives against the nomads between 73 and 91, accepted Xiongnu allegiance, and even assisted the Xiongnu against other nomadic tribes. As we have seen, the use of barbarians against other barbarians was a well-established tactic of sedentary states.

In the first century C.E., the Xiongnu belonged to two groups: the Southern Xiongnu, allied with the empire, and the Northern Xiongnu, hostile to the Chinese. In the second century, the empire faced internal quarrels and weakened. The Xiongnu then took the offensive again. When the Han dynasty collapsed (220 C.E.) in civil war, the nomads remained relatively well controlled. However, a century later, the Southern Xiongnu, who had become sinicized, overthrew the Chinese Ch'in dynasty and established a dynasty of nomad origin, the Wei. They occupied the capitals of Louyang and Chang An. A member of the Chinese imperial family who had escaped founded a new capital in Nanjing, creating a new dynasty, the Southern Ch'in, who ruled for three centuries (317–589).

While this Chinese dynasty ruled in the south, one of the nomad tribes surging in the northern borders, the Turkish-speaking Tuoba, captured Luoyang (422) and created the Northern Wei dynasty. The Wei state became sinicized and Buddhist, creating the masterly Buddhist sculptures of the Longmen Grottoes. The process of assimilation and sinicization is a recurrent feature of Chinese history, up to the Manchu. After a century and a half of their rule, however, erosion of their warrior culture and succession quarrels weakened the Northern Wei. New nomads would later invade China, including the Khitans in the eleventh century, the Jurchen in the twelfth century, the Mongols in the thirteenth century, and finally the Manchus in the seventeenth century.

Around the middle of the sixth century, the northern Eurasian steppes were dominated by three groups: the Juan-Juan, who controlled the area extending from Manchuria to the oasis of Turpan; the Hephthalite Huns, who occupied Turkestan, eastern Persia (Khorasan), and Afghanistan; and the Black Huns, who were established in the Ukraine.

The Turkish-speaking Göktürk nomads established a vast but ephemeral empire across northern Asia (552–83) after defeating the Juan-Juan, who had been their allies. They subsequently divided into western and eastern empires. The western empire allied with the Sassanids to crush the Hephthalite Huns and split Baskiria and Sogdiana with the Persians. Their kagan ruled from the region around the Orkhon River. The western Göktürks then allied themselves with the Byzantines against the Sassanids.

In 629, the eastern Göktürks tried to capture Chang An, the capital of the powerful Tang Empire (618–907), but were repelled. This was a period of Chinese expansion. China established a protectorate over Tarim under Emperor Taizong (624–49) and controlled northern Asia as far as Turkestan.

However, after a generation of decline, a new kagan, Elterish, reconstituted the Göktürk tribes into a powerful khaganate (682–744). Raids recurred, but the Tang resisted. Finally, the Göktürks made an alliance with China to confront two powerful nomad adversaries: first the Khitans, then the Uighurs, a Turkish-speaking people, who conquered the Göktürks in 744.

Central Asia changed significantly in the sixth and seventh centuries. The Tibetans defeated Tang troops in eastern Turkestan and expanded. At the same time, the Arabs reached Bukhara and advanced to Ferghana.

The Tibetans sought an alliance with the Abbasids against China in 732. A few years later, the Tibetans fought the Chinese for the control of Gilgit (northern Pakistan). In 751, Muslim Arabs allied to the Karluk Turks defeated Tang troops in the battle of Talas (751).

Besides the considerable expansion of the Arabs and the still robust Chinese Empire, two new Central Asian powers arose in the middle of the eighth century: the Tibetans, who continued to expand until their collapse in 842, and the Uighurs, who created a powerful empire, with its capital of Karabalghasun, who were allied with the Chinese in their conflicts with the Tibetans. The Uighurs were Manichaeans, and introduced an alphabet that was later adopted by the Mongols and the Manchus. The Uighurs were finally defeated by the Kirghiz in 840 after they had sought Kirghiz help in a fight for succession. The Ming would commit the same error with the Manchus in the seventeenth century.

Waves of Central Asian nomads followed one upon another. However, despite the loss of its western possessions along the Silk Road, China was able to resist the Göktürks and the Tibetans thanks to its superior administrative skills and powerful army.

The Kirghiz, who controlled High Mongolia, were soon displaced by the Khitai natives of the Orkhon region. The Chinese had arranged a treaty with the Khitai through marriage between the Khitai sovereign and a Chinese princess. However, such treaties were fragile. The Khitai had first accepted Uighur domination and later the suzerainty of the Chinese. However, the Khitan great khan, Abaoji, succeeded in rallying the Khitai tribes and proclaimed himself emperor, founding the Liao dynasty (907–1125) in northern China. As Chinese power weakened, the Khitai defeated the Chinese army and obtained annual tribute from the Song dynasty (960). As the Khitai themselves became sinicized, adopted Buddhism, and ruled a state patterned after the Chinese model, they soon had to face other nomad invaders. The Jurchens, former vassals of the Khitai in Manchuria, captured the capital of the Liao state and founded the Chin dynasty, which would rule all of northern China

(1115–1234). After their defeat, the Khitai were driven west and defeated the Seljuk Turks to create the Kara-Khitan khanate centered in modern Kyrgyzstan, which extended from the borders of China to the Sea of Aral, and would last until the thirteenth century. This Buddhist victory over the Muslims was the origin of the legend of Prester John, seen by Christians as a providential ally who would help the crusaders against the Muslims through an alliance with the Khitai.

Like other nomad groups, the Jurchens were mounted archers organized by the Mongol decimal system into units of 10, 100, 1,000 and 10,000 men. The first Jurchen emperor inherited the Liao Empire from the Khitai, but the Jurchens were unable to defeat the Chinese. The sinicized Jurchens would finally retreat to Manchuria, where they founded the "post-Chin" dynasty (1616) that would later lead the Manchu conquest of China (1644).

In the meantime, over a twenty-year period, beginning in 1206, the Mongols would occupy most of Eurasia, from Hungary to Java, from China to Muscovy, and from Syria to Afghanistan.

WESTERN ASIA

India was not spared nomad invasions, beginning with the Hephthalite Huns in the fifth century. Later, from the tenth to the sixteenth centuries, turcophone Muslim nomads resumed their attacks on northern India (the Delhi sultanate). Then, the Mughals, Muslims from central Asia conquered nearly all of the Indian subcontinent and maintained their control until the arrival of the British in the eighteenth century.

The nomads also played an important role in Persia. Ferdowsi's *Shahnameh,* a Persian epic written in the tenth century, recalled the struggles between the Sassanids and their nomadic Turan (Turkic) neighbors, who inhabited the area north of the Oxus River (Amu Darya).

In the seventh century, Persia converted to Islam, and Islamic cultural influences became very important under the Abbasid caliphate of Baghdad at the end of the eighth century. The Samanids in western Persia became a Muslim bulwark against the turcophone nomads of the steppe. From 875 to 999, the caliph's Samanid emirs expanded their rule north of the Oxus to Transoxiana, making war on the Karluk Turks. It was at that time that the Abbasids started using captured Turkish boys from Central Asia as slave-warriors, called *ghilman.* These eventually became aware of their strength, and in the second part of the tenth century, the *gulham* Alp Tigin took control of the Khorasan army and exercised a de facto power in Ghazni, Afghanistan (969). His successor, Mahmoud of Ghazni, became governor of the Khorasan and helped the Samanids defeat the Karakhanid Turks, who were threatening Bukhara (992).

The Persian Samanid dynasty was Sunni and fought the Shiite Buyid throughout the eleventh century. Then the Seljuk Turks advanced toward the Khorasan and defeated the Ghaznavids, who retreated to occupy the Punjab. The Seljuks controlled eastern Persia and helped the caliph defeat the Buyids (1055). Tughril Beg created the Turco-Persian Seljuk sultanate, which represented the caliph and was a guarantor of Sunni orthodoxy. His successor, Alp Arslan (1063–72), expanded Seljuk rule to all of Persia. He also defeated the Byzantines at the famous battle of Manzikert (1071), which opened Anatolia to Turkish domination. The Seljuk Empire reached its zenith under his successor, Malik Shah, and the great Persian counselor, Nizam al Mulk (1018–92). The Seljuks defeated the Karakhanids and captured Samarkand and Bukhara. However, their dominance was short-lived, as the Seljuks were defeated in turn by the Kara-Khitan khanate, leaving only scattered Seljuk emirates by the time of the first crusades.

Like China, Iran was a melting pot for nomadic invaders, who gradually adapted Persian culture. Iran's cultural traditions allowed it to maintain a strong identity, which was spread by the Abbasids to the Safavids. Although demographic assimilation was less important than in China because of Persia's smaller population, Persia's culture would soon dominate its conquerors. As a result, the Persian language became the lingua franca of a vast area, from Central Asia to Delhi and Uttar Pradesh, and remained the dominant language in these regions throughout the eighteenth century. Historical atlases show that throughout history, from the Achaemenids (fifth century B.C.E.) to Tamerlane and Nadir Shah, the great empires of this region have traditionally dominated an area that extends from Samarkand to Delhi.

CHAPTER 6

The Seljuks, the Mamluks, and the Crusades

The Seljuks created an empire soon after leaving the steppes. By the middle of the eleventh century, when they reached their zenith, these Turkish-speaking people had created a Persianized sultanate that acted as the champions of the caliph and Sunni orthodoxy. They played an important role during the Crusades, particularly the First Crusade, where their military prowess made them the Christians' most feared adversaries.

FACING THE FIRST CRUSADERS

When they advanced in the Orient, the crusaders had little idea that these territories had just been conquered by recently settled nomadic conquerors: the Seljuk emirs of Syria. After the death of Malik Shah (1092), the Seljuk Empire had splintered. This fragmentation helped the First Crusade (1095–99) succeed in Anatolia, as well as in Syria-Palestine.

The First Crusade was led by Godefroi de Bouillon; Hughes of Vermandois, the brother of the king of France; Raymond IV, comte de Toulouse; Normans from Sicily, Tancrede and Bohemond of Taranto; and Robert of Flanders. The European knights and their horses wore heavy armor, designed for frontal charges, but in Asia Minor, they found themselves harassed by swift, mobile mounted archers, a different type of adversary. In 1097, aided by Byzantine troops, they besieged and took

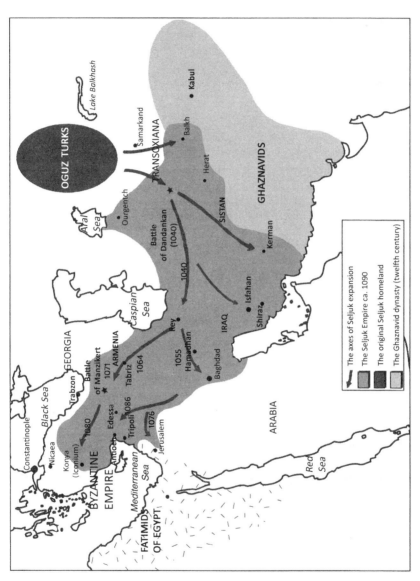

MAP 5. The Seljuk Empire at its apogee, ca. 1090.

Nicaea, defeating the Seljuk sultan Kilic Arslan I. Then, after passing through the Seljuk territory of Iconium (modern Konya) in central Anatolia, they advanced toward Antioch, divided into two armies, ten kilometers apart. Godefroi de Bouillon, Raymond IV of Toulouse, and Hughes of Vermandois led one; the other was under the command of the Normans and Robert of Flanders. There was little communication between the two armies.

The Normans' army caught first sight of the enemy near Dorylaeum in central Anatolia. As they were setting up camp to prepare for combat, they were attacked by the Seljuk cavalry, led by Arslan. From a distance, the mounted archers harassed the crusaders with their arrows. The knights were surprised and taken aback by this tactic, which did not allow them to retaliate, but they were well protected by their armor and had only limited casualties during the five-hour battle. However, that was not the case for either their infantry or their horses. The battle would have ended in a disaster if the other army had not arrived. Godefroi de Bouillon and his knights surprised the Turks from the rear and the flanks and forced them to withdraw. The victory of Dorylaeum was unexpected. It allowed the crusaders to continue their march to Antioch, which they captured after a siege of several weeks with the help of the collaboration of the Christian inhabitants of the city. The Seljuks tried twice more to attack the crusaders on unfavorable terrain, but were unable to withstand the knights' frontal charge.

Both the Seljuks and the crusaders were perplexed by their enemy's style of battle. The Seljuks understood quickly that they must avoid frontal clashes with the knights by dispersing before the crusader heavy cavalry charged. Then, before the knights could regroup, the mounted archers would harass them from a distance.

As soon as Antioch was captured, the crusaders confronted another large Seljuk army. The crusaders had lost a great many horses and had to depend on their infantry, who were armed with crossbows. The crossbowmen, shooting in ranks, were an effective response to the mounted archers, because the crossbow had a longer range than the enemies' bows. The crusaders won the battle at Antioch. The crusaders had learned that their crossbows could keep the mounted archers at a distance and so permit the knights to charge effectively.

Later, the crusaders remained in their castles along the coast and the interior of Syria-Palestine because Seljuk harassment rendered travel dangerous. After their initial victories, the crusaders largely limited themselves to defense. The crusaders also learned to move in large formations, staying on ridges to avoid ambushes. They were too few in number to risk large battles where significant losses would decimate the Christian forces.

In the twelfth century, the sultan of Egypt and Syria, Salah Ad-din Yusuf ibn Ayyub (1138–93), a Kurd whom we now know as Saladin, eliminated the Shia Fatimid dynasty and restored Sunnism. He launched a counteroffensive against the crusaders and won the important battle of Hittin (1187).

Hittin was a severe blow to the crusaders. The citadel at Tiberias, the capital of Galilee, was under attack by the Muslims and sought reinforcements from Guy de Lusignan, king of Jerusalem. Raymond of Tripoli advised waiting for Saladin's army to get nearer. However, Guy de Lusignan advanced toward Tiberias to meet him. When the crusaders' army, partly consisting of Templar and Hospitaller knights, set out, it was harassed by contingents of mounted archers. After an exhausting march in the summer heat, the crusaders met the Seljuks. The Templars and Hospitallers formed the rear guard at some distance from the infantry. The crusaders spent a difficult night, thirsty and harassed by the Muslims.

In the morning, the rear guard could not disengage, but the Christian troops nevertheless attempted to charge. The mounted archers avoided the clash and encircled the crusaders, weakening them with arrows. The crusaders, who held a position on a hill, tried again and again to charge and break the encirclement, but were forced to surrender. Several crusader castles surrendered and Jerusalem itself was captured after a twelve-day siege. The battle of Hittin was a decisive defeat for the Franks. The Arab historian Ali ibn al-Athīr, a contemporary of Saladin's, writes:

> While the reunited Franks were on their way to Saffuriyya [Tzippori in present-day Israel], Saladin called a council of his emirs. Most of them advised him not to fight, but to weaken the enemy by repeated skirmishes and raids. Others however advised him to pillage the Frankish territories, and to give battle to any Frankish army that might appear in their path, "Because in the East people are cursing us, saying that we no longer fight the infidels but have begun to fight Muslims instead. So we must do something to justify ourselves and silence our critics." But Saladin said: "My feeling is that we should confront all the enemy's forces with all the forces of Islam; for events do not turn out according to man's will and we do not know how long a life is left to us, so it is foolish to dissipate this concentration of troops without striking a tremendous blow in the Holy War." So on Thursday, 2 July 1187, the fifth day after we encamped at Uqhuwana, he struck camp and

moved off up the hill outside Tiberias, leaving the city behind him. When he drew near to the Franks, however, there was no one to be seen, for they had not yet left their tents. So he went back down the hill with his army. At night he positioned troops where they would prevent the enemy from giving battle and then attacked Tiberias with a small force, breached the wall and took the city by storm during the night. The inhabitants fled for refuge to the citadel, where the Countess and her children were, and defended themselves there while the lower town was sacked and burned.

When the Franks learned that Saladin had attacked Tiberias and taken it and everything in it, burning the houses and anything they could not remove, they met to take counsel. Some advised the King [Guy of Lusignan] to meet the Muslims in battle and chase them out of Tiberias, but the Count [Raymond of Tripoli] intervened to say: "Tiberias belongs to me and my wife [Eschiva of Bures, princess of Galilee and lady of Tiberias]. There is no question that Saladin is master there now and that only the citadel remains, where my wife is immured. For my part, if he takes the citadel, my wife and all my possessions there and then goes away I shall be happy enough. By God, I have observed the armies of Islam over the course of the years and I have never seen one equal to Saladin's army here in numbers or in fighting power. If he takes Tiberias he will not be able to stay there, and when he has left it and gone away we will retake it; for if he chooses to stay there he will be unable to keep his army together, for they will not put up for long with being kept away from their homes and families. He will be forced to evacuate the city, and we will free our prisoners." But Prince Arnat of al-Karak [Reginald of Châtillon] replied: "You have tried hard to make us afraid of the Muslims. Clearly you take their side and your sympathies are with them, otherwise you would not have spoken in this way. As for the size of their army, a large load of fuel will be good for the fires of Hell." "I am one of you," said the Count, "and if you advance then I shall advance with you, and if you retreat I shall retreat. You will see what will happen." The generals decided to advance and give battle to the Muslims, so they left the place where they had been encamped until now and advanced on the Muslim army. When Saladin received the news he ordered his army to withdraw from its position near Tiberias; his only reason for besieging Tiberias was to make the Franks abandon their position and offer battle. The Muslims went down to the water [of the lake]. The weather was blazingly hot and the Franks, who were suffering greatly from thirst, were prevented by the Muslims from reaching the water. They had drained all the local cisterns, but could not turn back for fear of the Muslims. So they passed that night tormented with thirst. The Muslims for their part had lost their first fear of the enemy and were in high spirits, and spent the night inciting one another to battle. They could smell victory in the air, and the more they saw of the unexpectedly low morale of the Franks the more aggressive and daring they became; throughout the night the cries "Allah akbar" (God is great) and "There is no God but Allah" rose up to heaven. Meanwhile the Sultan was deploying the vanguard of archers and distributing the arrows.

On Saturday, 4 July 1187, Saladin and his Muslims mounted their horses and advanced on the Franks. They too were mounted, and the two armies came to blows. The Franks were suffering badly from thirst, and had lost confidence. The battle raged furiously, both sides putting up a tenacious resistance. The Muslim archers sent up clouds of arrows like thick swarms of locusts, killing many of the Frankish horses. The Franks, surrounding themselves with their infantry, tried to fight their way toward Tiberias in the hope of reaching water, but Saladin realized their objective and forestalled them by planting himself and his army in the way. He himself rode up and down the Muslim lines encouraging and restraining his troops where necessary. The whole army obeyed his commands and respected his prohibitions. One of his young mamluks led a terrifying charge on the Franks and performed prodigious feats of valor until he was overwhelmed by numbers and killed, when all the Muslims charged the enemy lines and almost broke through, slaying many Franks in the process. The Count saw that the situation was desperate and realized that he could not withstand the Muslim army, so by agreement with his companions he charged the lines before him. The commander of that section of the Muslim army was . . . Saladin's nephew. When he saw that the Franks charging his lines were desperate and that they were going to try to break through, he sent orders for a passage to be made for them through the ranks.

One of the volunteers had set fire to the dry grass that covered the ground; it took fire and the wind carried the heat and smoke down on to the enemy. They had to endure thirst, the summer's heat, the blazing fire and smoke and the fury of battle. When the Count fled the Franks lost heart and were on the verge of surrender, but seeing that the only way to save their lives was to defy death they made a series of charges that almost dislodged the Muslims from their position in spite of their numbers, had not the grace of God been wtih them. As each wave of attackers fell back they left their dead behind them; their numbers diminished rapidly, while the Muslims were all around them like a circle about its diameter. The surviving Franks made for a hill near Hittin, where they hoped to pitch their tents and defend themselves. They were vigorously attacked from all sides and prevented from pitching more than one tent, that of the King. The Muslims captured their great cross, called the "True Cross," in which they say is a piece of the wood upon which, according to them, the Messiah was crucified. This was one of the heaviest blows that could be inflicted on them and made their death and destruction certain. Large numbers of their cavalry and infantry were killed or captured. The King stayed on the hillside with five hundred of the most gallant and famous knights.

I was told that . . . Saladin's son said: "I was at my father Saladin's side during that battle, the first that I saw with my own eyes. The Frankish King had retreated to the hill with his band, and from there he led a furious charge against the Muslims facing him, forcing them back upon my father. I saw that he was alarmed and distraught, and he tugged at his beard as he went forward crying: 'Away with the Devil's lie!' The Muslims turned to counter-attack and drove the Franks back up the hill. When I saw the Franks retreating before the Muslim onslaught I cried out for joy: 'We have conquered them!' But they returned to the charge with undiminished ardour and drove

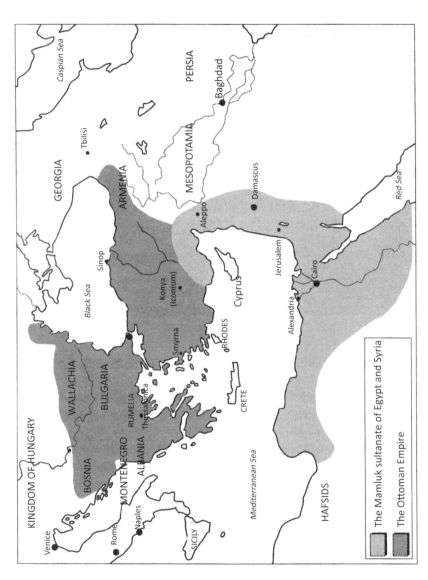

MAP 6. Ottomans and Mamluks, ca. 1470.

The Mamluk sultanate of Egypt and Syria

The Ottoman Empire

KINGDOM OF HUNGARY

Venice

Rome

Naples

SICILY

BOSNIA

MONTENEGRO

ALBANIA

WALLACHIA

BULGARIA

RUMELIA

Thessalonica

Mediterranean Sea

CRETE

Smyrna

RHODES

Konya
(Iconium)

Cyprus

Black Sea

Sinop

GEORGIA

ARMENIA

Tbilisi

Caspian Sea

PERSIA

MESOPOTAMIA

Baghdad

Aleppo

Damascus

Jerusalem

Alexandria

Cairo

Red Sea

HAFSIDS

our army back toward my father. His response was the same as before, and the Muslims counterattacked and drove the Franks back to the hill. Again I cried: 'We have beaten them!' but my father turned to me and said: 'Be quiet; we shall not have beaten them until that tent falls!' As he spoke the tent fell, and the Sultan dismounted and prostrated himself in thanks to God, weeping for joy." This was how the tent fell: the Franks had been suffering terribly from thirst during that charge, which they hoped would win them a way out of their distress, but the way of escape was blocked. They dismounted and sat down on the ground and the Muslims fell upon them, pulled down the King's tent and captured every one of them, including the King, his brother, and Prince Arnat of Karak, Islam's most hated enemy. They also took the ruler of Jubáil, the son of Humphrey (of Toron), the Grand Master of the Templars, one of the Franks' greatest dignitaries, and a band of Templars and Hospitallers. The number of dead and captured was so large that those who saw the slain could not believe that anyone could have been taken alive, and those who saw the prisoners could not believe that any had been killed. From the time of their first assault on Palestine in 1908 until now the Franks had never suffered such a defeat.*

Following the battle of Hittin, the Third Crusade returned and consolidated Christian control over the coastal regions of northern Palestine near the Frankish capital in Acre. However, they were never able to recapture Jerusalem or extend their control to the interior of Palestine. The Ayyubid dynasty founded by Saladin ruled Egypt until 1249 and Syria until 1260. After Saladin's death in 1193, the Ayyubids maintained a fragile peace with the crusaders. Europe, however, still remained fixated on the reconquest of Jerusalem.

MAMLUK RULE

By the ninth and tenth centuries, the Mamluks of Egypt—originally turcophone soldier-slaves from Central Asia known as *ghilman*—had become a major force for Islam. After they took over Egypt in 1250, it became the center of Islamic influence. They expelled the crusaders from the lands they had occupied in the Levant and were a dominant power in the region for more than 250 years (1250–1517). A large number of

---

* Francesco Gabrieli, *Arab Historians of the Crusades,* translated from the Italian by E.J. Costello (Berkeley: University of California Press, 1984), 119–23. Al-Athīr (1160–1233) witnessed and described both the counteroffensive against the crusaders of the Third Crusade and the Mongol invasion of 1220–21. For an alternative translation of the cited text, see *The Chronicle of Ibn al-Athīr for the Crusading Period from al-Kāmil fi'l-ta'rīkh,* pt. 2: *The Years 541–589/1146–1193: The Age of Nur al-Din and Saladin* (Burlington, VT: Ashgate, 2007).

ghilman were brought to Egypt by the last Ayyubid sultan, a descendant of Saladin's. In Egypt, they constituted the elite Bahri regiment and formed the sultan's bodyguard. However, the Mamluks soon took power and established a military empire of their own.

In contrast to the crusaders' armies of the thirteenth century, with the exception of the Knights Templar or Hospitaller, the Mamluks were highly disciplined. Many Mamluks in Egypt were Kipchak slaves from Central Asia, who had been expelled by the Mongols from Russia between 1236 and 1240. Like all military castes, the Mamluks were a closed society. They were turcophone and preferred to marry within their clan. They were one of the best armies in the world. The Mamluk troops were skilled in both nomad forms of combat and classic Muslim tactics. They defeated the Christian states of the Levant and Cilicia (crusaders and Armenians), and later the Mongols at Ain Jalut in Syria (1260).

The Mamluk army was perfected by Sultan Baybars (1260–77), who was of modest origins and had attained power through his own merit. His rise was remarkable and his army was to become an unmatched military machine for a hundred years (mid-thirteenth to mid-fourteenth centuries). He was born on the steppes of southern Russia around 1228, into a turcophone Kipchak family. Like other Kipchaks, he was caught up in the Mongol turmoil from 1236 to 1240. Some Kipchaks joined the Mongol army, others fled, while others, like Baybars, were sold as slaves. He was first sold in Aleppo, then sold again and found his way to Egypt, where he was sent to royal school for the Mamluks. The strict Mamluk military training included instruction in weapons use (riding, archery, shooting, saber, and lance practice) and the study of military strategy. The young Mamluks learned to combine their native nomad form of combat with the Ayyubid style of fighting, becoming highly trained professionals.

Baybars, a slave twice sold and despised, became an important commander in the Ayyubid army. Before he became sultan, Baybars and his Mamluk army defeated the crusaders. Jerusalem had been captured by the Muslims, and the leader of the Seventh Crusade, King Louis IX of France (Saint Louis), aimed to defeat the Ayyubids, who held Jerusalem. The crusaders arrived in Egypt in 1249 at Damietta, and the crucial battle against the Mamluks was fought the following year in Mansoura (1250). The indiscipline of the Frankish army, in which feats of valor were more important than following orders, is evident from the account of the battle of Mansoura provided by Jean de Joinville (1224?–1317):

It had been decided that the Templars would be the vanguard and that Count d'Artois would lead the second division behind the Templars. But as soon as Count d'Artois had crossed the river, he rushed with his army upon the Turks who were fleeing ahead of him. The Templars sent word that he was gravely insulting them by preceding them when it had been decided that he was to follow, and asked the count to let them move ahead of him as agreed with the king. Count d'Artois did not venture to answer, because Sir Fourcaud du Merle, who was a very good knight, was keeping a tight rein on his horse, and could not hear anything of what the Templars were saying to the count, because he was deaf, and was yelling "Get them! Get them!" Upon hearing this, the Templars thought that they would be dishonored if they let Count d'Artois move ahead of them. They spurred their horses as much as they could and pursued the Turks who were fleeing through the city of Mansoura toward the plain surrounding Cairo. When the Templars tried to go back, the Turks threw girders and joists at them in the narrow streets. And it was there that Count d'Artois and Sir de Couci, named Raoul, were killed, together with an estimated 300 knights. The Templars, as the Templar master told me later, lost 280 armed men, all cavalrymen.

My knights and I decided that we would pursue some Turks who were loading their equipment in their camp on our left, and we attacked them. While we were pursuing them throughout the camp, I caught sight of a Saracen who was climbing on his horse; one of his knights was holding the bridle. At the moment when he had his two hands on the saddle to get on the horse, I struck him with my spear under the armpit and knocked him over dead. When he saw that, the knight left his liege and, when I was riding by, pushed his spear between my shoulders and squeezed me against the neck of my horse, holding me so tight that I could not draw the sword hanging at my side, so that I had to take the sword which was tied to my horse's saddle. When the Turk saw that I had drawn my sword, he removed his spear and let me go.

When I arrived outside the Saracens' camp with my knights, we found at least six thousand Turks who had gathered for the campaign. As soon as they saw us, they ran towards us and killed Sir Hugues de Til-Châtel, lord of Conflans, who was under my command and carried the banner. We spurred our horses and went to rescue Sir Raoul de Vanault, who was also under my command and whom the enemy had thrown on the ground. As I was coming back, the Turks assaulted me with their spears, my horse knelt down under their assault and I was thrown over his head. I stood up as soon as I could with my shield hanging from my neck and my sword drawn. Sir Érard de Sivri, God save him, who was near, came closer and told us to retreat near the ruins of a house and to wait there for the king, who was coming up. As we were going, walking or riding, a large band of Turks came to strike us, threw me down and rode over me, pulling away my shield. When the Turks had moved on, Sir Érard de Sivri came back to me and took me to the ruined walls of the house, where we met Sir Ferry de Loupy and Sir Renaud de Menoncourt. Here the Turks attacked us on every side, as many of them had entered the house and they jabbed us with their spears from above the walls.

My knights asked me to hold the reins of their horses so that they would not scatter, and so I did. They then fought so bravely that they were praised by all who witnessed them or heard it told. Sir Hughes d'Écot was speared three times in the face, Sir Farry de Loupy was felled by a spear blow between the shoulders; his wound was so deep that blood was gushing out like wine from a barrel. Sir Érard de Sivri was hit on the face with a sword with such a severe blow that his nose was falling to his lip. Then I thought of Saint John and prayed to him: "Kind Sir Saint John, help me and save me at this hour of need!" As soon as I finished praying, Sir Érard de Sivri told me: "Sire, if you thought that neither myself nor my men would be blamed for it, I would go to the Count d'Anjou, whom I see there in the midst of the field, and ask for help." I answered: "Sir Érard, I think you would be most honored if you went to seek help to save our lives, as it seems to me that your own life is in great danger." And I spoke the truth, since he died of this wound. He took counsel from all the present knights and all approved what I had just said. Then, he asked me to let his horse go and I did so.

He went to Count d'Anjou and asked him to help me and my knights. A high-ranking squire who was with Count d'Anjou discouraged him, but the count answered that he would do what my knight had asked. He turned around to come to our help and several of his sergeants spurred their horses. When the Saracens saw them, they left us. Sir Pierre d'Auberive was leading these sergeants. When he saw that the Saracens had left us, he ran toward a group who were holding Sir Raoul de Vanault and delivered him.

As I was on foot and as my knights lay wounded, the king came up with his division, all trumpets blaring. He stopped on a road. I had never seen such a beautiful warrior. He seemed a head taller than all his men; he wore a golden helmet and held a German sword in his hand.

When he stopped, his good knights whom I have just named rushed at the Turks. Be assured that it was a real feat [of arms], since nobody was using bows or crossbows, but they were fighting the Turks with swords and maces. One of my horsemen who had run away with my banner, but had come back to me, gave me a Flemish nag which I mounted and rode to place myself near the king.

However, Sir Jean de Valeri, that good man, came to the king and advised him to bear to the right, by the river, to get help from the duke of Burgundy and others whom we had left to guard the camp, and to get water for his men, since the heat was already intense. The king ordered his sergeants to go and look for his knights who were part of his council and called them all by their names. The sergeants went to meet them in the battlefield, where the mêlée between them and the Turks was intense. They came to the king, who asked them their advice and they said that Sir Jean de Valeri's advice was very good. Then the king ordered the bearer of the standard of Saint-Denis and his ensigns to move to the right toward the river.

When the king's troops started moving, the horns, drums, and Saracen's horns rang again. The king had not moved far when he received several messages from the count of Poitiers, his brother, from the count of Flanders and several other powerful barons who had their troops there and all prayed the king not to move away too far, because they were surrounded by the Turks and could not follow him. The king called back the good knights of his counsel and everyone advised him to wait. Soon after, Sir Jean de Valeri came back and reproached the king and his councilors for not moving. Then, all the councilors advised the king to move toward the river, as he had been advised by Sir Jean de Valeri. At that moment, Sir Humbert de Beaujeu, the High Constable, came to the king to tell him that the count of Artois and his brother were defending themselves in a house in Mansoura and that they needed help. The king answered: "Constable, go ahead, and I will follow you." I offered to serve as the High Constable's knight, and he thanked me. We started on our way toward Mansoura. Soon a sergeant with a mace came to the constable very upset, and told him that the king had been stopped, and that the Turks were between him and us. We rode back and saw that there were more than a thousand between the king and us, and we were only six. I told the Constable: "Sire, we cannot get to the king through all these people, but let's move ahead of the group and let's put this ditch that you see in front of us between them and us, and we shall be able to rejoin the king." The Constable did what I advised. You understand that if the Turks had noticed us, they would have killed all of us; but they were occupied with the king and the other battalions and thought that we were their own men.

As we were going down along the river, between the river and an adjacent brook, we saw that the king had reached the river. The Turks were chasing the battalions ahead of them with great blows of swords and maces and were pushing them back upon the king near the river. Then the confusion was such that many of our men wanted to swim across the river to meet the duke of Burgundy, but they could not do it, because the horses were tired and the heat was intense, so that all we could see, going downstream, was the river full of spears and shields, horses and people who were drowning.*

After the battle, the Ayyubid sultan was assassinated and the Mamluk Baybars ascended the throne. Baybars followed up his victory at Mansoura with the systematic destruction of the remaining Frankish states in the Levant. In 1260, at Ain Jalut in southeastern Galilee, the Mamluks defeated a Mongol contingent. It was perhaps the turning point in Mongol expansion. The Mongol style of fighting was well known to the Mamluks. For the first time, the Mongols confronted a force whose discipline and unity were equal to theirs, but who had more familiarity with the geography and climate.

The Mamluks went on capturing crusaders in fortress after fortress, including those held by the Knights Templar and Hospitaller. Most of the Frankish kingdoms in the Levant had small populations, and the fights were mostly sieges, ending with the siege of Saint Jean d'Acre in

---

* Jean de Joinville, *La Vie de Saint Louis,* ed. Jacques Monfrin (Paris: Livre de Poche, 2002).

1291. In the fourteenth century, the Mamluks would go on to conquer Armenian Cilicia (1375), which had allied itself with the crusaders. In the region, only Cyprus escaped Muslim domination.

The relationship between the foreign military caste that dominated Egypt and the native population was entrusted to high-ranking intermediaries who were both guardians of the regime and spokesmen of the civilian population. The sultanate levied high taxes on the people. However, the regime endured for three centuries thanks, in part, to the prosperity brought by international trade. Egypt kept a virtual monopoly on trade with the Orient until the beginning of the fifteenth century. Trade with the Italians and other Europeans became particularly lucrative after the elimination of the Latin states of Levant and Cilicia reinforced the Mamluk monopoly.

In the fifteenth century, plague ravaged the Middle East, most seriously in 1459–60. Later, the Turkish Mamluks and the Circassian Mamluks (Cherkess), native to the Caucasus, fought each other bitterly. The only serious external threat was Tamerlane, who defeated the Mamluk sultanate in 1401.

In 1390, the Circassian Mamluks, called the Burji (the Tower), the name of their barracks, defeated the Turkish Mamluks. Slaves from Africa were also integrated into the Mamluk army, including Ethiopian eunuchs, who taught in the military schools.

The Mamluks' main theater of operations was Syria. The army started marching in the spring, with each soldier carrying his equipment on the back of a dromedary. Their horses, bigger than those of the steppes, were fewer because of the scarcity of pastureland. To reach Aleppo, in the north of Syria, from Cairo took thirty to forty days. The Royal Mamluks, an elite force used for frontal attacks, which numbered four to five thousand men, were the most important Mamluk regiment. The Mamluk order of battle was along traditional lines, consisting of two flanks, with the Royal Mamluks, led by the sultan himself, occupying the center.

Mamluk military power reached its zenith between 1250 and 1375 under the Bahri regiment. Military discipline deteriorated under the Circassian Mamluks. After the war against Tamerlane, the Mamluks lost their eagerness for combat, and their pride in their profession disappeared. They regarded firearms, then recently introduced, with haughty contempt. This attitude was not unique: it was shared by warrior castes in Europe, Japan, and the Middle East. However, some societies learned the advantages of firearms and cannons more quickly than others. For example, the Ottomans adopted cannons as early as 1453 and defeated the Mamluks in 1517 with the help of artillery.

The fame of the Mongol Empire has tended to eclipse the major role played by turcophone warrior peoples in North Asia in the sixth and seventh centuries. They harassed Persian-speaking nomads and were the backbone of Islam in the Middle East in the ninth century. The Seljuk and Ghaznavid empires were Turkish, as was the Ottoman Empire in the fourteenth century. Turkish domination extended from Central Asia to North India from the tenth century to the arrival of the Mongols.

The Mongol Empire was the apogee of nomad power. After the Mongols, Tamerlane, a Persianized Chagatai Turk, created almost as great an empire, but after his death, his conquests split up into a number of smaller kingdoms. The Safavid Empire succeeded the Mongol ilkhanate in Persia. In India, the Mughals consolidated their rule. Ruling from Istanbul, the Ottomans created a long-lived empire. In the Far East, the Mongol Yuan dynasty in China was replaced by the Ming. And, finally, Muscovite Russia threw off the Tatar (Mongol) yoke and began a march of conquest from west to east that would reach the Pacific Ocean. The era of nomad dominance had come to an end.*

* Gérard Chaliand, *Nomadic Empires: From Mongolia to the Danube* (New Brunswick, New Jersey: Transaction, 2003).

CHAPTER 7

The Mongol Empire

From the age of eighteen, it would take Genghis Khan (born around 1165) nearly twenty years to subjugate all of the Mongol tribes under his authority.* Until then, the Mongols, riven by interclan rivalries, played only a modest role in the steppes of North Asia.

The Mongol army was divided into clan-based fighting units using a decimal system (10, 100, 1,000). A man who left his group risked his life. After he was selected as supreme chief by the Kurultai, or great assembly of the Mongols, Genghis Khan was concerned with eliminating the tribal divisions that had traditionally weakened the Mongols. He therefore created intertribal fighting units meant to loosen tribal allegiance. He also harshly imposed the *yasa* code: severe penalties for infractions. He promoted commanders of humble origins who would be indebted to him. He also created a personal guard of ten thousand men, composed of high-ranking nobles and dedicated foot soldiers.

At the beginning of the thirteenth century, the major centers of the civilized world were weakening:

- The Islamic world, disunited for several centuries, was crumbling. The Seljuk Empire had collapsed and was replaced by the unstable Khwarezm Empire, whose capital was Samarkand,

---

* Paul Ratchnevsky, *Gengis Khan: His Life and Legacy* (Oxford: Blackwell, 1992).

which extended to the borders of India. Its ruler, Alla al-Din Mohamed II, was supported by a mercenary army.

· China was also divided. In the south, the Song dynasty was a formidable military power. However, a weak Tangut dynasty ruled in the north, and there was a Tibetan kingdom in the northwest.

· The Christian world was also divided. Armed with their broadswords, Teutonic and Swedish armies fought Orthodox Christians. The quarrel between the pope and the Holy Roman Empire raged.

Genghis Khan's conquests were gradual. First, he subjugated the steppes: the Kirghiz of the high Yenisei River, the Oirots of the Lake Baikal (1207), the Uighurs (1209), and finally the Xia Xia nomads north of China. Then the assault on China itself began. The Mongols initially lacked the knowledge and material for sieges, and so could not capture cities. However, the Mongols allied with Khitai, who brought the techniques of siegecraft, and by 1212, they had captured and sacked Peking. Genghis Khan withdrew from China, leaving twenty thousand soldiers and his Chinese possessions in the hands of his trusted general Muqali, who had once been a slave.

Next, Genghis Khan turned his attention to the Khwarezm Empire. He prepared his campaign carefully. First spies, disguised as merchants, gathered information, reconnoitered the terrain, and spread rumors.

All able-bodied Mongols were warriors, and their army was organized on the decimal system: ten men formed an *arav*; ten *arav*s, or a hundred men, formed a *zuut*; ten *zuut*s, or a thousand men, formed a *mingham;* and ten *mingham*s, or ten thousand men, formed a *tumen.*

At the top of this organization was the imperial *tumen.* Genghis Khan's nomads were as robust and frugal as any nomads of the steppe. Since childhood, they had been trained to ride and hunt, and they were accustomed to harsh climates in winter and summer. Their military superiority over other nomad groups was due to the discipline and cohesion imposed by Genghis Khan. The discipline was egalitarian: soldiers and officers received the same food, and abusive treatment was forbidden.

If in a group of ten, one deserted, the remaining nine would be put to death. The same went for the *zuut:* if an *arav* of ten fled, the remaining ninety were put to death. Similarly, if part of a group of ten advanced and the others stayed behind, those who did not attack were put to

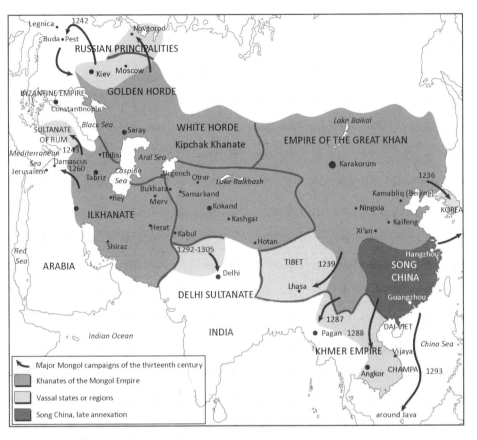

MAP 7. The Mongol Empire, thirteenth century.

death. If a warrior was captured and not rescued, his companions were put to death. Such rigorous discipline resulted in exceptional cohesion.

Military strategy was similar to that of other nomads: harassment of the enemy, flanking maneuvers, and simulated flight, sometimes lasting several days, to trap the enemy.

The superiority of the nomad army lay in its logistics and the fact that it could advance at the speed of the horses. Each mounted archer typically traveled with at least four horses. These small Mongol horses were robust and frugal and resistant to cold and heat. By switching mounts, Mongol troops could travel more than two hundred kilometers a day. Each nomad warrior carried two bows, a short bow to use from horseback and a long bow that was deployed on foot. The bows' ranges differed: the long bow's range was reputedly two hundred meters.

The entire Mongol army was mounted, with two rows of heavy cavalry followed by three rows of mounted archers. The heavy cavaliers wore laminated armor and carried hooked lances used to strike or unhorse enemy cavalry. They also carried sabers. Groups of one hundred widely spaced men formed the heavy cavalry. When the battle started, the mounted archers rode through the gaps between the heavy cavaliers. The archers tried to outflank the enemy while pelting them with arrows to break their formation. The Mongol army moved in silence, with orders given by colored banners that were raised or lowered. At night, lanterns replaced the banners. Once the adversary was in disarray, the Mongols would beat drums to signal for the final heavy cavalry charge, which would be accompanied by battle cries. The light cavalry would continue to harass the enemy from the flanks and the rear. The enemy was never completely surrounded. There was always an exit, but once the enemy fled, they would be pursued and annihilated by the Mongols. The imperial guard was kept in reserve to lead a final attack or to repel a possible counterattack.

With their multiple horses the Mongols could advance or flee faster than their adversaries. The Mongol army was never attacked by surprise. The mobility of the Mongol armies enabled them to maintain communications over large distances, so that separate armies could unite in concentrated attacks. Unless the commanders were the sons of Genghis, the strategy and tactics were left to professional generals, usually generals of humble origins whose success was based on merit, such as Subutai, Jebe, and Mukali.

The decision to attack the Khwarezm was taken at the *Kurultai* of 1218 in response to the execution of Mongol envoys at Otrar, on the Amu Darya. In the Khwarezm campaign, two nomadic armies faced each other: the Mongols on one side and the Turk Kara-Khitan nomads on the other. However, the Mongols, unlike the Kara-Khitan, had acquired siege techniques during their Chinese campaigns.

It is estimated that the Mongol army numbered a hundred thousand, although this seems highly exaggerated. Genghis sent two of his sons, Chagatai and Ögedei, to capture Otrar. During the siege of Otrar, Genghis sent his eldest son, Jochi, south of the Amu Darya River, while he marched with his youngest son, Tolui, north toward Bukhara, where they arrived in February 1220. The small Turkish garrison attempted to flee but was overcome, and Bukhara surrendered. The inhabitants were evacuated, but the city was systematically plundered then burned to the ground, with only a few buildings spared.

Then Genghis marched on Samarkand, taking with him the prisoners from Bukhara, who would be used for the siege. Otrar had been captured, permitting Chagatai and Ögedei's armies to rejoin their father's. The Turkish garrison of Samarkand fell to the Mongols and the city surrendered. Once again, the population was expelled and the city was pillaged. Part of the population was killed, but some were allowed to return to Samarkand, while the artisans were sent to Mongolia. The garrison that had surrendered was massacred. Next, the capital, Urgench, was besieged. To spare their men, the Mongols used the prisoners to build siege walls and man the front lines. Mohamed II had lost trust in his mercenary army and retreated to the Khorasan, pursued by two of Genghis Khan's generals: Jebe and Subutai. The generals and their twenty thousand men pursued him for nearly two years until his death.

The campaign continued throughout the Khorasan and Afghanistan until the summer of 1221. The cities of Balkh, Merv, and Nishapur were captured and the inhabitants massacred. In Herat, the inhabitants opened the doors of the city rather than face extermination. Their lives were spared, but the garrison was massacred. The Mongols' calculated use of terror reduced the need for long sieges and heavy casualties.

Genghis and his troops next crossed the Hindu Kush and laid siege to Bamyan, where Genghis's favorite grandson was killed. When the city was captured, Genghis showed no mercy. The city was razed without even being plundered.

The son of Mohamed II raised another army and defeated the Mongol garrison at Ghazni. Genghis launched a pursuit and crushed his army. Mohamed II's son escaped and battled for control of the Khorasan and part of Afghanistan. In a few months, the Khorasan was subjugated. However, during this turmoil, a small Turkish tribe fled to the west and settled in Asia Minor. Its chief was the father of Osman, the founder of the future Ottoman Empire.

The Mongols next turned their attention toward Europe. Jebe and Subutai, each at the head of two *tumen* (twenty thousand men), raided the Caucasus and Russia. The generals and their *tumen* ravaged Armenia, Georgia, and southern Russia before returning to Mongolia. For Russia, divided into many principalities (Souzdal, Riazan, Chernikov, Novgorod, Kiev), the battle of Khalka was a disaster, despite their alliance with the Turkic Kipchak nomads. The Kipchak vanguard was pushed back to the Russian camp. Many fled and were killed, including several Russian princes (1223). The *Novgorod Chronicle* vividly relates this event and the terror that the Mongol invasion inspired.

After the Mongols' victory over the Kipchak army, the Mongols integrated some of the Kipchak soldiers into their army. The Mongols would return twelve years later.

The last campaign of Genghis Khan was directed against the Tangut rebellion (1227) in northwestern China, where he executed the entire Tangut imperial family. However, he was reportedly wounded by a Tangut princess during an attempted rape and died in 1227 at the age of 62.

AFTER GENGHIS KHAN

In the absence of primogeniture, battles over succession occurred frequently in both nomadic and sedentary societies, as will be seen in the Ottoman Empire. Because uncles, brothers, and sons could all claim the throne, the death of a sovereign often led to civil war. Genghis Khan had therefore specified who was to succeed him.

At the death of Genghis Khan (1227), the Mongol Empire included all North Asia, northern Persia and Afghanistan, and northern China. His empire was nominally inherited by his chosen heir, his second son, Ögedei. Ögedei, besides his title of Great Khan, received Dzungaria. Following tradition, parts of the empire were divided between his other sons; Chagatai received Transoxiana, Jochi took the western part of the empire, and the youngest son, Tolui, received Mongolia. After Ögedei's death, the empire passed first to his eldest son, Güyük, then to a leader from a new clan, Möngke. The empire remained unified until 1259.

The different countries of this empire were connected by a system of communication, called *yam*, with relays providing horses and food every fifty kilometers. The *yam* system allowed the couriers to travel from two to three hundred kilometers a day. Under the reign of Kublai, the Great Khan and founder of the Yuan dynasty (1259–94), the Mongol Empire extended from Ukraine to the Pacific.

The fertile lands of Kievan Rus—present-day Ukraine—were the northwestern endpoint of the Eurasian steppe. This region, which extends southwest to Walachia, and Hungary, was crossed by successive nomad invaders, including the Huns, Avars, Pechenegs, Kipchaks, Oguz Turks, and the Hungarians. At the beginning of the tenth century, wooden fortifications were built to protect against nomad raids by the Pechenegs. The Russian princes who controlled Kiev competed with the nomads for domination and control of the Don and Dnieper Rivers, routes of access to Constantinople.

Later, the Russians forged an alliance with the Kipchaks to expel the Pechenegs. Still later, at the end of the eleventh century, the Oguz were repelled to the south. However, the continuous threat of steppe nomads encouraged Russian migration to the northern forests, where they founded Suzdal, Ryazan, and, in the twelfth century, Vladimir and Moscow.

When the Mongols undertook the conquest of Russia, the Kipchaks and Russians, longtime adversaries, united to face the common Mongol threat. The invasion of Russia was led by Batu, the grandson of Genghis Khan, through his son Joshi, and hence the nephew of Ögedei. Subutai was his commander in chief. Before the Mongols invaded Russia, they first dealt with the Kipchaks and Bulgarians. Batu and Subutai attacked the Bulgarians, while his uncle Möngke attacked and defeated the Kipchaks on the Volga. Some of the Kipchaks were incorporated into the Mongol army, while others fled with their khan to Hungary.

In 1237, Subutai crossed the Volga not far from Ryazan. The four Russian principalities were permanent rivals and remained disunited. Although Ryazan was a vassal of Suzdal, Suzdal refused to send reinforcements. The Mongols devastated the neighboring lands. Ryazan tried to counterattack, but its troops were routed. The Russian troops took refuge in Ryazan, which the Mongols then besieged. The Mongols erected wooden fortifications around Ryazan to block assistance and escape. The Russian princes quarreled with each other and remained more preoccupied with protecting their own territory than with supporting Ryazan against the Mongols. Ryazan fell in five days and was burned to the ground. Some of the population were massacred, others fled.

During the winter of 1237–38, the Mongols attacked the principality of Suzdal, whose prince resided in Vladimir. Subutai troops took Suzdal in the first assault. The Mongols then built a stockade around Vladimir, which they captured in February 1238, and massacred the population.

Then the Mongol army divided in two, with Subutai going north to attack Prince Yuri in Muscovy, and Batu advancing to the northwest toward Novgorod. Subutai captured Rostov and Yaroslavl, and Batu took Tver. Grand Prince Yuri, who did not receive support from Novgorod, waged battle near the river Sit, where he died with most of his army. During the winter, much of Russia had been conquered. Although the Russians had destroyed bridges, in the winter the rivers froze and could be easily crossed on horseback. However, by spring, the ice melted and the Mongols gave up their attack on Novgorod. They retreated south, devastating the principalities of Chernigov and Pereyaslav.

Kiev was the main objective of the southern Russia campaign. The prince of Kiev had fled, leaving the defense of the city to a nobleman named Dmitri. Batu captured the city and spared Dmitri, but the population was massacred and the town razed to the ground. After Kiev, Halych and Volodymyr-Volyns'kyi were ravaged. Batu's horde, known as the Golden Horde, left a lasting imprint on Russia.

In 1241, the Golden Horde invaded Hungary. Bela, the king of Hungary, was struggling with his nobles. Poland was divided into four dukedoms. To isolate Hungary, the Mongols decided to strike Poland first, using the same strategy they had used with the attack of the Bulgarians, and then the Kipchaks, before they confronted Russia.

The Mongol army divided in two. The smaller contingent consisted of two *tumen,* or twenty thousand men, and advanced toward Poland. The larger contingent included four *tumen* under the command of Batu and Subutai. It crossed the Carpathians and advanced toward Hungary. In Poland, besides the local army, there were French and German troops, the Knights Templars, the Teutonic Knights, and the Knights of St. John of Jerusalem. Together, with the forces of the duke of Silesia, Poland fielded around sixty thousand men. After defeating the prince of Galicia's troops, the Mongols captured Kraków and Breslau, and clashed with the duke of Silesia, who was awaiting reinforcement from the king of Bohemia. The Mongol armies reunited and decided to attack the Polish army in Legnica before the Bohemians could arrive. The duke of Silesia's knights led a charge, but were overwhelmed by the Mongols' arrows. However, a second charge was apparently victorious. The Poles, ignorant of the Mongol tactic of simulated retreat, pursued the retreating Mongol troops. However, when the Polish cavalry dispersed, the Mongols turned and charged. The defeat was total and the duke himself was killed. Batu and Subutai sent nine sacks filled with ears to Joshi to testify to their massive victory. When the king of Bohemia heard of the defeat, he ordered his army to retreat.

During that time, the Mongols advanced toward Hungary while the European forces were disunited. The alliance between King Bela IV and the Kipchaks ended after a group of Hungarian nobles aided by Frederick of Austria executed the Kipchaks' leaders. The Kipchaks retreated to Bulgaria and King Bela lost a precious ally, while Frederick of Austria, Bela's rival, gave no support.

The Hungarians arrived after an exhausting march on April 9, 1241, the day of the Mongol victory at Legnica. Bela had not heard of the Mongol victory when he left Pest. The Mongols pulled back slowly in the face of the advancing Hungarians. This retreat lasted several days until the troops arrived on the Mohi plain, where the Tisza and the Sajo Rivers connect. Bela's troops camped in the plain. The Hungarians chained their chariots together to form a circle and prepared to bivouac. At dawn, Subutai forded the Sajo River and Batu seized the only bridge, and crossed with his forces.

King Bela counterattacked. The Mongol archers had little space to maneuver, and suffered great casualties. However, Batu caught sight of Subutai attacking the enemy from the rear, and charged. The Hungarians retreated behind their chariots and tried to escape, but their flight turned into a debacle. King Bela managed to escape, but left most of his army on the battleground.

The Great Khan, Ögedei, had given the Mongols permission to conquer the remainder of Europe to the "Great Sea." However, at Ögedei's death in 1241, the Mongol armies were called back for his funeral, and the Mongol advance in Europe ended.

Möngke was elected Great Khan. His reign inaugurated important changes in Europe and in Muslim countries. In 1251, the young brother of Möngke, Hulagu, was named Ilkhan of Persia and instructed to put an end to the political assassinations of the Ismaili "Assassin" sect. Hulagu arrived in Persia in 1256 and besieged the Ismaili fortresses. The most remarkable, Alamut Castle, fell at the end of that year.

The Abbasid caliph, Al-Musta'sim, refused to cede power to the Mongols. In February 1258, Baghdad was surrounded by the Mongols, captured, and its garrison put to the sword. The caliph met Hulagu and accepted his order to evacuate the unarmed population. All those who evacuated the city were killed. Hulagu then massacred all those who had stayed in Baghdad, with the exception of Christians (Hulagu had two Nestorian wives).

Hulagu then killed the caliph. Hulagu made an incursion in Azerbaijan before marching toward Syria. His army was joined by Christian troops, including those of King Hethum I of Cilicia ("Little Armenia"), who had long tried to forge an alliance with the Mongols against the caliph. Hulagu captured Edessa and besieged Aleppo. Hulagu and Hethum were joined by Bohemond IV and his army. Aleppo fell and its population was massacred. In March 1260, Damascus surrendered. Only the garrison resisted. The entire city was massacred nevertheless.

After Hulagu left with a large part of his army in order to be present at the election of the next khan, the remaining Mongol forces were defeated by the Mamluks at Aïn Jalut in Syria.

By 1264, the Mongol Empire had lost its unity, and its center of gravity shifted to the east. After the death of Möngke, the new Great Khan was Kublai. After conquering China, he moved the Mongol capital from Karakorum to Peking. His conquest of Korea (1272) was followed by failures to conquer Japan (1274 and 1281) and Vietnam, but by the successful conquests of Cambodia (1296) and Burma (1297). His dynasty would last ninety years.

Everywhere, the Mongols ended up converting to the religion of the country they occupied. The Golden Horde and its Tatar descendants would endure in Russia until the middle of the sixteenth century.

CHAPTER 8

Timur the Lame

Timur the Lame, or Tamerlane, was a Muslim, born in 1336 into the turcophone Mongol Barlas tribe in Transoxiana (present-day Uzbekistan). He was not of royal lineage and paid allegiance to a Chagatai prince. As customary, in his rise to power, he first had to gain the support of his fellow tribesmen, then seek alliance with others. That done, the rest of the nomad tribes would join whoever possessed power and prestige.

Timur established his authority over the Barlas population, which was sedentary, whereas most neighboring tribes remained nomadic. His ascension to power was gradual. To ensure the loyalty of his new subjects, he took them on campaigns where they could find booty and glory. After 1370, he would spend the majority of his life outside Transoxiana. He progressively eliminated the tribal chiefs and replaced them with supporters or members of his family. He installed the Chagatai nomad armies permanently in the recently conquered provinces. He made his sons and grandsons governors of provinces, even though they were not always trusted by the occupying armies. He was careful that no governor could establish a power base strong enough to compete for the empire. Timur also moved nomad tribes from one region to another, for example from Anatolia and Azerbaijan into Transoxiana. He would deprive defeated tribes of their chiefs and install them in territories where they would find little support from the indigenous people.

Timur's army followed the nomad model, with a majority of mounted archers supplemented by heavy cavalry and infantry. The nomads were the backbone of the army, but they were nomads who had become sedentary and had learned siege techniques. Among the sedentary populations, Timur also had the support of Persian-speaking populations in Khorasan and Transoxiana. He also enlisted Armenians and Turkomans, including the Kara Koyunlu and the Ak Koyunlu, who supported him in 1402 in his fight against Bayezid.

Like all tribal leaders, Timur sought to exclude the most independent chiefs and to entrust the command of their troops to his trusted people. He gave lands to the tribal chiefs, but the land grants could not be transmitted to descendants and remained the property of the state. This system of land possession, *suyurgal,* was similar to the *timar* system of assigning conquered land to soldiers that would later be used by the Ottomans.

The troops were paid regularly, and soldiers received pensions after their service. Throughout his campaigns, Timur liberally adopted the successful military techniques of his adversaries. For instance, from India he adopted the use of elephants to scare the adversary and break through their lines. He kept the traditional nomad decimal system of organization of the army. Discipline was strict and his army proved invincible in spite of his multiple adversaries. Timur took power in Transoxiana in 1370, when the Mongol ilkhanate of Persia was moribund. In China, the Yuan dynasty, of nomadic origins, had been overthrown by the Ming two years earlier. Timur launched a raid into Chagatai territory that led him to the borders of Mongolia (1375–76). Soon, however, the Turkmen Kara Koyunlu and Ak Koyunlu took power in eastern Anatolia, the southern Caucasus, and western Iran. The steppe of the Golden Horde gained a remarkable new chief, Toktamysh (1378), who would be a formidable adversary.

Timur conquered Khwarezm, then eastern Persia (1380–81), and Afghanistan. Later, he captured Herat, Iraq, Azerbaijan, and western Persia (1385–88). Tabriz, Isfahan, and Shiraz also fell. In 1387, he also defeated Toktamysh for the first time. His struggle with Toktamysh was to last four years without clear resolution. Toktamysh, a direct descendant of Genghis Khan, was a master of nomad tactics. However, Timur was a military genius who combined the techniques of his sedentary enemies with the traditional nomad style of fighting. Timur and Toktamysh may have commanded as many as two hundred thousand troops each, but probably about half that number. Timur never delegated authority, and remained in direct command of his armies in all of his battles.

Timur finally defeated Toktamysh in his third campaign in 1395. Then, Timur had to defeat the adversaries that he had already previously defeated. He had to reconquer Persia, twenty years after his initial campaign. Again, he used the same techniques of terror and brutal repression as Genghis Khan.

After defeating Toktamysh, Timur marched on India. His troops were first terrified by the Indian battle elephants. However, Timur built camouflaged pits to serve as traps and ordered his cavalry to scatter sharp tripods to damage the feet of the elephants. Then he let loose a herd of buffalo with burning bundles attached to their backs. Terror changed sides as the frightened elephants turned against their own camp. Later, Timur would incorporate elephants into his army to fight the Mamluks in Syria (1400).

The Mamluks, who had been a powerful military force, had been in the wane since the ascension to power of the Circassians. Timur attacked and was victorious. He captured Damascus (1401) and Baghdad, where he erected pyramids of thousands of severed heads. After his victory over the Mamluks, Timur refrained, however, from attacking Egypt, the principal base of the Mamluk power.

The confrontation between Timur and the Mamluks took place in Syria. Timur was a Muslim fighting against Muslims, but he was also fighting Nestorianism in Central Asia.

Timur's next victory, over the Ottoman sultan Bayezid I, known as the Thunderbolt, was very important. Bayezid had been victorious in the Balkans, particularly at Nicopolis against the crusaders in 1396. He had also defeated the major Turkish principalities of Anatolia and seemed close to capturing Constantinople. Timur established his fortified camp close to Ankara and poisoned the wells on the road there, enabling him to defeat Bayezid's thirsty army nearby after only one day of battle. Bayezid was made prisoner (1402). Timur thus prolonged what was left of the Byzantine Empire—now reduced to its capital—for another fifty years.

Having defeated all his enemies, Timur then embarked on his last conquest, the one that would make him the equal to the Mongols: China. He died on his way there in 1405. He was the last of the great nomad conquerors, one of history's great conquerors.

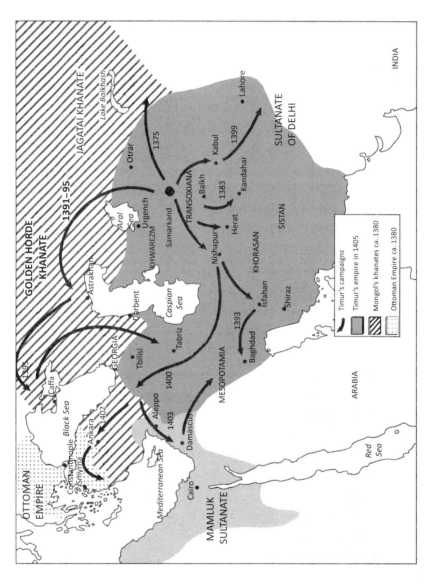

MAP 8. Timur's Empire, 1370–1405.

TIMUR'S HEIRS

In his campaigns, Timur changed the traditional order of battle consisting of a center with two flanks. To counter Toktamysh's crescent formations, he divided his army into seven brigades that could act independently. Thus, Timur enjoyed increased freedom of action and maneuverability to exploit the adversary's weakness or to redress failure in his own lines. One of these brigades was always held in reserve, usually to pursue the retreating enemy. Siege technique adapted from the Chinese and the Muslims was one of the strengths of Timur's army.

However, Timur's legacy was less lasting than that of Genghis Khan. Timur's son, Shah Rukh, maintained power over the heart of the empire, in the region between Transoxiana and Persia. He defeated the Kara Koyunlu, who contested his hegemony and transferred the capital from Samarkand, which Timur had never stopped embellishing, to Herat, where he also built remarkable monuments. After his death, the Timurid Empire fragmented, but the dynasty continued in Persia and Transoxiana. Its sovereigns encouraged the development of culture and science, as with Ulugh Beg, a passionate astronomer.

Anarchy reigned in Transoxiana at the end of the fifteenth century, but the Timurid dynasty survived until the death of the last powerful Timurid sultan, Hussein Bayqarah of Khorasan, in 1506. The descendant of Timur's who left the strongest historical imprint was Babur (1483–1531), who, after being expelled from Samarkand by the Uzbeks, conquered first Afghanistan in 1505 and then northern India, where he founded the Mughal dynasty (1526).

CHAPTER 9

The Ottomans

While the Byzantine Empire was confronting rival states in the Balkans, Turkic principalities were growing in power in Asia Minor, including the Karasids in the south, near Constantinople, and the Osmanlis or Ottomans who had been expelled from Central Asia during the Mongol invasions of the thirteenth century.

A PATIENT ENTERPRISE

After the decline of the Mongol Empire, the Anatolian Turks assumed the leadership of military expeditions and raids undertaken by so-called *ghazis* to extend Islamic domination through conquest. The modest Ottoman principality of the thirteenth century was enlarged across the Dardanelles in the fourteenth century with the complicity of the Byzantines. Although the Byzantines thought that this expansion would be temporary, it became permanent. The new capital of the Ottomans became Adrianople (Edirne). Thus, the Byzantine Empire was surrounded by Anatolian Turks, even if its maritime routes remained open to commerce and exchanges.

By the end of the fourteenth century, the Ottomans had conquered and annexed several Christian Balkan states, including Bulgaria and Serbia (battle of Kosovo, 1389). Ottoman diplomacy found allies among Christian knights who were hostile to the influence of the Holy Roman Empire and divided by feudal quarrels. The Ottomans were dissatisfied with the independent and frequently insubordinate *ghazi* armies, and so decided to raise imperial troops from among the prisoners of war. They soon replaced the recruitment of adults with *devşirme*, the selection of boys from Christian families to be trained to serve the empire as janissaries.

At the end of the fourteenth century, the Ottomans annexed the rival Turkoman principalities of western and central Anatolia. Under Bayezid, the Ottomans already possessed a nascent fleet. However, their empire almost collapsed when Timur crushed the Ottomans near Ankara (1402). Constantinople was no longer besieged and the Turkoman principalities rebelled. Bayezid's sons quarreled over the succession for more than a decade, further weakening the empire, until Mehmed I emerged as sultan (1413).

After they defeated the Kara Koyunlu, the Turkoman confederation of the Ak Koyunlu became a regional power in eastern Anatolia and northern Iraq, which Venice sought to use as an ally against the Ottomans. Shiite religious uprisings such as those of the Kizilbash and Sheik Bedreddin's adherents also shook the Ottoman state. However, the Byzantine Empire was too weak to benefit from Ottoman disarray, and the Latin states were dealing with other problems. In 1453, Constantinople, by then an underpopulated city, fell to the Ottomans.

No other post-Mongol empire, with the exception of Muscovite Russia, has influenced history as much as the Ottoman Empire. At the beginning of the fourteenth century, the Ottoman state was a small principality waging war against the infidels. It gained strength in the second part of the fourteenth century with its expansion into Anatolia and the Balkans. The capture of Constantinople (1453) and later, the domination of the Near East (1517), gradually expanded the Ottoman territories into a great empire, which reached its zenith under Suleiman the Magnificent (1520–66). However, in the sixteenth century, the naval superiority of western European states increased. The contemporary Turkish historian Halil Inalcik identifies 1590 as the beginning of the Ottoman Empire's decline.

The Seljuk sultanate of Anatolia, defeated by the Mongols (1234), became a vassal of the Persian ilkhanate. This led the Turkoman to migrate into western Anatolia. The Byzantine Empire, which had been briefly controlled by the Latins after the sack of Constantinople (1204), returned to Greek rule (1261).

Nomad incursions into Byzantine Anatolia became more frequent with the development of *ghazi* ideology. The small Ottoman state expanded significantly when the Ottomans reached Gallipoli (1352) and conquered Adrianople (1361). The Turks of Anatolia were invited to join the Ottomans and were sent to Europe to strengthen Ottoman domination. The Ottoman invasion of Europe occurred at a time of European fragmentation, with western principalities constantly making and breaking alliances. The Ottomans profited from this political instability. They had originally entered Thrace as allies of the Byzantines against the Serbs and the Bulgarians. Christendom was not only divided between Greeks and Latins, but also fragmented within religious communities by competing regional interests.

The Ottomans practiced the usual Islamic policy of religious tolerance and readily accepted the enlistment of the Balkan Christian troops in their ranks. In time, religious conversions occurred, particularly in Albania, Thrace, and Bosnia. With the disintegration of the Serbian and Bulgarian kingdoms and the Ottoman victory in Kosovo in 1389, the Ottomans became the principal power south of the Danube. They also subjugated the rival Turkish principalities of Anatolia, including the Karamans, Germyans, and Hamidili.

The real architect of the Ottoman power was Sultan Bayezid. He annexed the Turkmen principalities of Anatolia, dominated the Balkans as far as Albania in the west and Walachia in the north, and crushed Bulgaria. He tried to implement a centralized empire on both sides of the Dardanelles. In 1396, Bayezid defeated the crusaders' army in Nicopolis, which gave him great prestige. He annexed the last important principality of the Karaman in Anatolia and laid siege to Constantinople. But all his accomplishments were threatened by the destruction of Ankara and his capture by Timur (1402).

Bayezid's sons fought for the succession, and the Byzantines supported the weaker sons against the most dangerous pretenders. The struggle for the succession lasted about twenty years and ended with the victory of Murad II (1453). The new sultan turned his attention to the Balkans, where the Hungarian power represented the greatest threat.

The Ottomans captured Thessalonica, which the Byzantines had ceded to Venice. The goal of the Ottomans was to expel Venice from the region and to force the Hungarians to retreat north of the Danube. However, János Hunyadi won victories over the Ottomans in Transylvania and again south of the Danube (1441–42).

Shortly thereafter, at Varna (1444), Murad II defeated an army of Hungarian and Walachian crusaders who had crossed the Danube. This victory revealed the superiority of the Ottoman army and its elite janissary troops, who were to seal the destiny of Constantinople and the Balkans.

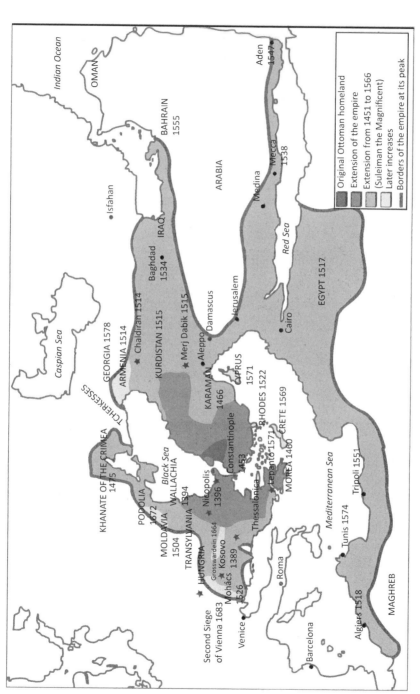

Indian Ocean

OMAN

BAHRAIN
1555

ARABIA

Aden
1547

Mecca
1538

Medina

Red Sea

EGYPT 1517

Cairo

Jerusalem

•Isfahan

IRAQ

Baghdad
1534•

Chaldiran 1514 ★

KURDISTAN 1515

Merj Dabik 1515 ★

•Damascus

•Aleppo

Caspian Sea

GEORGIA 1578

ARMENIA 1514

TCHERKESSES

KARAMAN
1466

CYPRUS
1571

RHODES 1522

CRETE 1569

KHANATE OF THE CRIMEA
1475

Black Sea

PODOLIA
1672

WALLACHIA

Nicopolis
1396 ★

Constantinople
1453

Lepanto 1571

MOREA 1460

Mediterranean Sea

MOLDAVIA
1504

TRANSYLVANIA 1394

HUNGRIA

Grosswardein 1664

Mohács 1526 ★ Kosovo 1389 ★

Thessalonica

Second Siege
of Vienna 1683

Venice

•Roma

Tunis 1574

Tripoli 1551

Algiers 1518

MAGHREB

Barcelona

Original Ottoman homeland
Extension of the empire
Extension from 1451 to 1566
(Suleiman the Magnificent)
Later increases
Borders of the empire at its peak

MAP 9. The Ottoman Empire, fourteenth–seventeenth centuries.

In 1448, Murad II won a difficult battle in Kosovo over Hungarian forces led by János Hunyadi. The Ottoman Empire, which had been shaken by Timur's victory at Ankara in 1402, had largely regained its power.

The sultan's power derived from the *kapikulu,* the sultan's personal slave army, which included the janissary corps. The army also included the cavalry, led by nobles but including a *kapikulu* contingent. The *kapikulu* increased in importance from the fifteenth century until the seventeenth, since it served as a check on the independence of the provincial *tımarlı.* Under Suleiman, the *kapikulu* numbered 48,000, including 20,000 janissaries. The janissaries and *kapikulu* were paid by the treasury and were under the direct control of the sultan. A new corps of cannoneers and musketeers was added under Murad II. The janissaries were given the most efficient arms, while the cavalry of noblemen continued using bows and swords.

The Ottoman cavalry—which in the late sixteenth century included six thousand *kapikulu, tımarlı,* and allied Tatars—was always the most prestigious and important branch of the military. The *akincis,* or light cavalry, who specialized in raids, were especially feared by European armies until countered by musketeer units at the end of the sixteenth century. They were disbanded in 1595. The use of firearms by European armies led the Ottomans to create a corps armed with muskets and crossbows, the *tufenkji.* Artillerymen, sappers and other specialists were part of the *kapikulu,* but formed a distinct group, the *topcu ocagi.*

Murad II's son, Mehmet II, led the siege of Constantinople in 1453, which lasted fifty-four days. The Ottoman Army of 50,000–80,000 soldiers faced 8,000 Christians, primarily Greeks and Genoans. A giant new Turkish cannon fired 1,200-pound cannonballs and was instrumental in the destruction of the city's fortifications. The Genoan commander was injured and the emperor died fighting. From then on, Mehmet II was famed as the conqueror of the "Rum" empire. The Christian states recognized Ottoman domination of the Black Sea, whose western border was now the Danube. Mehmet had defeated all the Anatolian dynasties that could have challenged his power.

In the north, Hungary remained a powerful adversary and forced the Ottomans to abandon the siege of Belgrade in 1456. Venice retained maritime superiority and supported the twenty-year war for Albania led by Skanderbeg. The Venetians also formed an alliance with Uzun Hassan, the leader of the rival Ak Koyunlu (White Sheep Turkmen) in eastern Anatolia. Uzun Hassan controlled western Persia, and marched with the allied troops of Karaman toward central Anatolia. Mehmet defeated

Uzun's army on the Euphrates in 1473 and next eliminated the coastal bases of Venice in the Morea and Albania, and expelled the Hungarians from Bosnia and Belgrade. Then Mehmet organized an expedition against the Knights of Rhodes, and in parallel captured Otranto at the heel of Italy.

Mehmet II was the true founder of the Ottoman Empire. After his death, his sons quarreled over the succession and their struggle was accompanied by a rebellion of the janissaries. The eldest son, Bayezid II, acceded to power. He campaigned in Moldavia, then against the Mamluks, who had been the supreme power of the Muslim world. The initial struggle (1485–91) remained inconclusive.

The next threat to the Ottomans came from the east in the form of a militant Shiite sect, led by Sheik Haydar and encouraged by Uzun Hassan. The adherents wore a red cap that gave them the name of Kizilbash (red heads). Uzun's successors vainly opposed the sect, while one of its faithful, Ismael, took power in Persia. Kizilbash influence in Anatolia and the Balkans was considerable. Ismael also tried to make an alliance with Venice.

Bayezid II became ill and was replaced by his son, Selim, in 1512, with the support of the janissaries. Two years later, Selim defeated Ismael at Chaldiran. This victory gave Selim control of the mountainous region of Armenia, extending from Erzurum to Lake Van. After his victory over Persia, Selim defeated the Mamluks in Syria and then in Egypt (1517). Soon after, the *sharif* of Mecca gave him the keys of the city and declared him to be the Guardian of the Faith. The Ottoman Empire had become a caliphate, and the Ottomans were now the protectors of the Muslim world.

The Ottomans remained a world power and played an important role in European political struggles until the end of the sixteenth century. They formed an alliance with the French king François I in his struggle for control of Italy with Charles V, the Holy Roman Emperor. The Ottomans wanted to prevent a single power from dominating Europe. Suleiman the Magnificent assumed the Ottoman sultanate in 1520. He captured Belgrade in 1521 and Rhodes the following year. A few years later, he defeated the Hungarians at Mohács (1526) and occupied Buda. Soon afterward, Hungary became an Ottoman province. On his side, Charles V attempted to form an alliance with the Safavids. However, Suleiman's campaign against Persia was victorious and he captured Tabriz, Baghdad, and Azerbaijan (1534–35). The French king François I became an ally of the Ottomans to weaken the Hapsburgs.

However, while the Ottomans campaigned in Europe, the Persians counterattacked. The war lasted seven years. In 1555, the treaty of

Amasya established the border between Persia and the Ottoman Empire along today's Iranian-Turkish border. Baghdad remained Ottoman.

The Ottomans maintained their alliance with the French under the new king, Henri II. They also supported Protestant rebellions against Charles V until the beginning of the seventeenth century, and helped to avert a unified crusade of Protestants and Catholics.

The Ottomans controlled the Persian Gulf and the Red Sea, and consequently the routes to the Orient and India. However, the Portuguese had already established a presence in the Red Sea, India, Diu, and the strait of Hormuz. After the Ottomans added Yemen to their territories (1547), they built a large fleet, which explored the Indian Ocean. Piri Reis, the commander of the Egyptian fleet and the author of the *Kitab-ı Bahriye* (Book of Navigation), expelled the Portuguese from Muscat. Although the Persian Gulf and the Indian Ocean remained under the control of the Portuguese, the Ottomans would retain control of the Red Sea until the end of the sixteenth century. The conquest of Cyprus (1570) was the last important Ottoman military victory.

Struggles in Europe resumed and the Ottomans suffered a terrible naval defeat at Lepanto in the Ionian Sea, off western Greece, in 1571, where their fleet confronted a naval coalition of Catholic Spain, Venice, and Austria. The Ottomans lost 200 galleys out of the 230 ships that took part in the battle. However, within a year the Ottoman fleet had been rebuilt and was strong enough to force Venice to sign a peace treaty renouncing Cyprus.

Between 1578 and 1606, the Ottomans waged war against the Hapsburgs in the west and against the Safavids in the east. From 1578 to 1590, the Safavids lost eastern Anatolia and part of western Persia and the Caucasus. However, the Persians received assistance from Russia, which was trying to expand into the Caucasus. At the end of the sixteenth century, the Ottomans were becoming isolated: they faced the Hapsburgs, Moldovans, and Walachians to the west, and the Cossacks of the Dnieper to the north. In the east, the Ottomans faced Abbas Shah, a formidable Safavid adversary, who had formed alliances with the Hapsburgs. States' interests had become more important than religious oppositions.

THE CAUSES OF OTTOMAN DECLINE

Although the Ottoman Empire was at its height in the late sixteenth century, it was fighting on two fronts and overstretched. After Lepanto, maritime supremacy gradually belonged to Europe. The pirates of the

Maghreb (North Africa) were independent of the Sublime Porte, and the Knights of Malta also threatened Ottoman ships. At the beginning of the seventeenth century, Mamluk influence in Egypt had strengthened and reduced Ottoman control. The Cossacks harassed the Ottoman fleet on the Black Sea. At that time, the French, English, and Dutch ships had all surpassed the Ottoman fleet, and the Dutch East India Company began direct trade with India as early as 1600.

The economic situation deteriorated at the end of Suleiman's reign. Inflation increased, imperial taxes oppressed the populations, and peasants were forced to borrow from usurers. Rural populations migrated to the cities, where they remained unemployed. The janissaries controlled and extorted the rebellious population.

The Europeans dominated commercial routes. The Ottoman treasury dwindled with the rise of English and Dutch commerce. The Christian world gradually encircled the empire on the Mediterranean, the Red Sea, and the Persian Gulf.

However, the causes of the Ottoman Empire's decline had more to do with domestic problems. For more than a century, since the capture of Constantinople until 1580, the empire had existed as a military enterprise, whose economy was based on expansion and predation. Necessary resources were always available, come spring, for new campaigns. The salaries of administrators and soldiers were guaranteed by the booty taken from captured cities. The sovereign, his counselors, and the army all believed in the permanency of continued Ottoman conquests and the survival of the empire depended on it.

The causes of the decline of the Ottoman Empire have long been debated among historians: Was it demographic? Did it reflect the deterioration of the slave system, or of the *timar* system of assigning conquered land to military officers on a standby basis? Courtiers began acquiring timars and converting them into private property. The number of soldiers disposing of *timars* was therefore reduced, despite their essential role in the army. Contemporary observers of the crisis wanted to return to the old practices and attributed the decline of the empire to the deterioration of the sultans' power and increased corruption. In fact, whatever the internal causes of the decline, two major external factors were of paramount importance. First, the conquests were, in large part, finished, and no more predation was possible. Constant wars had exhausted the empire. Second, capitalist and mercantile Europe destroyed the mercantile foundation of the empire by controlling Asian trade routes and introducing new models of commerce. Next to dynamic

Europe, the Ottoman Empire remained an increasingly anachronistic war machine, frozen in the past. Nevertheless, the empire maintained its paralyzing sense of superiority until the end of the eighteenth century.

THE OTTOMAN ARMY

In the late fifteenth and sixteenth centuries, Ottoman campaigns occurred yearly from April to October. The main Ottoman force was the cavalry, including a vanguard of light horses composed of Turkmen (*akincis*) and Tatars (*delis*), but the janissary infantry was increasingly important. By the seventeenth century, the Ottoman army remained formidable, but its dominance had ended. The last great offensive ended in defeat in Vienna, in 1683, and Raimondo Montecuccoli's Hapsburg troops had previously defeated the Ottomans at the battle of Saint Gotthard in western Hungary in 1664.*

In the late sixteenth and early seventeenth centuries, the Ottomans still had some success against small Hungarian and Croat forces. What changed in the seventeenth century was the constitution of larger European armies. In the seventeenth century, the Ottomans had to confront a united army from Venice, Austria, Poland, and Russia. The empire, twice humiliated on two fronts in sixteenth-century wars, tried to win decisive battles only on one front. The Turks received help from the Crimea Tatars, who provided the empire with cavalry contingents of up to fifty thousand men. However, with the increasing Russian attacks, the Tatars first had to defend themselves. By the end of the seventeenth century, the cumulative effects of wars on the Mediterranean, Central European, and Black Sea fronts (1684–99) had exhausted the empire.

The weakening of Ottoman power became evident in the series of defeats that led to the Karlowitz treaty of 1699 and to the loss of Hungary, Transylvania, Croatia, and Slavonia to the Hapsburgs, the loss of Dalmatia and the coastal Peloponnese to Venice, and the loss of Podolia to Poland. Elsewhere, the Russians advanced toward the south. The Ottomans lost Azov to Peter the Great in 1696. As for maritime control, the Barbary States acted independently, and local dynasties in Oman and in Yemen expelled Ottoman garrisons.

The influence of Christians from the Balkans and the Byzantine Empire on the Ottoman art of the siege is clear. From the Hungarians,

* See Rhoads Murphey, *Ottoman Warfare, 1500–1700* (New Brunswick, NJ: Rutgers University Press, 1999).

the Ottoman troops adopted the device of chariots set in a circle and chained together, which dated back at least to Attila and had been used by the Czech Hussite leader Jan Žižka (ca. 1360–1424).

In 1438, the Ottomans institutionalized the system of *devşirme* ("collecting"), the recruiting of young Christian boys, mostly from the Balkans, to bring up as janissary soldiers. The best were trained in an annex of the royal palace in Istanbul called the Enderun Kolej. Although they were slaves, they could neither be bought nor sold. The system had strict rules. The son of a widow could not be taken, and there were quotas for each village. Because married men could not be enrolled, Christian parents would marry their sons at twelve years of age to avoid enlistment.

Collection under the *devşirme* system usually occurred every seven years, but every four when necessary. Albanians, Montenegrins, Serbs, Croats, and Bulgarians were preferred, but Greeks could also be enrolled, and a *firman* (edict) by the sultan in 1564 allowed Bosnian boys to be taken even if they were Muslims. Since they were vassals, not subjects, Romanians, Moldavians, and Walachians were excluded, as were urban Jews and the despised Gypsies. In 1573, 80,000 young boys were selected in the Balkans and in Anatolia, where the empire drafted Armenian boys.

The training started at thirteen and lasted five years. It was strict and included the handling of cold steel weapons, and later of firearms, as well as horsemanship and archery. Wrestling was also part of the training. At first, the boys were not allowed to marry. Once they converted, the boys changed names. Out of 5,000 draftees, 1,000 to 1,200 were selected for the royal schools. Besides physical training, the boys learned Turkish as well as some Arabic and Persian. They were also taught how to read and write and practiced calligraphy. After training was complete at the age of eighteen, a boy would be enrolled in a company (*orta*) and would be tattooed on his leg and arm with his number and symbol. At forty-five, if he had survived, the janissary could retire with a pension.

The janissaries accepted the use of firearms, which the *sipahis* despised. Under Mehmet II they included archers, crossbowmen, and musketeers and could fight on foot as well as on horseback. Their number increased from 7,800 at Mohács in 1526, to 12,800 in 1567, and reached 40,000 by 1609. However, the economic crisis and provincial unrest in the middle of the sixteenth century led to the posting of janissaries throughout Anatolia, and their efficiency had declined by the end of the century.

The army had a cavalry three times larger than the infantry, and it expanded to four times the size of the infantry when the Crimean Tatars were included. Supplies and food were required for these men and their horses during the 180 days that constituted each yearly campaign. Between 1450 and 1550, the rapid territorial expansion of the empire created new logistical problems. It took fifty-two marching days, including stops, to go from Edirne to Hungary, and four months to march from the Asiatic shore at Constantinople to Baghdad.

The light cavalry (*akinci*) was the spearhead of the Ottoman Army during the fifteenth century. Under Mehmet II (1451–80), fifty thousand mounted archers fought in the nomad style and shared in the booty of battle. In the sixteenth century, armament and tactics changed. Two new groups emerged: the provincial cavalry, who were granted land titles by the sultan under the *tımar* system, and the *kapikulu*, paid by the sultan's treasury.

The *tımar* system allowed the sultan to demand military service in exchange for revenue generated by the allocated lands. It was thus possible to count on 50,000 to 70,000 cavalrymen, or "timariots," without direct expenditure from the treasury. This was a substantial army compared to the size of contemporary Central European armies, at least until the middle of the seventeenth century.

The Ottoman army was unrivaled in siegecraft and technically equal to European armies, despite some decline in the later seventeenth century, and could field as many as 100,000 men. On the European front, it probably numbered 50,000 to 70,000 men. We are better informed of the Hapsburg headcount: Montecuccoli, in the victorious battle of Saint Gotthard, had only 40,000 troops. The Holy League at the end of the seventeenth century could field a maximum of 70,000 men.

Given the importance of logistics, the organization of the Ottoman army was remarkable for its time. Its light cavalry of 20,000 to 30,000 Tatars knew all the techniques of nomadic warfare: surprise attack, encirclement, and rapid retreat. The army also had an artillery corps. The most commonly used cannon was the *darbzen*, weighing only 60 kilos and therefore highly mobile, but with limited firepower. Heavier cannons were used for sieges, in which the Ottoman sappers were very skilled. Ottoman muskets were similar to European ones. Battles were thus not won because of a technological superiority, but because of leadership and the quality of the troops. Until the end of the sixteenth century, battles were fought with the sultan present in person. Later, the grand vizier led.

The Ottomans were not firmly established in the Balkans until the annexation of the kingdom of Serbia (1459). Their domination in the east was not final until the elimination of their most dangerous adversary, Uzun Hassan, leader of the Ak Koyunlu (1473). In short, the greatest period of the Ottoman Empire, militarily, was between 1480 and 1590, and more particularly between 1521, the date of the fall of Belgrade, and 1590.

Peace between the Hapsburgs and the Ottomans lasted from 1606 to 1660. Hostilities resumed and were followed by Ottoman defeats (e.g., in the second siege of Vienna in 1683), culminating in the peace treaty of Karlowitz (1699), which marks the beginning of the Ottoman Empire's military retreat.

During this period, one must acknowledge the critical social and economic role played by war in the Ottoman Empire. The end of expansionism was also the beginning of the crisis in the empire, and one of its main causes.

In his book *Der Türkenkrieg* (1822), the Prussian general Georg Wilhelm von Valentini (1775–1834) has an excellent chapter on the Turkish army at the time of Montecuccoli's victory in the battle of Saint Gotthard (1664). Montecuccoli, he notes, presents the Turks as models to be imitated in war. After the battle of Saint Gotthard, they had performed a very daring maneuver, never repeated in their history. Although they had been defeated and pushed back with great casualties beyond the Rába River, they withdrew in good order, along the right bank of this river until Gran, where they crossed the Danube. There, they suddenly took the offensive and advanced toward the Váh River, threatening Moravia. Having learned about the crossing of the Gran by the Turks, Montecuccoli advanced to Pressburg (Bratislava), where he crossed the river and arrived on the Váh before the enemy. The vizier was surprised to find the Christian troops there already, and said that they must have been in direct communication with spirits who had revealed his plans to them. Nevertheless, the vizier held his position on the Hungarian border and concluded an advantageous peace treaty, which allowed him to keep the Neuhausel fortress (present-day Nové Zámky in Slovakia) and several other places that he had captured.

"The possession of Hungary opened the way to Western Europe, and the Turks twice arrived at the gates of Vienna," Valentini observes.

Dissatisfied with Austrian rule, the Transylvanians and Hungarians abased themselves, becoming allies and scouts for the Muslims. But the German princes rallied under the banner of Austria and, with the help of Jan Sobieski and his forty thousand Poles fighting in the Turkish style, stopped this invasion. Europe's future would have been like that of the Greeks were it not for this victory.

The Turks then had the excellent policy of fighting their enemies separately, and making peace with one so that they could attack the other. Thus, they took advantage of the twenty-year truce with Austria, after Montecuccoli's victory, to take Candia [present-day Heraklion on the island of Crete] from the Venetians and start a new war against Poland and Russia. . . .

They started the next war against Austria at the instigation of the French, and before the expiration of the truce, contrary to their custom. It began with the siege of Vienna, lasted sixteen years and ended in 1699 with the treaty of Karlowitz and the loss of Hungary, Dalmatia, and Transylvania. They were also forced to return the countries that they had conquered from the Venetians and the Poles, and to cede Azov to the Russians. . . .

The Turks then were constantly at war, and had no difficulty fielding armies of a hundred thousand men or more. Their artillery was considerable. In successful battles, the Christians would capture hundreds of artillery pieces. . . . Unable to rely on their Hungarian light cavalry, the Austrians could deploy neither support nor scouts. They felt secure only when in ranks six deep, including two ranks of pikemen. They surrounded themselves with *chevaux de frise* [horse barricades]. . . . the cavalry was mixed with the infantry, for instance, a battalion alternating with four squadrons. This organization was motivated by the impetuous attacks of the Turks and their superiority in the mêlée. According to the tactics of the time, the cavalry was trained to shoot, and dragoons often fought on foot. Montecuccoli at the Saint Gotthard battle disposed platoons of thirty musketeers on the flanks of his squadrons and was successful. It was important for the platoons or divisions to maintain a continuous fire against the janissaries, who advanced on all sides in tight formations and attempted to cut through the *chevaux de frise* with their axes. Prince Louis of Baden, who trained the great Eugène of Savoy, had the brilliant idea of employing sharpshooters from his battalions to distract the enemy until the moment of the attack. In the battle plan, the two lines were usually closed on the flanks by other troops arranged in columns, which gave the formation the appearance of a long square. The generals recommended never breaking formation, not even to pursue the enemy. . . . The Turks were cunning enough to launch false attacks and to place reserve units, one behind the other, which would suddenly stop the pursuit of the unwary Christians, and then counterattack through breaches in their lines. To counter these techniques, one could only use light cavalry held in reserve between the lines . . . [which] repelled the disorderly Turkish throng, while the European lines . . . moved en masse, always ready to assemble their cavalry to confront the assault of the Turkish cavalry, which came back to charge as rapidly as it was dispersed.

The Turks of that time . . . did not have a line organized for a frontal assault, but always had great masses of troops that surrounded the large Christian square on all sides. This style of fighting was probably the natural consequence of the superior numbers of the Muslim troops and of the vehement attacks of this furious multitude. . . .

Montecuccoli's main criticism of Christian armies was their size. He modestly only asked for fifty thousand men (half infantry, half cavalry) to confront a Turkish army twice that size. In Prince Eugène's wars [in the late seventeenth century], the armies were already more equal. The larger size of permanent armies allowed larger numbers of combat troops.*

* Georg Wilhelm von Valentini, *Der Türkenkrieg* (Berlin: Boicke, 1822); trans. Eugène de la Coste as *Précis des dernières guerres Russes contre les Turcs* (Paris: Firmin Didot, 1825).

CHAPTER 10

Safavid Persia

The Safavid dynasty began with the victory of Shah Ismael in 1501 over the Ak Koyunlu, a tribal Turkic confederation that was powerful in Persia until it was defeated by the Ottomans in 1473. After the death of its leader, Uzun Hassan, this confederation was torn apart by internal struggles.

Like that of the Kara Koyunlu, a rival Turkic confederation based in eastern Anatolia, which Timur had defeated, the Ak Koyunlu army was the last army in Persia based on the Turco-Mongol nomad model. It consisted essentially of a cavalry of mounted archers supported by a more modest infantry (in a ratio of 2.5:1). After being defeated by Ottoman artillery, the Ak Koyunlu would be further marginalized by the Safavids.

The Safavids had become Shiite two centuries earlier, after having previously adhered to a Sunni Sufi order. The most powerful local army was composed of Turkmen, and an Ak Koyunlu heir came to power. The Safavid capital was in Tabriz. Shah Ismael, the founder of the Safavids, fought to gain control of eastern Anatolia, Azerbaijan, western Persia, and Iraq. Shah Ismael quickly consolidated his power in western Persia and eastern Anatolia (1503–7) and began the conquest of Iraq. After he took Baghdad in 1508, he ruled the entire area once dominated by the Ak Koyunlu. Starting in 1510–14, however, the Safavids had to confront Mohamed Shaybani's Uzbeks and the Ottoman Empire on several occasions.

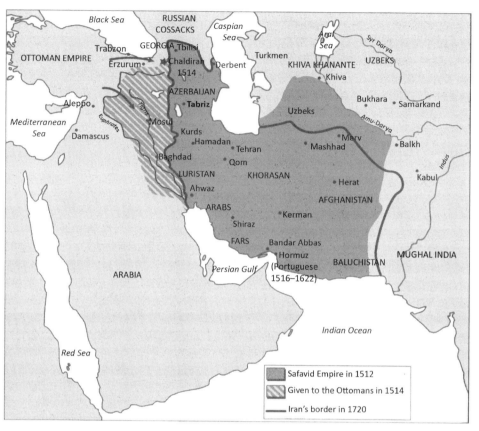

MAP 10. Safavid Persia, 1512–1720.

TWO POWERFUL ADVERSARIES

The Uzbeks appeared in the Kazak steppes toward the end of the four-teenth century. They were displaced in the fifteenth century by the Oirot Mongols, but then gathered strength under a remarkable chief, Mohamed Shaybani, and occupied Transoxiana. The steppes were henceforth occu-pied by the Kazaks.

Samarkand proved difficult to capture, and Shaybani tried three times (1499–1501) before finally succeeding. The Timurid Babur opposed a fierce resistance, but was finally expelled from Samarkand in 1501. Babur tried to recapture the city before retreating to Kabul in 1504. By 1509, Shaybani had conquered territories extending from the south of the Kazak steppes to eastern Persia. He would soon be confronted by an equally powerful adversary: Ismael Shah.

The battle took place near Merv. Shaybani was killed. As was the custom, his skull was made into a goblet banded in gold. The Oxus became the border between the Uzbek and Safavid possessions. Taking advantage of the situation, Babur reconquered Samarkand, but held it only briefly and was expelled again in 1511. Babur then looked east and invaded northern India (1525). Ismael had taken effective control of Persia, including Khorasan, eastern Anatolia, and Azerbaijan, but this expansion would inevitably lead to a confrontation with the Ottomans. Many Turkmen from Anatolia, including the Kizil Bash, were sympathizers of the Shiite Safavids and saw the Ottoman Empire as the defender of the Sunni. A great religious rebellion erupted among the Shiite Kizil Bash in Ottoman Anatolia in 1512, which was supported by the Safavids. The Ottoman sultan, Bayezid, abdicated in favor of his son, Selim, who inaugurated his reign with a harsh repression of the Kizil Bash, before attacking the Safavids. The latter practiced a scorched earth policy, which created logistical problems for the Ottomans. The Ottoman forces were victorious in a battle at Chaldiran in 1514, however, and established a new border between the two empires.

Is seems that the Ottoman army was numerically larger than the Safavids'. The Safavids had retained the Turco-Mongol form of combat, and their army was largely dependent on mounted archers. The Ottomans also had an infantry composed of janissaries and, more important, artillery. The Safavids' lack of firepower led to a crushing defeat, and the shah had to flee.

The Ottomans marched on Tabriz after their victory, but the Ottoman troops expressed the wish to retreat to Anatolia, so the shah was able to reoccupy his capital. Eastern Anatolia, once the domain of the Kara Koyunlu and the Ak Koyunlu, became Ottoman. Historical Armenia was integrated into the Ottoman territory in 1514, and this new border would become permanent.

The Chaldiran victory signaled the end of the nomadic style of combat, which became obsolete with the introduction of firearms. Artillery had already proven conclusive in the Ottomans' war against the Ak Koyunlu in 1473. It would also ensure the success of the Ottomans against the Mamluks of Egypt and Syria in 1517. However, Safavid Persia remained in control of part of the Caucasus and western Afghanistan. Tabriz was now close to the enemy border, which led Shah Ismael to move the capital to Qazvin. In Khorasan, in the east, the Uzbeks threatened Persia, but the Safavids, who had by then acquired cannons from the Portuguese, defeated them.

Ismael's status, almost godlike to the Kizil Bash, was only slightly diminished by his defeat at the hands of the Ottomans: the Kizil Bash continued to revere him and to consider him Ali's heir. Consequently, the rise to power of the Safavids represents the birth of a Shiite theocracy, with the shah as the leader. Most of the administrative posts were held by Persians, while Turkmen held the majority of military positions. In spite of his defeat at Chaldiran, Ismael, who died in 1524, created a dynasty that lasted two centuries and gave Persia its national identity.

Until 1533, Suleiman the Magnificent had concentrated on expansion in Europe (siege of Vienna, 1529), but peace with the Holy Roman Empire allowed him to turn against Persia. The Ottomans were a more serious threat than the Uzbeks, but even the Ottoman victory at Chaldiran did not result in the occupation of Persia.

Suleiman the Magnificent launched three offensives against Safavid Persia (1534, 1537, 1548). None of these was a lasting success, even though he captured Tabriz. Each time, the Safavids practiced a scorched earth policy, which ultimately forced the Ottomans to retreat. In 1555, Suleiman signed the peace treaty of Amasya. The Safavids lost Iraq and the holy Shiite cities of Najaf and Karbala, but retained Azerbaijan and a large part of the Caucasus.

For a century and a half, the Ottoman Empire and Safavid Persia would confront each other. Since the Ottoman Empire also confronted the Hapsburg Holy Roman Empire, Suleiman sought an alliance of the French in their fight against the Hapsburgs. This alliance led to a counteralliance between the Safavids and the Hapsburgs.

In addition, the Safavids led a jihad against the Christians in the Caucasus, with four large expeditions to capture Georgian and Armenian slaves in the mid-sixteenth century.

THE REIGN OF SHAH ABBAS

When Shah Abbas (1587–1629) came to power, the Safavid dynasty was in crisis: half of the empire was occupied by its adversaries, and internal quarrels and factions threatened civil war.

It was impossible for the shah to fight on two fronts, against both the Ottomans and the Uzbeks. He first had to reorganize his empire. He chose to attack his weakest adversary first. To this end, he signed a humiliating treaty with the Ottomans (1590), ceding them western Persia, Tabriz, and most of Azerbaijan. It took ten years to defeat the Uzbeks, who clung to the Khorasan. Herat and western Afghanistan would not be recaptured until 1598, and the eastern border would not be pacified until the seventeenth century. In 1603, Shah Abbas began his counteroffensive against the Ottomans. In a series of campaigns (1605–7), the Persians expelled the Ottomans from western Persia and in 1620, Shah Abbas captured Diyarbakir. He took Baghdad three years later.

Throughout his reign, Shah Abbas tried to reduce the power of the Kizil Bash's emirs bit by bit. It was a delicate task, since his dynasty had reached power with their support. Abbas found allies in the Caucasus: Georgians, Armenians, and Circassians joined his campaign in Armenia in 1603, and in Georgia, in 1614 and 1616. The shah even transferred several thousand Armenian artisans to settle them near Isfahan.

Shah Abbas's army was composed of Caucasian *ghilman* (slave-soldiers). It included ten thousand horsemen, twelve thousand artillery-men (with five hundred cannons), and twelve thousand infantrymen armed with muskets, all of whom were directly and regularly paid by the shah himself. In addition, the shah also had a bodyguard of three thousand men. The Safavids' regular army thus numbered thirty-seven thousand.

In addition, Shah Abbas could count on the support of some fifty thousand Kizil Bash to take part in campaigns. These provincial troops were not paid by the shah but by the tribal chiefs, using the revenues from their provinces. Each tribal chief who administered a province was required to supply a specific number of troops.

At the end of his reign, Shah Abbas progressively modified this system in order to weaken the tribal chiefs. The provinces, which retained their autonomy, were at the periphery of the empire: Georgia, Khuzestan, Kurdistan, and Loristan. He reorganized the army to make it a permanent force and adapted to the progressive increase in the firepower of cannons and muskets. He reduced the political and military importance of the tribal chiefs by introducing new ethnic elements and centralizing the administration. The commander of the new army was a Georgian, who became governor of the important province of Fars. He owed everything to the shah except his talent. However, the Kizil Bash continued to maintain their independence. The Khanat tribe, seen as too powerful, was divided in three and settled in Azerbaijan, Merv, and Astarabad, each several hundred kilometers distant from the other. Shah

Abbas also moved the Safavid capital to Isfahan and made it into one of the most beautiful cities in the world.

Safavid Persia reached its zenith under Shah Abbas, becoming one of the three great Muslim powers, along with the Ottoman and Mughal Empires, and one of the world's great powers.

CHAPTER 11

The Ming and Chinese
Politico-Military Traditions

China's foreign policy was for a long time defined by its long and vulnerable northern border, which was subject to frequent incursions from the nomads of the steppes. The nomads would often settle in the northern areas of the country, taking advantage of Chinese domestic problems. They would then gradually become sinicized, before being themselves swept away by other new nomadic invaders. China endured because of its cultural solidity and demography. Chinese influence in the north would expand under energetic dynasties such as the Han, the Tang, and the early Ming, the first post-Mongol dynasty (1368–1644).

China, that is, the China of eighteen provinces, extended to the north and to the east and developed considerable influence over Vietnam, Korea, and, through Korea, Japan. It is not surprising that China considered itself the Middle Kingdom. Some highlights of early imperial Chinese history include

- Unification under the Qin dynasty in 221 B.C.E.
- Under the Han dynasty (206 B.C.E. to 24 C.E.), new institutions emerged, as well as a strategy to control the bend of the Ordos and the oases of the northwest in order to repel nomad invasions. From the time of the Han dynasty, Confucianism formed the basis of social relations.
- The progressive occupation of more southern regions occurred as a result of gradual migrations during the first and second

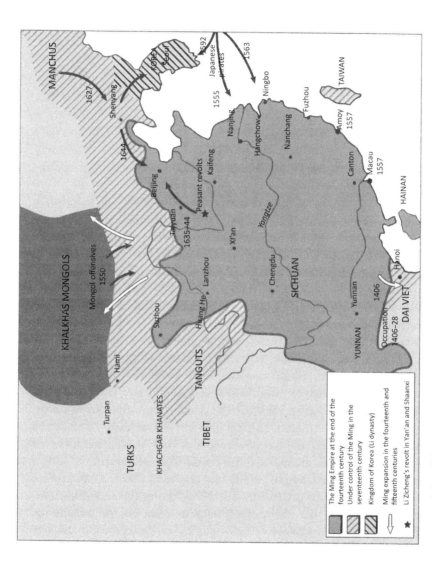

MAP 11. Ming China, 1368–1644.

centuries C.E. and again at the beginning of the Song dynasty (960–1279).

- Finally, from the seventh century on, China developed the system of mandarin bureaucracy, where bureaucrats were recruited based on competitive exams under a sovereign whose rule was based on the "mandate of heaven."

THE PRINCIPLES OF CHINA'S BORDER POLICY

During auspicious periods, the Chinese Empire received tribute from nomadic tribes at its borders. Conversely, China would withdraw and sometimes pay tribute in times of difficulty. Twice, China was totally occupied by nomads: by the Mongols (1279–1368) and by the Manchus (1644–1911).

Historically, all the Chinese dynasties, whether Han (i.e., indigenous Chinese) or non-Han (nomad), tried to maximize their influence over the periphery of the empire. This policy required a stable government and a strong army. That was the case under the Han, Tang, and (early) Ming dynasties, and also during the Mongol (Yuan) and Manchu (Qing) dynasties.

Under the Han, the dynasty sought to control Xinjiang in the north, South China, Southeast Asia, southern Manchuria, and northern Korea. Under the Tang, the dynasty extended its control to Central Asia as far as present-day Kazakhstan, Mongolia, Tibet, northeastern India, and the north of Korea. Under the Yuan, the Mongols were even more expansionist and tried to extend Chinese dominance to Japan, Vietnam (unsuccessfully), Java, and Burma. The Ming were victorious in southern Manchuria, Central Asia, Mongolia, Burma and the north of Korea. Finally, the Manchu dynasty resumed the traditional geopolitics of China and launched campaigns to increase Chinese control in Central Asia and Tibet. The Chinese Empire had reached its largest extension.

The last nomad threat to China was crushed in the eighteenth century. Nevertheless, the north of China was occupied by nomads for almost half of Chinese history after its unification under the Qin dynasty (206 B.C.E.). The nomads, however, invariably adopted Chinese manners and customs. Similar acculturation of nomads also occurred in Persia.

China specialists, including experts within China, tend to see the military policy of China as defensive and founded on political negotiation, with violence used only as a last resort when the adversary had already been largely defeated. This perspective owes much to Sun Zi's sixth-century B.C.E. treatise *The Art of War.* However, if we study Chinese history, rather than the writings of Sun Zi, Confucius, or Mencius, we see that force was constantly required both inside and outside China. Under the Han, the Tang, the Sui, the Ming, and the Qing, China fought offensive and defensive wars beyond its borders. At their inception, many new dynasties tried to establish or reestablish control over China's borders. Most of the military campaigns were directed toward the north and the northeast against nomads who raided and pillaged sedentary regions whenever they could. The famous fifteenth-century naval expeditions of Zheng He under the Ming (1405–33) explored East Africa and Southeast Asia, but did not attempt to conquer newly discovered regions, although the Chinese nevertheless considered them tributary states.*

The nomads remained a constant menace throughout more than two thousand years, from the fourth century B.C.E. to the seventeenth century C.E. When Chinese dynasties were weak, they would typically try to pacify the northern nomads with tribute. Waves of nomad invasions recurred, as well as counteroffensives, which periodically succeeded in expelling the nomads, but without ever subduing or destroying them. On the other hand, in countries to the south of China with sedentary populations, like Vietnam and Korea, Chinese occupation was culturally and institutionally very significant. It should be noted that the northern dynasties, of nomad origins, were also adept at fighting other nomads, whose style of combat was familiar to them.

Chinese strategy, generally speaking, followed a few basic rules:

- Cooperate with distant countries and strike the closer enemy.
- Use a barbarian people against another barbarian people.
- Avoid strong enemies; attack the weaker.†

Those axioms constitute a basic corpus elaborated by Sun Zi and were also followed by Persia and the Byzantine Empire. However, such subtle stratagems were poorly suited to the conditions in northern China created by the nomad raids: avoidance of battle would lead to predation. Many observers of Chinese military strategy have placed too much emphasis on military history as seen through the eyes of Sun Zi

---

* See Edward L. Dreyer, *Zheng He: China and the Oceans in the Early Ming Dynasty, 1405–1433* (New York: Pearson Longman, 2007).

† Edward L. Dreyer et al., *Chinese Ways in Warfare,* ed. Frank A. Kierman Jr. and John K. Fairbank (Cambridge, MA: Harvard University Press, 1974).

and readings of Mao Zedong.* In fact, Mao did not address conventional war at all in his major works, but focused on guerrilla strategy, which naturally seeks to avoid frontal attacks and gain time before an offensive confrontation. Mao wrote little about the period of conventional war from 1946 to 1949.

The Qin (221–207 B.C.E.), Han (206 B.C.E.–24 C.E.), Sui (581–618 C.E.), and Tang (618–907 C.E.) systematically used force to unify the country and impose Chinese domination on the periphery. Early Ming rulers did likewise, but the Ming dynasty later embraced a siege mentality, sheltering behind the Great Wall, and withdrew from coastal China.

THE CHANGING STRATEGY OF THE MING

The Ming dynasty embraced different strategies during the three centuries of its reign. For centuries, northern China was either fighting the nomads or being conquered by them, while subjugating them culturally. In the south, dynasties like the Song were specifically Chinese. The north and south had distinct methods of combat. It was the Yuan Mongols who united the two Chinas. A century after the Mongol invasion, the Chinese founded the Ming dynasty and forced the Mongols back to the steppe. They were faced with a problem: which military tradition should they adopt? The northern tradition, forged through centuries of combat, or the southern one, that of a classic sedentary state?

During the first period of their reign, the Ming adopted the Yuan style, with its nomad techniques of combat. At the start of the dynasty, Ming military operations extended over an immense expanse, from Central Asia to Burma, and from the Xinxiang to Annam. This presented a considerable logistical challenge and required an excellent system of roads. The Ming army was initially organized according to the decimal Mongol system and based essentially on mounted archers who harassed the enemy with arrows before a frontal attack was attempted. Gradually, however, the Ming returned to more traditional Chinese ways and gave up their aggressive policy, which had, in any case, met with only partial success. The economy became the primary concern, with a focus on development in southern China.

The Ming army used gunpowder and bronze cannons starting in the early 1400s. In *Science and Civilisation in China* (1954–2008), Joseph Needham dates the introduction of bronze cannons in China to the

* See *Mao stratège*, ed. Gérard Chaliand (Paris: Le Félin, 2002).

beginning of the fourteenth century (they appeared later in Europe). However, cannons were used more as a strategic weapon than as field guns, and by 1400, Chinese military technology was beginning to lag, perhaps because of the Ming court's hostility to innovation.

A study of the Ming dynasty shows that in the absence of a great emperor, the state quickly fragmented. It was unable to make rapid decisions because of the multiple centers of power and unwieldy number of generals and ministers. In the fifteenth century, the military capacity of the dynasty declined. In fact, China's borders, which under the Yuan had equaled those of the Tang era, came under threat during the later Ming.

The Ming decided to strengthen the Great Wall and added to it from the mid-fifteenth century to the mid-seventeenth. At its beginning, Ming rulers sought to imitate the Mongols and control the north, a policy pursued with mixed success until 1425. In 1372, Ming troops campaigned in the vicinity of Karakorum, and in 1380, they fought and repelled northern nomads. In 1388, they conducted a victorious campaign against the Mongols. Then they invaded Vietnam (1406–27), but without success. Zheng He's seven expeditions of naval exploration occurred between 1405 and 1433. In the meantime, the Mongols waged victorious campaigns in the north (1410–24). In 1449, the Mongols defeated the Ming, and the emperor himself was captured. The Ming reorganized their military forces and continued to build the Great Wall (1473–85). A final expedition against the Mongols in 1498 was unsuccessful.

With the arrival of the Portuguese and increase in Japanese piracy, the Ming's policy was forced to change. The situation had deteriorated on all fronts. Invasions of Vietnam and Central Asia had failed. In 1420, an expedition to the Red River ended in defeat and the evacuation of Vietnam. China's coasts were threatened by Japanese pirates, and in the middle of the sixteenth century, to prevent smuggling and pirate raids, the Ming forbade all coastal trade.

At the time of the Mongol dynasty, Kublai Khan (1216–94) knew how to subdue the northern nomads: economic blockades were imposed to deprive the nomads of resources, combined with vigorous attacks in the spring when the nomads' horses were weakened by winter. These tactics were adopted by the early Ming emperors but had been gradually abandoned by the beginning of the sixteenth century. The Ming sought a modus vivendi with the nomads, even if temporary. China's main growing areas were in the south, and food had to be transported north to supply Ming garrisons numbering roughly a million men, a very costly operation.

With time, the Ming, a southern dynasty, lost interest in the northern steppes, which had been one of their major preoccupations at their dynasty's inception. Early on, they were advised by experienced Yuan counselors who were familiar with the steppes. However, as the Ming returned to the Southern Song's Confucian conception of China, they lost interest in the barbarian world and largely renounced the use of force, which had, in any case, led to failure. How could they expect to maintain the empire? Contradictory advice circulated, and weak emperors were unable to make bold decisions (1506–1620). Should they reconquer the Ordos, that vital bend of the Yellow River whose possession was essential for the control of northern China? Or should they fortify the Great Wall, an imaginary line of protection, like the French Maginot line, which might have vulnerabilities against a determined adversary?

Esen, an Oirat Mongol, rose to power and, with an iron grip, unified the steppes from the Xinjiang to Korea. That was a source of great concern to the Ming. The Oirat Mongols and the empire had established commercial relationships, which an emperor decided to reduce in the middle of the fifteenth century. The Oirat Mongols responded by preparing for war. The Chinese court and emperor decided to mount a punitive expedition in 1449, which ended in disaster. Not only was the battle lost, but the retreat turned to disaster and the Mongols captured the emperor.

This total defeat marked a turning point in Ming strategy. The Chinese garrisons withdrew, while the Oirat pushed ahead. Without army garrisons in the north, the Ming lost control over the steppes. The Yuan, like all the strong dynasties, had controlled the Ordos. After 1449, the Chinese attempted a counterattack to retake the Ordos, but failed. The Ming then fell back on the defensive policy of the Great Wall (1474).*

Meanwhile, in the steppe, a new chief emerged, Dayan-Khan, a descendant of Genghis Khan (1453–70). He launched raids on the northern and western borders of the empire and, like the Yuan, built a series of forts from which he could control the steppes and launch raids.

In the sixteenth century, the nomads retained considerable power. Another chief, Altan Khan (1507–82), succeeded Dayan-Khan and con-

---

* Arthur Waldron, *The Great Wall of China: From History to Myth* (Cambridge: Cambridge University Press, 1990).

tinued pressuring the Ming. His goal was not so much to conquer the empire, but rather to obtain greater concessions and tribute. The Ming continued their attempts to control the Ordos during the fifteenth century, but abandoned these in the sixteenth.

The ban on maritime trade and the evacuation of coastal cities started in 1523. The empire became isolated as it retreated in both the east and the north. Consequently, piracy increased, particularly on the southeastern coast. Debates about expansion versus isolationism generally favored the isolationists, who, nevertheless, were unable to control piracy or stop the nomad incursions. These policies weakened the empire and would lead to its fall in the following century. From the mid-sixteenth to the early seventeenth centuries, Ming China had to confront annual nomad incursions.

Ming dynasty strategy can be divided into three stages. The first resumed the Yuan strategy. Its goal was to keep the northern nomads in check through a combination of military, economic, and diplomatic pressure. In the second stage, from the mid-fifteenth to the mid-sixteenth centuries, inaction characterized Ming policy. The third stage, from the middle of the sixteenth century on, was decidedly isolationist.

During the first phase, the capital was moved to Peking (Beijing), facing the steppe. As the dynasty remained strong in the north, it also expanded in the south: Annam was invaded (1406) and transformed into a Chinese province, but Vietnamese guerrilla resistance compelled China to retreat (1427).

Meanwhile, the Muslim eunuch Zheng He commanded a series of tributary voyages to East Africa (1405–24) and the Indian Ocean. At a time when the Portuguese had not yet reached Madera, Zheng He commanded 317 ships and 28,000 men. His voyages were limited to exploration, the establishment of trade, and the recognition of Chinese power. The expeditions altered the royal succession in Java and Ceylon (Sri Lanka), and the Malay states became Chinese tributaries.

Five campaigns were launched against the Oirat Mongols during the first phase of the Ming Dynasty (1410–49). The first four campaigns were victorious but did not eliminate the Oirat threat. The final campaign was disastrous. By around 1540, the still formidable empire had been weakened militarily. A defensive mentality developed, following a series of defeats and internal troubles. The Ming had to confront Esen's attacks in the middle of the fifteenth century, then the incursions of Altan Khan.

Gradually, the infantry came to include more and more mercenaries, often recruited among vagabonds and criminals. In 1449, a conscript militia was organized to oppose the Oirat Mongol offensive against Peking. Since talented men chose to join the mandarin class rather than the army, the officers were mediocre, with the result that although discipline was strict, it was ineffective. Military decisions were made by the mandarins, who considered themselves superior to generals.

CHAPTER 12

The Manchu and the End of the Nomads

The Manchu were the last nomadic group to conquer a major sedentary civilization. They were descendants of the Jurchens, who had previously conquered northern China in the twelfth century. After forty-five years of war, the Manchu took Peking (Beijing) in 1644. They would remain in power until 1911.

Unlike other nomad populations that invaded China, the Manchu were neither Turks nor Mongols. They were hunters rather than shepherds. They occupied the area northeast of the Great Wall in present-day Manchuria. They were involved in a quarrel of succession and seized power from the Ming. An exceptional leader called Nurhaci (1559–1626) laid the basis for the conquest. He had unified the seven Jurchen tribes and had become their undisputed chief by 1615. The Ming dynasty was undergoing a crisis due to rebellions in the north as a result of famine, while on the eastern coast, Japanese pirates were creating havoc. Nurhaci controlled a large territory north and east of the Great Wall. In 1619, he proclaimed himself emperor and invaded China. The Ming launched a counteroffensive to capture Nurhaci's capital, Mukden. The large Chinese army advanced in four columns, and Nurhaci decided to attack them separately. The confrontation led to the annihilation of three columns, but the Manchu remained north of the Great Wall.

A series of mediocre emperors succeeded one another, and bureaucrats made most of the decisions. When Nurhaci died (1626), the

Manchu controlled an efficient military empire. One of Nurhaci's sons, Hong Taiji, took power and continued the incursions against the Ming. However, Ming cities remained unassailable.

After the Manchu had conquered Korea, they undertook their first large raid across the Great Wall (1629). Peking was well defended by a general, but the Ming executed him because of rumors of treason. Hong Taiji could not capture the city. For the nomads, unless helped by sedentary expertise and cannons, it was very difficult, if not impossible, to capture fortified cities.

The Manchu's first cannon was cast in 1631. In 1635, after they had incorporated Mongolia into their empire, they adopted the name of Manchu. Their mobility allowed them to harass the Chinese forces in the north, who were forced to remain behind their fortifications, and border towns fell to the Manchu.

Behind the Great Wall, the Ming dynasty faced a revolt. A Ming rebel commander, Li Zicheng, captured Loyang, then Kaifeng and Xian. When he finally marched toward Peking, the emperor committed suicide. The court, having no choice, accepted Li Zicheng as the new emperor. However, a provincial governor, Wu Sangui, refused to submit. He had troops and decided to seek the alliance of the Manchu to dispute the throne with the usurper.

Helped by the Manchu, Wu Sangui took Peking. However, once the Manchu were in the city, they refused to cede control. Thus, the Qing dynasty was created. It would last 268 years. Sinicized, the Manchu resumed the traditional geopolitics of conquering Chinese dynasties. They finally defeated the nomads of the steppe: the second Oirat khanate of Galdan Khan (1676–97) was crushed by the Qing emperor Ching K'ang-His in 1686 with the help of cannons that had been provided by Jesuits.

After the Mongol Empire and Tamerlane, the nomads' heirs and their sedentary descendants continued to dominate Eurasia in the fifteenth and sixteenth centuries. Nomad dominance in Europe had ended in the sixteenth century, but the descendants of nomads would rule China until the early twentieth.

CHAPTER 13

The Mughals and Islam in India

Muslims from Central Asia had dominated northern India since the tenth century. Persian cultural influence prevailed among them, and their military commanders were of Turkic or Mongol—or, more rarely, Persian or Afghan—descent. Their military strategy was typically nomad, with the addition of new techniques acquired from the sedentary populations of Persia. The military elite obtained lands from the sultan of Delhi and were expected in exchange to participate actively in his campaigns.

THE MUGHAL DYNASTY

The Mughal dynasty began with the Turco-Mongol leader Babur (1482–1530). Babur spoke and wrote Chagatai, a Turkish dialect influenced by Arabic and Persian.* The Uzbeks had expelled him from Samarkand and rebuffed his attempts at return. He retreated to Kabul (1504). From there he led a relatively small army of 15,000 men, equipped with cannons, into battle with the army of Sultan Ibrahim Lodi at Panipat (1526) on the plains near Delhi, where invaders of the subcontinent had fought for control of India for thousands of years.

---

* Babur's memoirs have been published as *Bābur-nāma*, trans. Annette Susannah Beveridge (New Delhi: Oriental Books Reprint Corp., 1970).

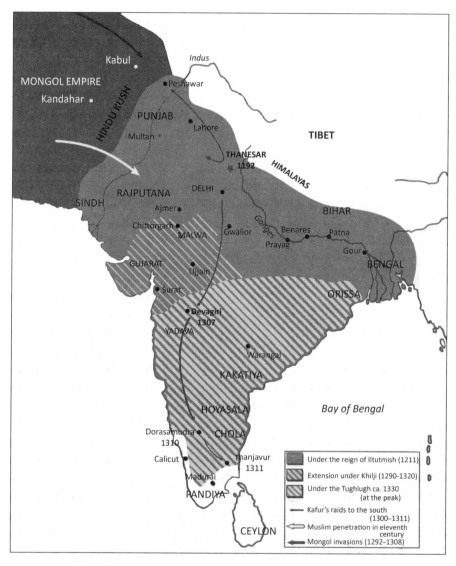

MAP 12. The Delhi Sultanate, 1211–1330.

Babur's army included different Muslim groups: Turks, Mongols, Persians, and Afghans. This highly disciplined army was composed of mounted archers, fighting in the traditional manner, helped by cannons and muskets. Babur's victory at Panipat was total, and gave him control of the Indo-Gangetic plain as far as Patna. After Babur's death, his son

Humayun was forced to withdraw to Afghanistan after a defeat at the hands of Sher Khan's cavalry (1540), but Humayun returned fifteen years later with a reorganized army and recaptured Delhi.

A year after Humayun's death, in 1556, the generals of the new thirteen-year-old emperor Akbar defeated the Indians in the second battle of Panipat. Akbar would become the greatest of the Mughal emperors. He showed exceptional religious tolerance and even attempted to establish a kind of Hindu-Muslim syncretism. He was an efficient administrator and reformed the army to create and maintain a permanent and regularly paid force with a complex organizational plan. This basic accomplishment was difficult to achieve in nomad armies because of their tribal structure and the fact that war was considered a seasonal activity.

The cavalry played the same crucial role in the Mughal army as it did in other Muslim armies. The elite units of the emperor were well paid but constituted only a few thousand men. The cavalry, which was not in the direct service of the emperor, kept growing in the seventeenth century.

The order of battle was the traditional one: heavy cavalry and infantry occupied the center, along with the sovereign, accompanied by his astrologers, doctors, and bodyguards, as well as elephants to break enemy lines (although they were infrequently used). The vanguard consisted entirely of light cavalry, which also held the flanks. Reserves to bolster the center in the event of a counterattack were at the rear, along with remounts and fresh supplies of food and weapons. Artillery increased in importance under the Mughals. Guns were mounted on heavy chariots, which were chained together to serve as defensive barriers against enemy assault. The gunners were mostly Ottoman Turks, but there were also Portuguese, Dutch, and Indians. Sharpshooters armed with muskets and flintlock rifles were interspersed between the chariots. Dromedaries carried other firearms. There were also grenadiers and grenade throwers. Then came the cavalry. For a large campaign up to forty thousand horsemen would be arranged on the flanks, in reserve, and at the center. Half a dozen elephants were positioned in front of the vanguard and twelve at the center, with others on the flanks and in reserve.

Under the reign of Akbar, the army included a mixture of Turkish-speakers, Rajputs, and Afghans. The battle plan was discussed by the sovereign and his counselors. Battles generally started at dawn and stopped at dusk. In Timur style, the vanguard, as well as the vanguard of the flanks, advanced first. Then, the two flanks would attack. If the enemy resisted this assault, the center intervened to deal a decisive blow.

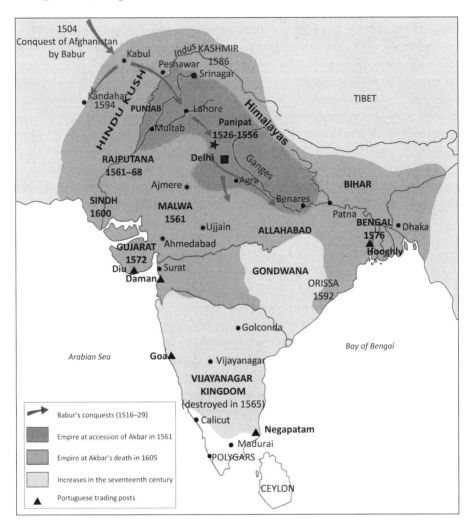

MAP 13. Mughal India, 1542–1605.

Over time, success depended increasingly on the damage inflicted by the artillery.

Cannons became very mobile in Akbar's reign, with each mounted on an individual carriage. However, the cavalry still remained critical because of its mobility and assault capacity. After the first signs of weakening by the cannonade, the cavalry charged. After letting fly their arrows, the cavalry attacked with sabers, a favorite Mughal weapon, although the redoubtable Rajput cavalry preferred lances. Besides the

Rajputs and the Sikhs, who appeared in the sixteenth century, the most fearsome Indian troops were the Marathis, who practiced guerrilla warfare, but were also formidable in regular combat.

The fiercest battles took place surrounding the enemy general's elephants. Since retreating was considered dishonorable, the commander's death signaled victory. To take advantage of their superior firepower, their numbers, and their excellent, disciplined cavalry, the Mughals favored classic battles on the Indo-Gangetic plain, which the river Ganges linked with Bengal. Military operations were more complicated in mountainous regions of the Deccan plateau or the swampy terrain of Bengal. It took a long time for the Mughals to develop a fleet, but they eventually understood the advantage of combining attacks on land and sea.

The Mughal infantry initially lacked prestige, but over time, and with the development of muskets and flintlock rifles, its importance increased. Under Akbar, it consisted of twelve thousand men. The infantry was used for sieges, which played a very significant role in many Mughal campaigns. The Mughals also built an exceptional network of forts.

Mughal logistics became more complex in the seventeenth century, in parallel with the development of a more classical army. Transportation was organized with elephants, Bactrian horses, dromedaries, and oxen. A convoy followed to supply the army.*

The decline of the empire began when Jahangir rebelled against his father, Akbar, who had conquered northern India and Afghanistan. Jahangir's rebellion was put down, but he nevertheless ascended to the throne six years later and ruled from 1605 to 1627. Fighting between Muslims and Sikhs started under Jahangir and lasted until Partition in 1947.

The English had established their first trading outpost in Machilipatam in 1611. Jahangir's son led a rebellion against his father in Afghanistan. At the death of Jahangir, his son, Shah Jahan, became emperor (1628) and invaded the Deccan Plateau, the south-central part of the subcontinent. His reign was munificent and greatly impressed Persian and Ottoman ambassadors. However, the Persians invaded Mughal Afghanistan in 1649. Soon afterward, a civil war arose from a crisis in succession. Shah Jahan was removed from power (1659). Aurangzeb, the last of the Mughal

---

* See *The Cambridge History of India*, vol. 4: *The Mughal Period*, ed. R. Burn and W. Haig (Cambridge: Cambridge University Press, 1937); *The Encyclopaedia of Islam*, 2nd ed., ed. P.J. Bearman et al. (Leiden: E.J. Brill, 1960–2005); Virginia Fass et al., *The Forts of India* (London: Collins, 1986).

emperors, acceded to the throne, captured the south of India with the exception of the Tamil areas, and pacified the Deccan region.

The English reinforced their presence (1686–90) and fought the Mughals. The Marathis (1699–1706) rebelled and shook the Mughal domination in the south of India. In the next twenty-five years, they became a serious threat, while the Europeans fought one another for the domination of India. By the time Aurangzeb died in 1707, Mughal grandeur was a thing of the past.

THE SEDENTARIZATION OF THE MUGHAL EMPIRE

After they had become sedentary and built successful empires, the Ottomans, Safavids, and Mughals ruled successfully for several centuries. The Ottomans were closer to Europe and benefited most from European military innovations. However, after their expansion, none of the nomad empires would be sufficiently innovative to perpetuate themselves. The nomads valued tradition over innovation. The first post-Mongol Empire, the Ming Empire (1368–1644), succeeded in eliminating the Mongol dynasty, but then withdrew upon itself and was finally swept away in the seventeenth century by the Manchu, the last great nomad wave.

The nomads remained a dominant power through the fourteenth century, but their power had declined by the middle of the sixteenth. From that time on, their role in Eurasian history was restricted to China. Elsewhere, the Ottomans had taken Constantinople and became, less than a century later, masters of a considerable empire. In Persia, the Safavids were a major power. In India, the Mughals created a prestigious empire in the sixteenth and seventeenth centuries. In the middle of the sixteenth century, Russia liberated itself from Tatar domination and took the offensive, eventually conquering Siberia.

CHAPTER 14

Russia and the End of the Tatars

The Mongols dominated Russia for two and a half centuries. The tide seemed to turn when Prince Dmitri won the battle of Kulikovo over the Golden Horde, or Kipchak khanate, in 1380, but it was an ephemeral victory. After Kulikovo, Tokhtamysh, the khan of the White and then the Blue Horde, assumed the leadership of the Golden Horde near the Sea of Azov. Having reunited the territories that the Horde had formerly ruled, Tokhtamysh then attacked Russia and demanded tribute. When it was refused, he ravaged Suzdal and Vladimir and then burned Moscow, Prince Dmitri's city, to teach him a lesson. The grand duke of Lithuania tried to intervene, but was also defeated. The Tatar yoke would last another century.

THE TATAR YOKE

In 1395, Timur defeated Tokhtamysh after a long struggle and reconstituted the Kipchak khanate. However, succession quarrels led to its disintegration a few years later. The Crimean khanate was founded in 1430 and the Kazan khanate in 1445. These khanates remained formidable military powers. In 1445, Moscow Grand Duke Vassily was crushed at the battle of Suzdal by the Kazan Tatars. The Tatars feigned a retreat, trapped the Russian cavalry, and captured the grand duke. However, the khanate was not powerful enough to subjugate the Russians. They exchanged the grand duke for ransom, but did not attempt to take Moscow.

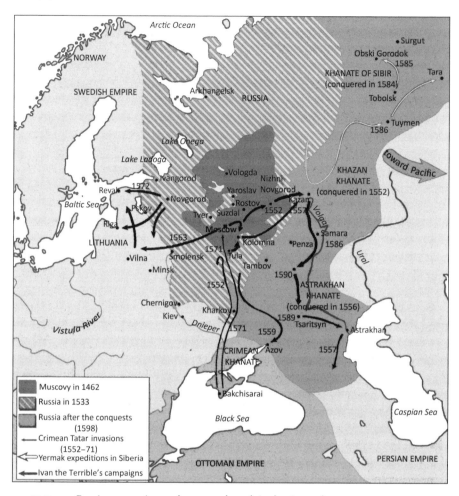

MAP 14. Russian expansion to the east and south in the sixteenth century.

Starting in the middle of the fifteenth century, the Russians ceased to pay tribute to the Horde. In 1480, Grand Duke Ivan III of Moscow formed an alliance with the khan of Crimea and refused to pay tribute to the Kipchak khanate. The Kipchak khan marched on Moscow. The two armies met at the Oka River and remained on opposite sides, observing each other without engaging in battle. After a few weeks, fearing that the Crimean khan would take advantage of his absence to capture his fiefdom, the Kipchak khan retreated. A year later, the Kipchak khan was killed by the khan of Sibir (Siberia), and the Crimean khan captured the Kipchak capital of Sarai, ending the Kipchak khanate. The remaining khanates were those of Crimea, Kazan, Astrakhan, and, though less important, Sibir. All were Muslim. The most combative was the Tatar khanate of Crimea.

After he ascended the throne, Ivan III's son, Ivan IV, known to history as Ivan the Terrible, overcame the khanates of Kazan (1552) and Astrakhan (1556) with the help of artillery. Muscovite Russia, already an immense territory, began to expand to the east and south. The menace of the nomads of the steppe had almost been eliminated.

THE MONGOLS IN RUSSIAN HISTORY

What role did the Mongols play in Russian history, and can we say that Muscovite Russia was a post-Mongol Empire? Pope Innocent IV's Franciscan emissary to the Great Khan, Friar Giovanni da Pian del Carpine (1182?–1252), describes the terrible depredations and massacres of the Mongols in Russia.* For many generations, their occupation of the southern steppe, including the lands surrounding the Black Sea, deprived Russia of its richest farmland. The Mongol occupation cut the ties that Russia had forged with Europe. Cultural regression is obvious, for instance, in comparing the architectural creativity of Suzdal and Vladimir at the beginning of the thirteenth century with the limited artistic production of the fourteenth and fifteenth centuries.

The Mongol contribution was mostly in the domain of military tactics and cavalry. In addition, the Mongol administration established a system of taxation, which the Russians would use to centralize the country. What is most striking, however, is the length of the Mongol occupation of Russia. Moscow was sacked by Mongols in 1237 and would be sacked again in 1571, after an interval of some 334 years, by the Crimean Tatars.

THE EXPANSION OF MUSCOVY

The beginnings of Moscow around 1150 were modest. It was small and backward compared to trading cities like Novgorod and older cities like Suzdal, Vladimir, and Rostov. But Moscow was located at the crossroad of the routes connecting these northern cities to Kiev and other cities to

---

* In Giovanni da Pian del Carpine, *Histoire des Mongols,* trans. and ed. Dom Jean Becquet and Louis Hambis (Paris: A. Maisonneuve, 1965).

the south, and was situated near the source of the Volga, Don, Dnieper, and Oka rivers.

Once Moscow had asserted its dominance in the northeast (Suzdal–Vladimir) there remained only two important independent Russian states: Novgorod and Ryazan. Moscow also knew how to negotiate with the Mongols, allying with them when they were powerful and rejecting them when they were weak. Finally, Moscow became the metropolitan center and the religious capital of all of Russia. Moscow's rulers would become more and more powerful, and they soon evolved into autocratic tsars. To the west, however, Lithuania and Poland also grew more powerful in the fourteenth and fifteenth centuries.

Ivan the Terrible was the first Muscovite ruler to be crowned tsar of Russia. Around 1550, the army was restructured to place greater emphasis on artillery and engineering, and a permanent force of musketeers was established. This allowed Ivan the Terrible to resume the centuries-old battles with the nomads of the steppes, but this time to the advantage of Russia. At the beginning of his campaigns, the khanate of Kazan was helped by the Crimean Tatars supported by Ottoman janissaries and artillery. In 1552, the Russians defeated the janissaries in the south and invested Kazan both on land and on the Volga River. After the conquest of Kazan, the Russians marched to Astrakhan and occupied it (1556). Of the three Tatar states, only Crimea remained, supported by the Sublime Porte. The forces of the Crimean khanate took the offensive but were repeatedly repelled (1554, 1557, and 1558). They also failed to recapture Astrakhan in 1569. However, in 1571, the Giray khan Devlet I led his troops to Moscow and burned parts of it to the ground, but was unable to take the Kremlin.

Meanwhile, after more than twenty years of fighting, Ivan the Terrible failed in his Baltic offensive. During the last years of his reign, the Cossack Yermak Timofeyevich began the conquest of Siberia. The Russians had already reached the source of the Yenisei River around the middle of the sixteenth century. Beyond the Urals, the khan of Sibir encouraged the resistance of local tribes to the Russian occupation. Around 1582, Yermak led an expedition of only 1,600 Cossacks east of the Urals. With his firepower and good organization, he occupied the capital of the khan of Sibir, but he was unable to hold it and was killed before reinforcements from Ivan could arrive (1584). Ivan's larger army defeated the khanate of Sibir and founded a fortified administrative center, Tobolsk, in 1587. Later, the Russians would continue to the Sea of Okhotsk. In the early to mid-seventeenth century, over a thirty-year period, the Russians advanced more than three thousand miles from the Ob River to the Pacific. They settled in Kamchatka in 1696. In the Amur region, they battled the Manchus until the Nerchinsk treaty (1689) established a temporary border between the two empires.

The Kazan and Astrakhan conquests gave the Russians access to the fertile lands of the southeast. The Russian government encouraged the occupation of these regions, but this offended the nobles. Migrations became illegal, but continued nonetheless. To escape serfdom, the migrating peasants often became Cossacks, that is, free warriors of the frontier.

The extension of Muscovite Russia to the Ukraine in 1654 was very significant. Since 1569, the Ukraine had been controlled by Poland. Poland considered the Eastern Uniate Catholic Church, with links to Rome, as the legitimate successor to the Orthodox Church. Though many Orthodox bishops had accepted the union, much of the population continued to support Orthodoxy, despite persecution.

The Cossacks intervened. Toward the middle of the sixteenth century, the Dnieper Cossacks had settled on an island in the Dnieper and launched raids against the Crimean Tatars and the Ottoman Empire, which supported the Tatars. From 1624 to 1638, a Cossack peasant rebellion occurred in Ukraine, which Poland contained with difficulty. In 1648, the population rose again, and under the leadership of Bogdan Khmelnytsky, created a Cossack state, which chose allegiance to Moscow.

The Muscovite expansion continued. Between 1610 and 1640, the Russian border moved over three hundred miles south, constantly expanding into lands previously controlled by the Crimean Tatars. With Peter the Great (1682–1725), Russia became a great power. Russia defeated Sweden at Poltava in 1709, but lost a war against the Ottomans in 1711. Under Catherine the Great, the Russians took Azov and finally defeated the khanate of Crimea in 1771. The Crimean Tatars were the last nomad heirs to the Mongol Empire. They had survived with the support of the Ottoman Empire, the enemy of Russia.

In the middle of the fifteenth century, the Russian cavalry fought with lances, sabers, and axes. As the Mongol khanates became divided, Ivan III's army gained strength and cannons were installed to defend Russian cities and fortified camps. The roads were not suitable for the transportation of cannons, and the cavalry preferred mobility and raids over firepower. Ivan the Terrible introduced mobile cannons suitable to Russia.

The Crimean khanate was created around 1430 by Hacı Devlet Giray, a grand-nephew of Batu Khan, the founder of the Golden Horde. This khanate lasted until 1771, when it was finally destroyed by the

Russians. The influence of the Crimean khanate extended as far as Tambov in the north, but its center of power was in the south, between the Don and the lower Dnieper. The nomadic Tatars had established their capital at Bakhchysarai in central Crimea. Several nomad groups, like the Nogai Horde, submitted to them, and they in turn became vassals of the Ottomans in the middle of the fifteenth century, enabling their khan to receive occasional help from Ottoman janissaries. Thus, Poles and Muscovites who attacked the Crimean Tatars would be considered to be attacking the Ottoman Empire directly. The Ottoman alliance, as well as the distance from Moscow, helps to explain the longevity of the Crimean khanate. Being in the vicinity of the Ottoman-controlled Black Sea, the Crimean khanate was ensured of impunity in spite of their raids on northern populations.

The nomads were traditionally organized under the decimal system and would start their raiding campaigns in the winter when rivers froze and could be easily crossed. The khan would seek approval from his "nobles" to raise troops, whose allegiance was to their tribal chiefs and not to the khan directly.

The Tatars could raise as many as a hundred thousand men, but in general their campaigns did not require more than fifteen or twenty thousand. They also provided the Ottomans with several thousand horsemen for their campaigns. The Tatar army was originally a classic nomad cavalry force, but in time, they added harquebusiers. The khan had some 600 harquebusiers who traveled on horseback but fought on foot. When campaigning, the Tatars had three horses apiece. The description of foreign travelers who crossed Crimea in the seventeenth century suggests that the Tatars used the same small horses that the Mongols had used in the thirteenth century. Their favorite weapon remained the bow until firearms came to dominate the battlefield. Most Tatars fought without armor, but their chiefs wore helmets and sometimes breastplates. Tatar horses were not shod, but could cover some thirty miles a day. When they arrived near Russian forts, they would divide into columns to advance unnoticed.

No fires were lit. If they met with a strong resistance, the columns would regroup. An army of twenty-five thousand Tatars with their seventy-five thousand horses was an impressive force when seen from a distance. However, their technique of approach usually consisted in dividing the army into three with two-thirds remaining stationary and one-third being divided in units of a hundred, which would raid villages. In case of strong resistance, they would regroup to strike together. The rearguard would only intervene when necessary, as for instance, when the enemy had received reinforcements.

The Tatars' raids were swift. Most of the time they remained unpunished, because their army would be gone by the time enemy reinforcements arrived. Between 1667 and 1672, John Sobieski's Poles, who contributed to the defeat of the Ottomans in Vienna, clashed several times with the Tatars. The Tatars were most vulnerable on their return to Crimea. In 1672, Sobieski surprised them as they returned with thousands of captives to be sold to the Ottomans.

When the raids were successful, as was usually the case, the booty was divided upon return. If captives were taken they were sold, women in particular, to Ottoman merchants who would resell them in Constantinople or the ports of the Black Sea.

The summer campaigns were usually fought with only ten to fifteen thousand men, using the same technique of dividing and regrouping when necessary. Surprise was the principal element of success. The Russian response was to build Cossack forts in the south to limit the territory where the Tatars could travel with impunity.

The Tatars fought either for booty or at the request of the Ottomans. They had the advantage of mobility and surprise. However, they were poorly equipped to assail fortifications, and were generally no match for the Polish cavalry. The formidable Polish heavy cavalry was composed of armored and helmeted hussars, armed with lances and swords. The Polish cavalry comprised some twenty thousand men, mostly hussars, who preferred frontal attacks. On their flanks were the light cavalry, uhlans, armed with sabers and pistols. The Polish cavalry under Sobieski was able to defeat the Tatars in the seventeenth century, but Russian troops would only take Crimea in 1771.

Catherine followed the same expansionist policy as Peter the Great and the earlier Muscovite tsars. The neutralization of the Crimean Tatars was a consequence of Russian victories over the Turks, resulting in the treaty of Küçük Kaynarca (1774). Crimea was declared independent, but the Tatars continued to recognize the religious authority of the Ottoman sultan, who, as caliph, was the spiritual leader of Islam. In 1783, the Russians annexed Crimea, and many Tatars relocated in Ottoman territories.

CHAPTER 15

The Ascent of Europe

The history of triumphant Europe might be said to start either with the discovery of America in 1492 by Christopher Columbus or with Hernán Cortés's conquest of Mexico in 1521. The latter date seems preferable, since the Reformation had begun (1517), and Magellan had just finished circumnavigating the world (1522). The European victory over the Ottomans at Lepanto in 1571 marked the beginning of the naval supremacy of Catholic Europe in the Mediterranean. In the sixteenth century, Europe took a lead that would increase remarkably during the following centuries, notwithstanding the continuing power of the Ottomans under Suleiman the Magnificent, the Safavids under Shah Abbas, and the Mughals under Akbar.

MARITIME POWER AND TRADE

The Portuguese king Henry the Navigator encouraged maritime exploration. Vasco da Gama arrived in India in 1499, after circumnavigating Africa. At this time, the sea routes in the Indian Ocean were controlled by Muslims. Ten years later, the Portuguese asserted their naval supremacy in the Indian Ocean by defeating a large Muslim fleet in front of the Indian port of Diu. The Portuguese established enclaves in Asia at Goa (1510), Malacca (1511), and Macao (1547). Spain followed in Portugal's wake and Spanish ships reached the Philippines in the same year as the battle of Lepanto. In the Americas, a handful of men, the Conquistadors,

MAP 15. Spanish conquests in America in the sixteenth century.

occupied Mexico (1519–21) and Peru (1531–35) and began a process that would result in a Christian Latin American continent that spoke Spanish and Portuguese.

It is noteworthy that more than a century before the Portuguese had even reached the Cape Verde Islands, a much larger Ming Chinese fleet had already explored the coasts of East Africa, Indonesia, and Malaya. However, the Ming navigators had not established naval bases or trading centers.

The North Asia steppe had long been the geopolitical fulcrum of Eurasia, but in the sixteenth century, the oceans began to assume this role. The rider of the steppe was replaced by the caravel. Europe would create a worldwide empire with the help of naval firepower. In the middle of the sixteenth century, Ivan the Terrible had defeated the Mongol khanates of Kazan and Astrakhan, reversing the trajectory of occupation from west to east and north to south against the Tatars of Crimea, who were allied with the Ottomans. The Russian expansion preceded the conquest of North America.

Silver and gold imported to Europe from America resulted in an increase in prices, which profited the merchants but penalized the population and caused great inflation. The potato made its appearance in Europe. Conversely, smallpox ravaged the New World. In the sixteenth century, new ideas that arose during the Renaissance led to important religious, cultural, and scientific innovations.

THE MOVEMENT OF IDEAS

The development of printing was fundamental. Christianity changed: the sixteenth century was a century of schisms within the Latin Church and between Catholics and Protestants. Ignatius of Loyola (1491–1556) founded the Jesuit Order, laying the basis for the Counter-Reformation. In his books *The Prince* and *Discourses on the First Ten Books of Titus Livy,* Niccolò Machiavelli (1469–1527) developed a political analysis free of the religious perspective that had clouded the vision of his predecessors. (Machiavelli recommended doing away with mercenary troops and drafting citizens.) Nikolaus Copernicus (1473–1543), a Pole trained at the University of Padua, questioned many established truths with his heliocentric theory of the planetary movement.

Christianity lost its monopoly on social theory. The dynasties of the fifteenth century developed an increased political independence defined by self-interest. For example, the alliance of François I of France and the

Ottomans against the Hapsburg Empire would have been unthinkable a century before. In military strategy, the Spanish general Gonzalo de Córdoba (1453–1515) instituted the *tercio,* a new battle formation that combined pikemen and musketeers, which proved enormously efficient on the European battlefield until the Spaniards encountered the more advanced techniques developed by the Protestant Prince Maurice of Nassau (1567–1625), who led the Dutch revolt against Spanish rule. From a cultural perspective, the sixteenth century produced Leonardo da Vinci, Michelangelo, Erasmus, Rabelais, Montaigne, and Shakespeare.

The Reformation played a major role, especially when it spread across Europe after Calvin settled in Geneva (1536). Northern Europe became Protestant. The Counter-Reformation regained Poland, Hungary, and Austria, and the large Reform movement in France was crushed.

Scripture became the sole religious authority for Protestants, but multiple scriptural interpretations gave rise to various sects, including the Puritans, who would settle New England a century later. With the Council of Trent (1545–63), the Catholic Church began essential reforms with the help of the Jesuits.

The religious conflicts between Catholics and Protestants came to an end with the resolution of the Thirty Years' War (1618–48). The Catholic Church was consolidated. Calvinism had spread, and Lutheranism was well established in Germany and Scandinavia. Anglicanism, a middle way, had been adopted in England; the Puritan revolution there led by Oliver Cromwell (1599–1658) ended in failure soon after his death.

Critical thinking developed at Europe's universities, which enjoyed considerable autonomy. Protestantism, which no longer could be regarded as heretical, challenged the dogmas of the Catholic Church. Classicism and the revival of the ideas of Greek antiquity in the Renaissance combined with critical thinking and religious emancipation to create an effervescent inauguration of the seventeenth century.

Galileo (1564–1642) defended Copernicus's astronomical theories. Descartes (1596–1650) reframed theological controversies and tried to provide answers through logic. Paracelsus (1493–1541) questioned the theoretical foundations of medicine, as did William Harvey (1578–1657) a century later. Kepler's discoveries advanced astronomy and Francis Bacon redefined the scientific method in the same century. The pendulum clock, thermometer, and microscope were invented at the end of the sixteenth century, and the barometer and telescope followed.

Military theories, long dormant in Europe, regained vigor together in combination with innovations in military organization linked to the

Protestant renewal. In the sixteenth century, the Swiss had laid new stress on the role of infantry, which was further enhanced by the mix of weapons, including the musket, in the Spanish *tercio*. The emperor Charles V's Lex Carolina (1532) helped define military law.

Despite the hostility of Richelieu's France—a Catholic state allied with Protestant states to weaken its main rival, Spain, another Catholic state—the Holy Roman Empire survived the Thirty Years' War. In that war, the Hapsburg supreme commander Albrecht von Wallenstein (1583–1634) laid the basis for modern logistics, and Montecuccoli above all further modernized the art of war, inflicting a defeat on the Turks at the battle of Saint Gotthard in 1664.

Protestant military thinking was based on close study of the Old Testament (Joshua, Judges, Samuel 1 and 2), using the first-century Roman-Jewish historian Flavius Josephus's *History of the Jews* as a manual. Jan Žižka, the Hussite leader in Bohemia, had been a precursor: it took two centuries to overcome the Hussites (1620). Meanwhile, the Reformation had become well established in Europe. In time, Plutarch's *Lives of the Noble Greeks and Romans* replaced the prophecies of the Old Testament. Agrippa d'Aubigné's *Histoire universelle* (Universal History; 1616–18), François de La Noue's *Discours politiques et militaires* (Political and Military Discourses), and *Le Parfait Capitaine* (The Perfect Captain) by Henri, duc de Rohan, laid the foundations of Protestant military thinking. In addition, important contributions to military thinking were made by Nassau in the Netherlands, Gustavus Adolphus in Sweden, and Cromwell in England.

Among the great commanders of the era were Turenne, Montecuccoli, and Eugène of Savoy (Petrovaradin, 1716; Belgrade 1717). The wars of religion cost Europe dearly, particularly in Germany, as recounted in Grimmelshausen's famous novel *Simplicius Simplicissimus* (1668), and ended in abolishing the possibility of validating a unique and absolute religious truth. Princes became more independent, and their power increased, as a result of the decline of the Catholic Church.

THE EUROPEAN EXPANSION

The exploration and colonization of the Americas continued in New England, Quebec, and in the South, where the demand for labor to harvest sugar, cotton, and tobacco supported the slave trade. The Portuguese, English, French, and Dutch had already begun slaving. Epidemics had ravaged the populations of Spanish America. In Asia, the Jesuit priest Matteo Ricci visited the court of Peking. The Russians had reached the Pacific and signed a treaty with China to define the frontier between the two empires (1689). Japan had closed itself to foreign powers for two centuries under the Togukawa shogunate. In Europe, between 1648 (the Peace of Westphalia) and 1789, changes accelerated in science, technology, and philosophy. From the middle of the seventeenth century until the French Revolution, Europe showed a dynamism, an eagerness for innovation, and a spirit of adventure that had never been seen before.

Trade, exploration, and the increased importance of sea routes transformed farming and manufacturing. European agriculture changed with the introduction of potatoes, maize, and turnips. Manufacturing developed in England. The use of steam energy (developed by Denis Papin, and then by James Watt) and the beginning of coal and steel production heralded England's future industrialization. Mathematics progressed rapidly and was applied to advances such as the telescope and the microscope. Analytical geometry advanced, and new ways of seeing the world emerged with Spinoza in Holland, Leibniz in Germany, and Hobbes, Locke, and Newton in England. The ancient Greek concept of democracy, which first reappeared in the Swiss cantons, was resurrected in the Netherlands, then in England with the British Parliament. Its influence would become momentous in the West, where it would give birth to the United States of America (1776).

After the bloody wars of religion and the Peace of Westphalia, monarchs fought limited wars with common rules for limited stakes. The progress of the art of fortification was remarkable, particularly among the Italians, the Dutch, and especially the French (Vauban), who came to dominate Europe under the monarchy of Louis XIV.

Prussia in the eighteenth century made a grand *entrée* with Frederick the Great. After Peter the Great and Catherine the Great, Russia joined the cohort of the great powers. France, England, and the Austrian Empire were already playing leading roles. After its Civil War, England settled into a government where the monarch's cabinet was named by the crown but was responsible to Parliament. While not yet fully democratic (neither those without property nor dissident religious minorities were represented), this new system put an end to absolutism, which continued to prevail in France. The maritime superiority of England allowed it gradually to dominate the seas and expand its empire to Canada and India.

The French, on the other hand, supported American aspirations for independence (1776–83). The Enlightenment produced ideas never articulated before, except perhaps in Étienne de La Boetie's *Discours de la servitude volontaire* (Discourse on Voluntary Servitude). These ideas had been developed by Voltaire, Diderot, Helvetius, d'Holbach, and Rousseau in France, Beccaria in Italy, Adam Smith and David Hume in England, Immanuel Kant in Prussia, and Thomas Jefferson and Thomas Paine in America.

European colonizers occupied North America, Spanish America, Brazil, and part of South Africa, and soon would occupy Australia and all of Siberia north of the Amur River. Slavery was a natural consequence of the American plantation economy, yet at the end of the eighteenth century, opposition to slavery was voiced in both England and France (by Condorcet, Olympe de Gouges, and Brissot). In Russia, serfdom would continue until 1861.

Exploration by land and sea continued, including expeditions led by Louis de Bougainville, James Cook, and Vitus Bering, a Dane in the service of the Russian navy, who explored Alaska and the strait that bears his name. The Russians now occupied the coast of Alaska, and continued south to establish forts down to Northern California (Fort Ross). Meanwhile, the Spanish moved north from Mexico to establish missions up the coast of California, including San Francisco (1775). On the eve of the French Revolution, the largest cities in the Americas were Mexico City, with nearly 100,000 inhabitants, followed by Lima, the seat of the Spanish viceroy of Peru.

The population of Europe continued to grow at the end of the seventeenth century and into the eighteenth. In 1774, Russia had overcome the Ottoman Empire, but it was prevented from capturing Constantinople by the Western powers, especially Britain, which feared a Russian advance to the Mediterranean. From this date on, the Ottoman Empire was supported by the British to assure that the Dardanelles would not fall to the Russians.

Control of India would soon pass from the Mughals to the British. The Safavids belonged to the past, and Islam was in decline. One solution was Muslim modernization of the sort attempted in Egypt by Mehmet Ali (1769–1849). On the other hand, the founder of the Wahhabite movement, Muhammad ibn Abd al-Wahhab (1703–92), who was from Basra (Iraq), wanted to restore Islam to the purity of its beginning and received support from the Saud clan in Arabia. Though unsuccessful in the beginning, Wahhabism, a strict observance of the Koranic precepts, would survive and see a revival with the foundation of a kingdom by Ibn Saud in Arabia (1932).

Russian troops had overcome the Ottoman forces during the war of 1768–74. A complete Ottoman reorganization, institutional and material, was necessary. The "Tanzimat" movement of 1826 attempted to modernize, but had little effect except on the military. Mehmet Ali's response to the crisis faced by the Muslims was impeded by British influence.

In 1761, the Mughals were only a shadow of their former glory, and the Marathas who controlled northwestern India were crushed by the Afghans under Ahmed Shah Durrani, who created the Afghan kingdom (1747). Mughal India was caught between the Afghans in the northwest and the British in the northeast. The British won. In Persia, the last of the Safavids was dethroned by Nader Shah, who was able to dominate Persia and the Caucasus and to take Delhi. His brutal career ended, however, with his assassination in 1747. All of the post-Mongol empires (Ming, Safavid, Mughal) had collapsed, while the Ottoman Empire was moribund, permitting the ascent of Britain and Russia in Asia and allowing the Austro-Hungarian Empire gradually to gain control of part of the Balkans.

In the Far East, Japan closed its doors after the massacre there of Christian converts in the seventeenth century. China remained powerful until the end of the eighteenth century and was admired by the Europeans who appreciated the fact that it had neither a dominant religion nor a hereditary aristocracy. In Europe, intra-Catholic quarrels resulted in the expulsion from most countries of the Jesuits, whose order the pope dissolved in 1773 (a decision reversed in 1814).

On a military level, the division system and the importance of artillery (Gribeauval) were universally recognized by the eve of the French Revolution. There was an abundance of strategic thinking (Folard, de Saxe, Lloyd, and Guibert). Mass conscription radically changed the concept of war. It became a mass war based on a democratic process, and war became absolute. Battles sought the annihilation of the adversary. The 1792–1815 conception of war heralded the hecatombs of the world wars of the twentieth century.

The Napoleonic Wars had direct and indirect consequences, including the maritime domination of the seas by Britain (Trafalgar, 1805), and the awakening of German nationalism (Jena, 1806). Military strategy was refined by Scharnhost and Gneisenau, along with the most influential of the strategic thinkers, Clausewitz, who witnessed the Napoleonic Wars. The Swiss-born general Antoine-Henri Jomini was also influential at the operational level.

The French Revolution's Declaration of the Rights of Man (1789) echoed through Europe until the Revolution of 1848. The Terror

(1793–94) ended the revolutionary process and led to the rise of the Napoleonic Empire, which ended in disaster for France. Subsequently, the Congress of Vienna (1815), chaired by the Austrian Klemens von Metternich, reorganized Europe, neutralized Russian expansionist aspirations, delayed the unification of Germany, and placed Italy under the control of Austria and the pope. National aspirations reappeared, but the Hapsburgs had gained a respite that would last a century.

Nationalist movements led to the unification of Germany and Italy, and later to the division of the Austrian Empire. In the twentieth century, nationalism would eventually spread throughout the world.

TRANSFORMATION BEFORE 1914

The consequences of the Industrial Revolution (ca. 1760–1840) and colonial expansion between 1815 and 1914 were significant.

The Industrial Revolution

The Industrial Revolution started in England in the latter part of the eighteenth century, and manufacturing using coal and steam power soon spread to the European continent. The railway and the steamship altered the speed with which goods were distributed, and advances in metallurgy and mechanization radically modified production. France, Belgium, the Netherlands, Germany, and the United States quickly industrialized. Basic innovations in chemistry and metallurgy often occurred first in Germany, but were notably transformed into mass-produced products in the United States (Ford). All sectors seemed to develop concurrently. Rail travel improved: the Union Pacific Railway linked the eastern United States to San Francisco Bay in 1869, the Trans-Siberian railway line was completed in 1903, and the Berlin-Baghdad line reached Syria in 1914. The United States extended its territorial reach from the Philippines to the Caribbean in 1898 after the Spanish-American War. The transatlantic cable (1866), telegraph, radio, and telephone revolutionized communication. The West became richer, and populations soared with better hygiene and a decline in infant mortality. In the course of the nineteenth century, Europe's population grew from one hundred and eighty-five million to four hundred million, with emigration of about sixty million to the New World. Rural migration to the cities provided an expanding workforce, which labored under strenuous conditions (fourteen hours a day was typical in 1880). The Civil War in the United States (1860–65), the first modern war, had demonstrated the terrible advances in firepower and communications that industrialization had created.

Karl Marx (1818–83) and Friedrich Engels (1820–95), whose Communist Manifesto appeared in 1848, were among those who promoted socialist ideas. After the revolutionary Paris Commune was harshly repressed in 1871, the governments of industrialized European countries introduced reforms in order to maintain stability in the face of social unrest. By the end of the nineteenth century, Germany had become a military superpower and also possessed Europe's most powerful industrial sector.

Colonial Expansion

There were many stages to the colonial expansion that started with the conquest of the Americas. Dutch colonization of Indonesia began in the seventeenth century, and the Dutch East India Company established a settlement at the Cape of Good Hope in South Africa (1652), only a few decades after the arrival of the *Mayflower* on the coast of Massachusetts (1620). The British East India Company controlled most of India by the end of the eighteenth century.

In the eighteenth century, the Russians extended their domination to the Kazak steppes. In 1731, a khan of the "Small Horde" sought the help of the Russians against an Oirat Mongol invasion. Russia obtained the allegiance of three Kazak hordes and established a line of forts close to Orenburg. In the nineteenth century, the Russians undertook the conquest of southern Kazakhstan, as well as Turkestan and the Uzbek emirates of Bukhara, Khiva, and Kokand. The Russian presence in the Caucasus started with Georgia in the south. Subsequently, Russia occupied territories ruled by Persia (1828), such as modern Azerbaijan and Armenia. Then, from Transcaucasia, Russia conquered the Caucasus proper, which was overwhelmingly Muslim. In Daghestan, the Russians faced the long resistance (1834–59) of Sheik Chamyl, a member of the Sufi Naqshbandi sect, founded in the sixteenth century.

Japan remained isolated until 1854, when American warships forced it to open its ports. Faced with the rise of the "White peril," Japan renounced isolationism. A few years later, the Meiji revolution overthrew the Togukawa shogunate (1868). Japan modernized rapidly in order to avoid European domination.

In 1839, the British, who purchased Chinese goods with the profits from the sale of illegally imported opium grown in India, quarreled with the Canton administration. A war followed, and the British obtained large concessions (Treaty of Nanking, 1842). In addition to Canton, four ports were opened, and Hong Kong was ceded to Great Britain. Extraterritoriality was also sought and granted to several other European nations. The Chinese were humiliated, but the balance of power was such that the concessions remained European possessions. In 1860, China lost another war against Anglo-French forces and had to concede additional territory. In 1895, China suffered an even greater humiliation: Chinese armies were defeated by modernized Japanese forces, and China lost Korea.

With the exception of French Indochina and Dutch Indonesia, much of the rest of Asia had been divided between tsarist Russia and Great Britain, with Afghanistan as a buffer state. Persia, on paper, was a sphere of influence divided between the Russians, in the north, and the British, in the south (1907). The economy and influence of the Ottoman Empire had long declined. The Ottoman Empire played off rivalries between European powers in order to survive, but it had continued to lose territories, Greece, Serbia, and Bulgaria among them.

In 1869, the Suez Canal opened sea routes to the Indian Ocean and benefited Great Britain by shortening the route to its major colony, India. In the middle of the nineteenth century, the United States vastly expanded its territory at the expense of Mexico, and asserted its hegemony over the Western Hemisphere, including the Caribbean (1898) and Central America. The Panama Canal (1903) was financed by the United States and would remain under its control for a century.

By 1914, thirty years after the Berlin Conference of 1884–85 that aimed to regulate the process, all of Africa, except Liberia and Ethiopia, had been colonized by the European powers.

WORLD WAR I AND ITS CONSEQUENCES

World War I not only triggered the collapse of the Ottoman Empire, whose Pan-Turkish ambitions led to the Armenian genocide (1915–16), but transformed the Arab Near East into states under French or British mandates. The Balfour Declaration (1917) granted a Jewish homeland and gave Zionists hope for the creation of a Jewish state. With Mustapha Kemal, Turkey avoided the dismemberment that would normally have been its fate. Modern Turkey was created on the model of the European nation-state. The caliphate was abolished in 1924 and secularism was officially adopted. Turkey was proclaimed the country of the Turks alone, despite the existence in it of a large Kurdish minority.

In Arabia, Abdul Aziz ibn Saud (1880–1953), an adherent of the puritanical Wahhabite sect, became king in 1932. Mecca and Medina were now controlled by the Saud and not the Hashemites, who ruled in Transjordan and Iraq. Oil exploitation began in the 1930s, and would bring considerable wealth to the austere Saud, who came to live opulently in spite of an ostentatious display of strict Wahhabism.

In India, the Congress Party was founded in 1885 and petitioned for self-rule. Between the two wars, Gandhi's India achieved independence without an armed struggle (1947). It was followed by Partition of the subcontinent into India and Pakistan (East and West). The Muslims, led by Mohammed Ali Jinnah, refused to be ruled by Hindus. Great Britain supervised a democratic vote, which led to Indian rule by its Hindu majority for the first time in centuries and the emigration of most of the Muslims. Partition was, however, extremely violent. Two wars over Kashmir, populated largely by Muslims but given to India, were lost by Pakistan in 1948 and 1965. East Pakistan, where troops from West Pakistan sought to crush dissent, became independent in 1971 with the help of India and was renamed Bangladesh. The economic and institutional contrasts between India and Pakistan are now considerable.

China struggled to regain territorial control and improve economic development from the moment it became a republic (1911). Japan became a colonial power, like the European countries, in Korea (1910) before extending its domination to China (1931 in Manchuria, and 1937 in coastal China).

Perhaps the most important Western concept, besides nationalism, was the idea of democracy: the notion that power is not granted by divine right or by a heavenly mandate, but by the will of the people. Today, citizens of the West live under democratic institutions. However, until the eighteenth century, despotism remained the standard even in most of western Europe. The invention of democracy was an exceptional change in political organization, even though women have long been and continue to be excluded from political power in many countries.

CHAPTER 16

The Time of Revolutions

With the exception of a few classical regional wars (e.g., the Indo-Pakistani, Israeli-Arab, Korean, and Iran-Iraq wars, and the Falkland conflict between Britain and Argentina), twentieth-century wars were mostly irregular conflicts. It was an era of decolonization, and revolutionary wars played a major role.

If guerrilla war is a war where bands of men wearing no uniform aim to use surprise and harassment to weaken a regular army, the revolutionary war tries, by the same military means, to take control of a population in order to seize power. The ideas of emancipation and modern nationalism, aided by improved organizational techniques, allowed colonial and semi-colonialized populations to liberate themselves from Western domination through violence. The legitimacy of colonial domination was questioned even within the colonializing nations. In the long run, liberation movements succeeded politically. During the Cold War, there were local crises like those of Berlin (1948) and Cuba (1962). The Cold War, based on a balance of terror, brought the superpowers indirectly to help client states or weaken the allies of the main rival.

CONFRONTING THE MODERNITY
OF THE WESTERN WORLD

At the time of colonial expansion, small European armies conquered and controlled most of Asia and Africa. Less than a century later, small bands of guerrillas managed to keep much larger Western armies in check. How did this transformation happen? The technological advance of the West was, in great part, responsible for the conquests. Its initial successes were made possible thanks to the steamship, telecommunications, the machine-gun, and control of malaria. But had the West lost its technological advantage in the twentieth century? With the exception of Dien Bien Phu, guerrillas almost never won a regular battle, but nevertheless won many wars despite their inferior armament and technology, even reaching a higher level of organization.

Western technological superiority does not alone explain European domination in the nineteenth century. The subjugation of colonized people was a reflection of a presumed natural superiority of European civilization that was accepted by both the colonizer and the colonized. It would take three generations for colonized peoples to develop and answer the challenge of modernity brought by Europeans. Western colonial expansion was spatially immense, including the extension of Russian imperialism to the Caucasus, Central Asia, Mongolia, and Manchuria; the expansion of the United States to incorporate large parts of Mexico, as well as Puerto Rico, the Philippines, and the northern Pacific Islands; and European conquests in Asia and Africa.

The ledger of colonialism remains ambiguous. In addition to oppressing and humiliating colonized peoples, colonialism also introduced essential elements of modernity. Among other ideas, modern nationalism spread around the world. The primary goal of colonial expansion was not, of course, to bring the advances of modernity to colonized peoples. However, as Western ideas spread among the local elites who spoke the language of the colonizer, colonialism became more difficult to justify morally and politically.

The depredations of the colonial period are well known: slavery and the slave trade, the decimation of Native American populations (both north and south of the Rio Grande, as far as Argentina), the disaggregation of the populations of the South Pacific, the opium trade in China (1840), and harsh repression, for instance in German Southwest Africa (1905–7). In the United States, the most democratic country in the world, slavery was abolished only in 1865, racial discrimination in public schools was declared unconstitutional by the Supreme Court only in 1954, and fully equal political rights were only legally acquired in the 1960s.

Asian and African societies were traditionally ruled by despotic chiefs or sovereigns who held absolute political power. The Ottoman Empire, the Manchu Empire, the Indian principalities, and the Malay sultanates were all corrupt, oppressive, and decadent to varying degrees. In Africa, village "communalism" was handicapped by superstition, tribal wars, and slavery.

The massive onslaught of European nations on Asia and Africa in the nineteenth century was a brutal shock. It was then that the clash of the civilizations really happened. In a large part of the Muslim world and in China and in other Asian countries, the first reaction was to take refuge in a return to traditional moral and religious values. After Great Britain defeated China in the Opium War (1840), China was forced to open its doors, but it still remained confident in the superiority of its culture. Progressively, however, as more humiliations were inflicted on China by Western powers, the ruling mandarinate became preoccupied with their country's weakness and Western scientific and technical accomplishments. Chinese students were sent to Europe and the United States to master science, but this new knowledge proved difficult for China to integrate with its political structure. It became evident with time that it would be necessary for colonized peoples to master the concepts, ideas, and institutions that contributed to Western superiority.

Japan was the only power that proved capable of modernizing in the face of colonialism. With a revolution from above, and helped by its insularity and ethnic and religious cohesion, Japan successfully completed indispensable reforms. In 1895, Japan won the first Sino-Japanese War, traumatizing the mandarinate. It was bad enough to be defeated by the English or French, but to be defeated by Japan, a country China considered a vassal centuries earlier, was a disaster.

China began efforts to redirect its Confucian outlook from the past toward the future. The most original theory was Yen Fu's, who, a year after the defeat by Japan, proposed four "manifestos" to correct China's weakness and backwardness. He stressed that the Manchu monarchy was powerless against foreigners and despotic toward its people, and argued that the mandarinate was too rigid, corrupt, and smug in its ignorance of the outside world. Yen Fu tried to introduce the idea of open-ended progress based on struggle, instead of a cyclical history in which the past constantly recurred.

Elsewhere, too, modernization proved more difficult than just adopting Western scientific and military techniques. The Ottoman Empire, for instance, which survived only because of the Anglo-Russian antagonism, was unable to modernize. The adoption of European military techniques was insufficient to stabilize the empire. In spite of their desire for modernization, even the so-called Young Turks failed to modernize the empire and define a new and sustainable ideology. They hesitated between a Muslim identity, an Ottoman-style empire, and the establishment of a state that would include all Turkic peoples, even those as far as Central Asia (Pan-Turanianism). Finally, Mustapha Kemal would save the country from a disaster by creating modern Turkey based on the European model of the nation-state.

The most difficult aspect of modernization for Asian and African elites was assimilating revolutionary new European ideas, elaborated in the late eighteenth and nineteenth centuries, whose preconditions were critical thinking and free expression. Unlocking the secret of Western superiority would require great efforts from them and would take three generations. What was there to discover? First, there was nationalism, a brand new idea. The arrogance of the colonizers and racial discrimination would feed the flames of nascent nationalism in the colonies. Maxime Rodinson writes:

> The Third World is not a single entity. It is composed of populations formed by different cultures, at various levels of technical, economic, and cultural development. However, in the past one hundred and fifty years, at different moments of their evolution, these populations were all placed in similar conditions of humiliation and servitude by the dominating power of the Euro-American West. These colonial societies collapsed in the same way. I call it the end of resignation. . . .
>
> At the same time as Europe was oppressing populations on several continents, it also offered several models of liberation. For the conformist societies of Asia and Africa, Europe offered the example of a world where debate was perpetual. As this aspect of the Western world was revealed to colonial elites, they understood that the struggle for a better society was possible. There was hope again.
>
> The situation of oppression and humiliation began to be analyzed within the framework of tradition. Was the success of the West due to its religion, which it championed so often? Should Western religion be attacked? Should their own religion be reformed according to Western religious principles and methods? This line of reasoning led to "colonial heresies" and syncretic religious movements. Then their analyses turned political. Should Western methods of political struggle be used? Should Western forms of government be adopted? In any case, the great European political ideology of the nineteenth century, nationalism, was embraced. It provided a perfectly adequate framework for the great revolt against Europe, waged with its own weapons.*

* Maxime Rodinson, "Marxisme et tiers-monde," in id., *Marxisme et monde musulman* (Paris: Éditions du Seuil, 1972).

Modern nationalism is a recent concept.* The French Revolution, for the first time, developed the idea that a nation had "natural rights," that the nation underwrote the state, and that the nationalist concept applied universally.† The revolutionary new idea that men possessed "natural rights" and should be equal under the law spread throughout Europe in the nineteenth century. The practical consequence was that if citizens— no longer mere subjects of the state—did not approve of the political organization of their society, they had the right and the power to replace it with a better system.

The new ideas of the French Revolution spread in Europe with the Napoleonic armies. Almost everywhere in Europe the creation of the nation-state became the goal of the people. The national awakening of the German elite happened after the catastrophic Prussian defeat in the battle of Jena in 1806. The generation of Herder, Fichte, Gneisenau, Scharnhorst, and Clausewitz saw Napoleon as an example as well as an adversary.

The Congress of Vienna (1815) denied the new legitimacy of the nation-state. A century later, the Austrian Empire would succumb to this refusal. The French Revolution brought with it the challenge of the nation in arms. How would the undemocratic regimes in Europe confront the dilemma? How could they retain the support of the people while holding on to their monopoly of power and privileges? In Russia, the despotic tradition allowed the empire to ignore the dilemma until World War I.

National unity and independence were central themes in the West in the nineteenth century. The models were the patriots like Kossuth and Garibaldi, fighting for the rights of their people. The ideas were those of Rousseau, Fichte, and Mazzini, to name only a few.

In 1900, the idea of a "nation" was very difficult to comprehend for the elites of most societies in Asia (in Africa, only Egypt had elites at this level). How could the elites, aware of the political lethargy of their countries, bring about the emergence of a national consciousness? There were various concepts that the African and Asian elites had to assimilate

---

* See Elie Kedourie, *Nationalism* (1960; 3rd ed., London: Hutchinson, 1966). In 1864, at least a third of the population of France did not understand French; see Eugen Weber, *Peasants into Frenchmen: The Modernization of Rural France, 1870–1914* (Stanford, CA: Stanford University Press, 1976).

† The American Declaration of Independence was formulated in terms of the natural rights of individuals, not in terms of the rights of nations, a concept that was developed in the nineteenth century.

before they could use them to liberate themselves from Europe. For traditional societies with despotic traditions, it seemed self-evident, however, that inequality was the order of things.

If nationalism and the concept of the nation-state constituted the dominant ideology of the nineteenth century, it also nurtured the idea of the republic, which motivated the Young Turk revolution in 1908 and the Chinese revolution that put an end to the Manchu dynasty in 1911. The idea also spread of allegiance to a political party (e.g., the Indian Congress party and the Egyptian Wafd) that embodied the aspirations of the elites and (potentially at least) of the people, and not just those of the sovereign and his representatives.

In the Afro-Asian world, colonial societies generally passed through a stage of refusal and withdrawal into religious ideology or traditional ethics, followed by a stage of acceptance of colonialism among the acculturated and urbanized elites. This acceptance of Western superiority was accompanied by humiliation. Some of the new elites were ashamed of the poverty and backwardness of their masses, but this phase did not last long. Other, more radical, nationalists surfaced and began the struggle for colonial identity and dignity. In the meantime, the colonial system generally disrupted the traditional economy, introduced private ownership of the previously collective land, and created new social classes.

The era of great traditional revolts, such as the Indian Mutiny (1857) and the Boxer Rebellion (1901), came to an end. Another generation of leaders seeking independence emerged with Gandhi in India and Sun Yat-sen in China. After World War I, new colonial elites emerged who had mastered the politics and ideas of the West. Further colonial expansion came to an end with British and French mandates in the Near East (1920), the colonization of Libya (1922–32) and Ethiopia (1935) by Italy, and the expansion of the Japanese empire (1931).

The assimilation of Western ideas first allowed limited emancipation and identity recognition among colonized peoples, and eventually led to the creation and the recognition of independent nation-states. European concepts spread, including the idea of a nation-state and the concept that any alternative to self-government was servitude. It was no longer possible for great societies like China to ignore the "Western Barbarians" or to underestimate them. Nor was it possible for Islamic powers to wait for the storm to pass by clinging to religious ideology.

In 1918, U.S. President Woodrow Wilson proclaimed the right to national self-determination. However, this "universal" right was limited to Central Europe. New European nation-states were established after the partition of the Hapsburg Empire: Czechoslovakia, Yugoslavia, and Poland, all with complex mixtures of different ethnic and linguistic minorities. With the exception of the mandates, colonial problems played a minor role at the Paris Peace Conference in 1919.

Until the beginning of the century, Darwinian theories seemed to lend scientific justification to claims of European superiority. Wilson recommended that colonized people's grievances be taken into consideration. However, although the founding fathers of modern nationalism spoke out against colonialism, the colonized peoples themselves were neither politically conscious nor politically active. The post–World War I era provided only a framework for future movements, which would result in post–World War II emancipation twenty-five years later. The Baku Congress of the Peoples of the East was hosted by the USSR in 1920. It was not an Asian initiative but a Bolshevik strategy seeking to compensate for the failure of the urban Marxist revolution in Germany. In the face of an acute crisis and increasing danger, Mustapha Kemal enabled Turkey to escape foreign domination with the help of the Bolsheviks and a tradition of a strong central state and a strong military (1922). Similarly, Ibn Saud forced the British to recognize Saudi independence in 1932.

In the aftermath of World War I, the promulgation of the right to self-determination in eastern Europe had little impact on the development of nationalism among colonized populations, owing primarily to the political backwardness of the indigenous colonial elites particularly in sub-Saharan Africa. The principle according to which the nations can freely decide their future was supported both by the liberal American President Wilson and by the Russian Bolshevik Lenin. The Soviet regime attempted to use the right to self-determination to incite colonized populations to shake off their imperialist yoke. A few communist parties appeared: in China, with the foundation of a communist party by twelve members in Shanghai in 1919; in Egypt, with a short-lived communist party founded in 1920; and in Vietnam, with a communist party founded in 1925. The 1920 Baku Congress, with its majority of Turkish-speaking attendees, proved to be of little consequence. It occurred too early in the century.

AFTER THE GREAT WAR

The application of the principle of self-determination to the colonies depended on colonial elites that were few in number. However, seditious ideas slowly started to circulate and take shape.

A wave of colonial revolts after World War I remained modest in scope. Unlike the resistance to the first phase of colonial conquest, these represented the first attempts at challenging the colonial order itself. The concessions made by the Chinese government were not accepted as legitimate by its citizens. In Afghanistan, Amānullāh expelled the British troops who controlled Afghanistan's borders (1919). Moroccan Berbers rose against the Spanish and, later, the French in the Rif War (1925–27). There were also armed rebellions in Burma, Indonesia (1926–27), Vietnam (1930), and Syria that attempted to reject the colonial rule. India, besides a few sporadic terrorist actions, saw the emergence of a nationalist movement, the Indian National Congress, which was joined by Gandhi. Great Britain tried to remain patient and to adhere to its liberal ideals. Gandhi, a brilliant tactician of nonviolence, increased political pressure and was able to rally the majority of the Indian masses. Nonviolence, of course, can only be effective when addressed to a democratic public opinion.

The end of World War I signaled the birth of nationalist ideas that would be fully implemented after 1945. While these ideas appeared slow to mature, in fact their spread was rapid given the limited political consciousness of colonized peoples and the risk of severe repression they faced.

The problem of the colonized societies facing the formidable West was to restore their independence and their culture. That was relatively easy for China because it had a long and brilliant history, and because it was only partially occupied. Besides, China never had a problem of identity: it suffered from a superiority complex rather than an inferiority complex. Independence was more problematic for India, which had long been occupied and was divided between Muslims and Hindus. India was more a collection of societies or a civilization with a common culture than a single state. It was even more difficult for Arab societies, where religious ideology could not hide the feeling of humiliation born from the contrast between the servitude of the present and the glorious past. It was also very difficult for the Africans, whose traditions were ill-suited to modern technology and Western political theory.

Western Orientalism, a much-disparaged field of study nowadays, restored this past, or at least fragments of it. In spite of the colonialist aspect of Orientalism, it rediscovered an Asian historical record that was sometimes lost or forgotten or misinterpreted, just as in the nineteenth century, western Europeans had restored classical Greece to the Ottomanized Greeks.

The new urban elites in colonial countries rejected the arrogant and humiliating West. Those elites were the most directly exposed to racism and well prepared to react, since they had mastered the ideas and concepts of the West. As a result, they most directly experienced the inferiority inherent in their colonial status. In their daily lives, they felt like second-class citizens in their own countries. All nationalist movements began in urban areas.* The unrest of the peasants was different. Local grievances sometimes became unbearable and caused sudden uprisings. These were mainly peasant rebellions to maintain traditions in the face of the modernizing pressures of colonialism. The peasants themselves did not have a coherent political goal and had little sense of a national identity. Colonized countries largely remained collections of regions. Thus, the aspirations and goals of the first nationalists were generally ignored by the peasants.

The social strata that would lead the nationalist movements were not the traditional elites, who had already been defeated or were actively collaborating with the colonialists. Thus, with two exceptions: in Morocco and Uganda (Buganda), the nationalist leaders were neither princes, mandarins, sultans, nor chiefs. The backbone of the nationalist movement was a segment of the urban petit bourgeoisie and upper middle class. However, in almost all cases (with the exception of Mao Zedong), nationalist leaders had studied in the West and had been influenced by Western political philosophy.†

In contrast, the countries that had not been colonized remained ruled by their traditional elites, as in Yemen, Ethiopia, and Afghanistan. In Siam (Thailand), the aristocracy kept power. In Persia (Iran), Reza Shah was installed as emperor by the British and managed to control the tribes but not the aristocrats or the landowners.

In 1904, the Russo-Japanese War ended in a Japanese victory and became an important milestone in East Asia, attracting many foreign students to Japan, Chinese included. They were eager to understand how an Asian country could defeat a European power. Western European power nonetheless remained largely intact until World War II. Tsarist Russia, after all, was seen as a backward country, often perceived as semi-Asian. The colonial insurrections between the two wars were crushed regardless of their degree of organization, including Abd al-Krim's revolt in Morocco (1925–27). Colonial wars were fought by professional European troops with the support or the indifference of

---

* Based on the supposition that the nation-state is the natural organization of societies throughout the world.

† Sun Yat-sen was a doctor; Gandhi and Jinnah were lawyers; Sukarno was an engineer; Bourguiba was a lawyer; Jomo Kenyatta studied in London, Nkrumah in the United States, Senghor in Paris, and Nyerere in Edinburgh.

European public opinion. The righteousness of the "civilizing mission" was not questioned. Colonialism was both seen as morally right and thought to improve the situation of the colonized countries.

On the eve of World War II, none of the great colonial powers were prepared for the possibility of a Japanese invasion in East Asia. The rapid Japanese victories against the Americans in the Philippines, the Dutch in Indonesia, the French in Indochina, and the British in Malaysia (1942) had considerable impact on colonial opinion. These victories showed that the destruction of the colonial order was possible, and that colonial powers could be defeated. Guerrilla movements started to organize. In Indochina, the lapse of time between the Japanese surrender and the arrival of the Allied forces allowed national liberation movements to arm themselves before the return of the French. So it was with the Dutch in Indonesia.

During World War II, the nonviolent anti-colonialist movement was very active in India. In 1942, Gandhi led the "Quit India" movement, which led to his imprisonment and the banning of the Congress Party. But independence had to be granted in 1947. A conference of newly independent Asian and African states held in Bandung in 1955, only ten years after a war that had left Europe anemic and ended its hegemony, marked the emancipation and political autonomy of the Asian world, which would soon be followed by African emancipation.

Unlike that of the Society of Nations created after World War I, the Charter of the United Nations included the right to self-determination for all colonized countries, not just those dominated in Central Europe. The principle had already been formulated by President Wilson and Lenin, but previously had exercised little influence on the colonized world. In theory, nobody opposed the principle of self-determination, that is, the right of people to decide for themselves. But there was no enforcement either among colonies or for minorities trying to secede in new nation-states.

Self-determination was complex. The Enlightenment philosophers had argued that governments should govern only with the consent of the governed. By the nineteenth century, it was thought that the government must represent the nation. Henceforth, each nation had the right to be an independent state. As a result, empires that governed disparate ethnic and national groups were considered illegitimate after World War I.* In fact, the right to self-determination had been expressed in various

* Wilson said of the centralized empires that they ruled foreign populations that they had no natural right to govern.

forms since the French Revolution: in European nationalism, Wilson's self-determination, Asian and African decolonization, and the ethno-nationalism of minorities.

With modern nationalism, at least for the West, the "divine right of kings" was replaced by the "natural rights" of citizens and nations. Modern nationalism also marked the transformation from a religious to a national identity. Religion declined progressively in Europe from the moment when nationalism and national wars replaced the Wars of Religion. This was not the case in all societies.

The recognition of the right to self-determination by the international community encouraged decolonization in Asia and Africa. These ideas were not new, but new elites appeared who refused to accept foreign rule.* These elites no longer proposed to improve colonial status or grant reforms. In World War II, fought by the Allies in the name of liberty, the Japanese defeat of colonial powers made colonized people realize that independence was possible. Times had changed in Asia and would soon do so in Africa. It was the end of European domination. The nation-state was the only model that could replace colonial domination, regardless of whether it suited the ethnic and religious composition of the newly liberated colonies.

The principle of self-determination was based on the concept that the state and the nation should coincide. In 1945, the United Nations, in San Francisco, declared "respect for the principle of equal rights and self-determination of the populations." Was it a principle that should be respected, or a right? In any case, the right to secession was excluded.†

In 1952, the United Nations issued a Declaration of Human Rights. All populations and all nations had the right to self-determination, that is, the right to freely determine their political, economic, social, and cultural system. Self-determination, however, was an international, not a national, law. Control within national boundaries was in the hands of each individual state. In fact, the right to self-determination within a state depended on the will of the leader, and sometimes on military force. Self-determination goes back to the tradition of Enlightenment philosophy: the right to rebellion against a government perceived as illegitimate because it does not respond to the aspirations of its citizens.

---

* On the psychology of colonialism, see Albert Memmi, *The Colonizer and the Colonized* (Boston: Beacon Press, 2007), originally published as *Portrait du colonisé, précédé de Portrait du colonisateur* (Paris: Corréa, 1957).

† The Universal Declaration of the Rights of Peoples promulgated in Algiers on July 4, 1976, was much more advanced but was never implemented.

The movements of liberation in Asia and Africa had to assimilate the ideas and concepts of modern Europe, including nationalism, in order to free themselves from European domination. It would only be possible to overcome European colonialism by learning Europe's lessons. The proclamation of nation-states followed the European model.

There were, however, two problems. First, the frontiers of the colonies, particularly in Africa, rarely reflected historical boundaries or boundaries between homogeneous ethnic groups. Was self-determination the exclusive right of the majority? The constitution of nation-states in the Afro-Asian world resulted in widespread oppression of and discrimination against minorities.

Second, core Western principles—democracy and the respect for human rights—were often poorly applied inside national boundaries. The list of states in Asia, Africa, and Latin America that had democratic governments, as we understand the concept, was very short. Parliamentary democracy was considered a symbolic institution for the colonized elites and was contemptuously dismissed by the dictators who built the new nation-states. There was, in fact, a regression of the Asian and African elites' aspirations.

AFTER WORLD WAR II

After World War II, independence was often gained through violent struggle. Guerrilla war proved to be a valuable politico-military instrument for movements of national liberation.

Democratic institutions were contemptuously dismissed by liberation movements under the pretext that the masses were not interested. Indeed, favorable preconditions for democracy were usually lacking in colonized societies, whose heritage was usually one of classic despotism prior to colonial domination. The problems were not exclusively those of colonialism. Some "elites" grabbed power and exercised it with cynicism. The lack of democratic tradition was a handicap, as were the poor economies and cultural backwardness of colonized societies.

But perhaps they were less of a handicap than the absence of critical thinking. In these countries, the world was understood as fundamentally hierarchical and unequal. What permitted the despotism of the new elites was rigid social stratification. As a result, independence usually benefited only a few segments of the population. Liberated colonies did not follow the American model, which privileged freedom and equality of opportunity and led to great social mobility. Rather, traditional societies and the regimes that they produced prioritized stability and did not encourage transformation and mobility regardless of their self-proclaimed ideologies. In classic despotism, as in the Ottoman Empire, autonomy and political power were not an option for the subjects of the state.

Given their historical traditions, the governmental authority of new nation-states often remained unchallenged. Frequently, the superficial semi-democratic style was only a simulacrum of democracy, with an enlightened despotic tradition persisting under a democratic façade, as with Mustapha Kemal.

The post–World War II history of new nation-states was often disrupted by revolts, which were usually repressed. Peasants frequently revolted against their difficult conditions. However, the peasants never thought that they had rights. In fact, many of the ideas and concepts that the West produced in the eighteenth and nineteenth centuries continued to remain novel in the new nation-states. For example, many elites or pseudo-elites of Asia, Africa, and Latin America never accepted that men and women should have equal rights. This idea seemed absurd to the ruling class. Force continued to be the main method of control between the state and its subjects, now called citizens, who generally had neither the dignity nor the rights of citizens in a democracy, and who lacked the concept of a civil society.

In many cases, it was also true that the masses mobilized for a nationalist, religious, or revolutionary cause often appeared to prefer a government that told them what to do rather than a government that gave them free choice. Where the apathy and passivity of the governed exist, they are largely the result of the mediocrity, complacency, and even cowardice of the enlightened class. The fundamental problem of establishing even a limited democracy persists in many African and Asian countries and in some countries in Latin America. In the absence of a stable democracy, the risk of tyranny, despotism, and insurrections will inevitably persist.

CHAPTER 17

Guerrilla Warfare

The origin of the word "guerrilla"—small war—derives from the Spanish rebellion against Napoleon's occupation (1807–14). Guerrilla war, as a technique, is immemorial, but whereas many ancient treatises were devoted to the art of conventional war in ancient China, Greece, Rome, and Constantinople, the first treatises on guerrilla war were published by French and German authors only in the nineteenth century. These were written in response, in part, to the impact of the bloody Spanish rebellion on the Napoleonic armies, and in response to other guerrilla-like insurrections faced by the French in the Vendée and Tyrol. It has been said that the Spanish partisans put about four hundred thousand of Napoleon's soldiers out of action. Without underestimating the importance of Wellington's classic army, the impact of the Spanish partisans was much more damaging to Napoleon's armies than were the wars against Prussia and Austria, and nearly as damaging as the classical campaign in Russia itself. The Russian partisans' role was less important (1812). However, it was efficient, because it hindered Napoleon's troops' food supply and decimated the forces in the rear during the winter retreat.

WEAPONRY AND MANPOWER

Why were guerrillas so successful in the nineteenth century? It cannot be attributed to nationalism, which had little influence in Spain or

Russia, and only moderate influence in Germany. Those who fought in the Tyrol, Russia, and Spain were peasants. Though they may have been partly motivated by patriotism and religion, the guerrillas' principal motivation, in the case both of the Spaniards and of the Russians, was to defend their crops and protect their means of existence and their faith.

"The two transformations that made modern armies vulnerable to guerrilla war were the importance of matériel and the increase in manpower," Camille Rougeron observes.* The French Revolution inaugurated mass enlistment; troops that had formerly lived off their own supply train now used the resources of the occupied country. Living off the land was possible in rich countries such as Italy or Central Europe, but became problematic in Russia and Spain.

Improved equipment (the artillery doubled in importance) and matériel combined with simplified logistics and smaller food convoys to make French troops more mobile and reduce their dependence on hard-to-defend supply lines. However, in Spain, the peasants refused to sell food or let it be requisitioned, and in the Russian winter, little food was available even for the local population.

Clausewitz, who covered the Russian campaign from the side of the Russians, argued that Napoleon's lack of foresight was responsible for the Grande Armée's annihilation: had provisions been stockpiled in the cities during the army's advance, they would have fed it during its retreat.[†]

J.-F.-A. Lemière de Corvey, who observed guerrilla tactics as an army officer in the Vendée and Spain, writes in his 1823 book *Des partisans et des corps irréguliers* (On Partisans and Irregular Forces):

> The goal of partisans is to have enough force to alarm the enemy, move wherever the need arises to harass the enemy, attack his supplies, destroy and capture his convoys, intercept his messages and his communications, and capture soldiers isolated from the army. Guerrilla war, led by a skilled chief inspires terror in the enemy. Even though the enemy may occupy the cities, he will have to cross roads to get from one city to the other, and he will be attacked on the road. He will have to skirmish at each pass and won't dare let a single vehicle go unescorted. His troops will tire, recruitment will become difficult, and the army will be destroyed progressively without having ever experienced a serious defeat on the battlefield.[‡]

---

* Camille Rougeron, *La prochaine guerre* (Paris: Berger-Levrault, 1948).
† Carl von Clausewitz, *The Russian Campaign of 1812* (New Brunswick, NJ: Transaction Publishers, 2007).
‡ Jean-Frédéric-Auguste Lemière de Corvey, *Des partisans et des corps irréguliers* (Paris: Anselin & Pochard, 1823).

After 1815, with the exceptions of the Greek War of Independence (1821–29), the Carlist wars in Spain (1833–40), Garibaldi's insurgency in Italy (1860), and Polish uprisings (1830–31, 1863–64), guerrilla war was less important. In Europe, it was the time of urban insurrections: 1830, 1848, and 1871. Political theorists of the time stressed the importance of the proletariat rather than the peasants.

Between the conquest of Algeria (1830–47) and World War I, when the colonial world had largely been "pacified," guerrilla conflicts occurred mostly in Asia and Africa. What characterized most of these guerrilla conflicts—the long resistance of the Caucasus against the Russians, resistance to the British in Burma, Javanese resistance to the Dutch, Filipino resistance to the Americans, and Indochinese and West African resistance to the French—was that the guerrillas were defeated. European defeats were few: Afghanistan (1842) and South Africa (1879) for British troops, Vietnam for the French (1895), and the Rif for the Spaniards (1922). The toughest war fought by the British in the colonial era was the Anglo-Boer War of 1899–1901. Despite overwhelming British superiority in manpower, the Boers proved themselves remarkably successful guerrilla fighters until the British commander in chief, Lord Kitchener, used internment camps and severe repression of the civilian population to defeat them. In addition, the Ashanti war (in present-day Ghana) and the Burmese wars fought by the British required several long campaigns. The only absolute defeat, in this period, was the result of a classic war when the Ethiopians almost destroyed an entire Italian army in the disastrous battle of Adowa (1896).

European armies of the West were finally victorious everywhere thanks to their superior armament. The machine gun (Gatling, 1862; Maxim, 1884) was decisive.

Some very tough wars occurred: in Algeria against Abd el-Kader (1830–47); in South Africa, against the Zulus; in Southwest Africa against Jacobus Morenga's insurgency;* in Sudan against the Mahdists (1885–98); in Somalia against Mohamed Abdel Hassan, who resisted the British for more than twenty years (1899–1920); and in the Caucasus, where Sheik Chamyl also resisted the Russians for several decades (1834–59). At the beginning of the Rif war, Abd el-Krim inflicted a

---

* Horst Dreschler, *Südwestafrika unter deutscher Kolonialherrschaft*, vol. 1: *Der Kampf der Herero und Nama gegen den deutschen Imperialismus* (Stuttgart: Steiner, 1966), translated as *"Let us die fighting": The Struggle of the Herero and Nama against German Imperialism (1884–1915)* (London: Zed Press 1980).

disastrous defeat on the Spanish at Anwal,* while Omar Mukhtar resisted the Italians in Cyrenaica for ten years (1922–32). René Pélissier lists more than a hundred insurrections in Angola and Mozambique between 1840 and 1930.† All these insurrections were bound to fail, despite occasional successes, given the superiority of the European arms and organization. Besides their obvious military superiority, Western armies were led by professionals with the backing or indifference of the state and public opinion and remained convinced of the righteousness of the war and of their so-called civilizing mission.

For most European strategists, guerrilla war remained a marginal phenomenon. Major military theoreticians from 1860 to 1930 were more interested in classic war and naval strategies. The American Civil War, the Franco-Prussian War, and World War I were closely studied, but guerrilla wars received little attention, with the exceptions of discussions of the role of partisan snipers in the Franco-Prussian War of 1870, and Lawrence in Arabia and General Paul von Lettow-Vorbeck in Tanganyika during World War I. However, guerrilla wars continued during this period, particularly within the Ottoman Empire: neither the Armenian Fedayees (1890–1908) nor the Internal Macedonian Revolutionary Organization (IMRO; 1869–1908) were successful.‡

Guerrillas such as Nestor Makhno and his Ukrainian anarchists, the counterrevolutionary Roman von Ungern-Sternberg in Mongolia, and the "Basmachis" of the Bukhara emirate also fought the Soviet Red Army during and after the Russian Revolution. The British also suppressed Arab guerrillas in Palestine (1936–39). However, there was no decisive guerrilla success in the Afro-Asian colonial world until after World War II.

Latin America was a very different context and faced only limited foreign interference. There were several ephemeral successes in Latin American civil wars that combined regular and irregular operations, as in the Mexican insurgency of Pancho Villa and Emiliano Zapata and

---

* See *Abd el-Krim et la république du Rif: Actes du Colloque international d'études historiques et sociologiques [Paris], 18–20 janvier 1973* (Paris: F. Maspero, 1966); David S. Woolman, *Rebels in the Rif: Abd el Krim and the Rif Rebellion* (Stanford, CA: Stanford University Press, 1968).

† René Pélissier, *Les guerres grises: Résistance et révoltes en Angola, 1845–1941* and *La colonie du minotaure: Nationalismes et révoltes en Angola, 1926–1961*, 2 vols. (both Montamets: R. Pélissier, 1978); id., *Naissance du Mozambique: Résistance et révoltes anticoloniales, 1854–1918*, 2 vols. (Orgeval: R. Pélissier, 1984).

‡ The only success was that of Ireland (1916–21), a country that struggled against a democracy.

the Nicaraguan insurgency of the populist leader Augusto Sandino (1927–33).

However, the greatest success of a guerrilla army was yet to come. After retreating over six thousand miles, the remnants of the Chinese Red Army established a sanctuary in Shanxi province (1935). The Japanese attacked in 1937, when Mao Zedong had just finished the first volume of his treatise on revolutionary war.*

NATIONALIST IDEOLOGY

To fight an anti-colonial war, the elites of the colonized society must have assimilated modern ideas and, in particular, the ideology of nationalism. This is a difficult process that rarely occurred spontaneously. The motto "Learn from the enemy" never made more sense than for colonized populations. In order to create their political organizations, whether mass political parties or vanguard parties, they copied European models.

Patriotic resistance generally begins spontaneously and only later becomes organized. In contrast, revolutionary guerrilla wars were planned and organized at the top and spread as a function of the support of the population. Typically, traditional guerrilla armies lacked professional soldiers; the Zulu army of Shaka (1787–1828) in South Africa was an exception. Fighting occurred more or less spontaneously, never during harvesting, and under the leadership of traditional chiefs. The traditional peasant guerrillas often fought against change and modernization. Innovation, except for military weaponry or tactics, was unknown.

While patriotic resistance aimed at expelling invaders and restoring traditional leaders from the past, revolutionary war sought to gain power in order to create a new order. At the beginning, a revolutionary guerrilla struggle may use rudimentary armaments, but it is often structured according to a sophisticated conceptual and strategic vision that has been elaborated in political, military, and organizational dimensions. Revolutionary guerrilla war embraces modernity, in the words of Amílcar Cabral (1924–73), "everything that the world has conquered to serve humanity."†

---

* Mao Zedong, *On Guerrilla Warfare* (1937; Urbana: University of Illinois Press, 2000).

† Amílcar Cabral, "L'arme de la théorie," in id., *Unité et lutte*, vol. 1, ed. Mario de Andrade, trans. Sophie Mayoux et al. (Paris: F. Maspero, 1975).

Modern guerrilla war developed in a specific historical framework: World War II, the rise of Asian and African nationalisms, and the progressive end of colonialism, with the weakening of political support for it in Europe. Guerrilla wars are a reflection of their time.

MAO'S ORIGINALITY

The term "revolutionary war" finds its origins in Mao Zedong. Mao's innovation, not directly apparent in his work, consisted of utilizing a Leninist vanguard party to mobilize and organize the peasants rather than the workers. This innovation was unorthodox, since according to Marxist theory, the vanguard party was supposed to mobilize and organize the urban proletariat. At the military strategic level, Mao's originality was to combine regular and irregular units within the framework of irregular operations. Once the conditions became propitious, the combined forces could fight classic conventional battles. Nationalism amplified these political and military innovations. The Japanese invasion (1937–45) allowed the Chinese Communist Party to wrest the nationalist mantle as the defenders of China from the corrupt Kuomintang, and China's identification with the Communists continued in the immediate postwar period (1945–49).

Mao's military conceptions were met with opposition both before and after the Long March. However, he resisted demands to create a conventional army: "We must not fight, in general, against the 'partisan spirit' but instead honestly recognize the partisan aspect of the Red Army. There is no shame in that. On the contrary, the partisan aspect constitutes our idiosyncrasy, our strong side, the instrument of our victory over the enemy. We should be prepared to renounce the partisan aspect of our army, one day, but now it is impossible." He later added: "We stand against a purely military point of view and against roaming bands of soldiers, but we consider the Red Army as a tool of propaganda and as a means to organize the people." *

Mao advocated a mobile war with a shallow rearguard. He avoided adventurism on the offensive and counseled retreat when faced with superior forces. The military command was centralized, but gave necessary flexibility to the corps of partisans. Finally, the Red Army included propagandists to further Communist party organization.

* Mao, *On Guerrilla Warfare.*

With these exceptions, Mao followed classical guerrilla strategy: gathering intelligence in order to choose a favorable time and place for battle, familiarity with the terrain, and strong local support. In addition, he used the traditional techniques of harassing the adversary while keeping the initiative and of demoralizing the enemy to create favorable conditions for victory before engaging in battle.

Mao's originality rests in the tight relation between political and military operations. The Japanese occupation helped to cement a strong alliance between the Communist Party and the peasants. The Japanese troops' terror and devastation, combined with the harshness of their occupation, forced the peasants to react (the Nazis committed the same error in Ukraine).

The traditional rural elites had fled, and without their collaboration, the Japanese occupation could never establish legitimacy. The sparse occupation left much terrain open to the Red Army, which organized an effective campaign of anti-Japanese propaganda. The Japanese themselves increased the nationalist prestige of the Communist Party by designating it as their main adversary.

The Chinese military had a tripartite structure: the Red Army, full-time regional partisan guerrillas, and local militias. This structure would be widely copied throughout the world, from Vietnam to the Portuguese colonies. In the army, each unit had a political commissar, who supervised its relationship with the population. It was an army that did not mistreat the peasants and claimed to be at the service of the people "through action." This was a new concept in a peasant society. The political and administrative tasks of the army were varied and depended on different components: military organization, propaganda and education, cooperation with the civilian population, and intelligence gathering. In war zones, the militia and its supporters built roads, scouted, and provided information and food to the peasants. In the contested zones, the population contributed in the organization of the resistance, liquidated traitors, and destroyed roads and supplies when necessary. In villages controlled by the Red Army, the army would explain the reasons for fighting and promulgate new programs: tax reductions (of 25 percent), free distribution of food to the poor, the recruitment of youth into the militia for self-defense, and the creation of mass organizations for anti-Japanese resistance. Propaganda units were dispatched to open new fronts and staffed by local officials who were natives of the targeted region.

Cadres needed precise knowledge of the local problems, including the economic conditions and the causes of dissatisfaction. This required serious preparation and cadres who spoke the local dialect. They would first infiltrate the village, dressed as peasants, in order to establish initial contact with the population. They identified potential supporters. At the regional level, other groups were recruited to provide support to the resistance, including artisans and students. Bandits were also used and sent to combat zones, but never to the Red bases. Finally, assemblies of representatives were elected. Although their political power was limited, the assemblies tied the masses psychologically to the resistance.

The eight years of fighting against the Japanese solidly established the Communists in their northern bastion. However, in 1945, nobody believed in the possibility of their nationwide success. Indeed, even the USSR negotiated with the Nationalists and recognized Chang Kai-shek's legitimacy in exchange for Outer Mongolia. The Chinese Communists won in spite of their isolation, their inferior weaponry, and their relative numerical inferiority. The foundation for their success was based on the organization that they had established during the Sino-Japanese war.

Mao's model of revolutionary war would be repeated in Vietnam, but Mao's concepts and techniques would be adopted by various movements, including non-Marxist-Leninist movements.

GUERRILLAS

The term "guerrilla movements" encompasses various types of guerrillas, including:

- Liberation movements fighting against a colonial power or foreign occupier
- Revolutionary movements within a country, motivated by religious or social grievances
- Minority movements, either ethnic or religious, with a desire to secede or become autonomous

Although nationalism is usually present in some degree, guerrilla ideologies are varied. They can be

- Marxist-Leninist
- Conservative, seeking to maintain or restore a previous society in the face of unwanted change

- Reactionary, with the goal of returning to a real or imagined past

Guerrilla movements occur because of unacceptable ethnic or religious oppression or as a consequence of social discontent that reaches a breaking point. However, since the end of World War II, the catalyst for most guerrilla conflicts has been a political movement that involves a small number of highly motivated volunteers whose goal is to incite and organize the population. These groups are initially very small. The Chinese Communist Party had only twelve members when it was founded in 1921. The APIGCV (African Party for the Independence of Guinea and Cape Verde) included only six founding members at its first meeting in 1956.

The first objective of this leadership group is to understand its own society: to determine the sociological imbalances, to develop an appropriate strategy for current conditions, to identify potential adherents and social sectors that can be mobilized, and to assess the political weaknesses of the adversary, both domestically and internationally. In the words of the revolutionary Amílcar Cabral:

> We know, indeed, that the progression of a phenomenon into a movement, whatever its external conditions, essentially depends of its internal characteristics. We also know that, at the political level, even when the reality of other societies looks better and more attractive, our reality can be transformed only by our concrete knowledge, by our efforts, and by our sacrifices. We should remember that in this tricontinental universe, where revolutionary experiences and examples abound, even with the great similarities of the cases and the identity of our enemies, national liberation and social revolution are not export goods. They are fundamentally, and each day more so, the product of local and national conditions, influenced by external factors (favorable or unfavorable) but essentially determined by the unique historic reality of each population.*

At the beginning, the founding members, the core of the party, are recruited. They are aware both of the nature of the oppression and of the vulnerabilities of the oppressors. Often it is easiest to recruit among the discontented semi-intellectual or half-educated urbanized youth, who are often marginalized and alienated from existing social classes and lack clear future prospects. It is more difficult to mobilize the most oppressed who, after their long servitude and misery, may initially have no hope of change and little taste for risk. It is vital to form mid-level

---

* Cabral, *Unité et lutte,* 1: 13.

cadres. High-level cadres already exist in the leadership and among the intellectuals, who will soon rally the movement. Mid-level cadres are essential. They are responsible for political work on the ground: day-to-day propaganda, recruiting, and organization. These cadres give the masses a reason to act and enable the creation of an organization that is capable of rebelling against the established power.

The next phase consists of securing what is called the "support of the masses," that is to say, a large segment of the population. Persuasion, agitation, indoctrination, intimidation, and the selective use of terror to eliminate the enemy's agents must all be employed. This difficult and delicate mobilization stage is designed to create a clandestine political infrastructure and to popularize the aims and slogans of the movement.

In the Leninist model, the organizational strategy consists of forming a popular base from a small group of disciplined militants. This strategy presupposes an unpopular state typical in colonized countries after World War II. On the other hand, it was much more difficult to mobilize within the general population or among struggling minorities in countries that already had won their independence, since nationalist themes could be used by the government.

The Maoist and Vietnamese version of the model had great influence on the rest of the colonized world. The Maoists and Vietnamese considered the support of the population and a prolonged armed struggle as the two fundamental factors leading to change. The support and the control of the population compensated for the state's advantages: control of the administration, the police, and the army. During the early phase, when the party was small and propaganda was critical, the cadres recruited individuals whose personalities or position might attract a significant part of the population. They also sought to infiltrate state institutions and instigate strikes and demonstrations whenever possible. It was better to organize these actions only when their success was assured, since failure could impact morale and cause the loss of months of patient work.

A guerrilla movement survived only with the support of part of the population, who were responsible for providing information, communication, food, and recruits. This support depended on a clandestine political infrastructure. The gradual increase in support for the guerrilla movement reflected the erosion of state authority.

The goal of selective terrorism against the state and its agents in the countryside and in the cities was not a military victory, but rather, a weakening of the state's authority. Assassinations and bombings also showed the masses that the enemy was vulnerable everywhere, even in the capital. In colonial situations, the combination of guerrilla actions and selective terrorism was aimed at forcing the imperialist state to negotiate.

Clandestine political infrastructure was fundamental and required work and organization, along with the passive support of the population. The population had to share the objectives and goals of those who fought. Actually, the political objective of revolutionary guerrilla actions was to win over the population itself. The demoralization of those who passively supported the government and the persuasion of neutral elements were the targets of guerrilla propaganda. The refusal of the masses to join the movement would often prove fatal.

In order to gain popular support, insurrectional movements usually tried to show the righteousness of their struggle, as well as the vulnerability of the supposedly invincible enemy. This was accomplished with dramatic acts of selective terrorism, and with sabotage, which demonstrated the revolutionary organization's efficiency.

When the leader was charismatic, popular support grew faster. The ideology for which he fought was also a powerful means to attract new membership. Marxist-Leninism provided a coherent explanation for world conflicts and often proved an effective ideology. To designate imperialism and its supporters as the enemy provided a clear and believable target. However, nationalism provided an even more powerful motivation for movements struggling against foreign domination.

The identification of friends and foes, the denunciation of corrupt systems, and the demonstration of the system's fundamental indifference to the needs and aspirations of the people all had one goal: motivating the masses. What were the goals of most liberation movements? To create disorder, disrupt the administrative machine, and disorganize the economy. In short, to undermine the authority of the state. It was easy to create disorder. The police and the army had to guard all possible targets, while the guerrillas needed to strike only one or two to achieve their desired effect.

At the military level, conflict would escalate slowly. At the beginning, the guerrillas usually had the initiative, and surprise would produce early victories that encouraged the combatants and demonstrated the existence and value of the movement to the peasants and to public opinion. The guerrillas' training was critical, not so much for its military aspect as for instilling motivation and ideology, along with strong discipline.

What were the social components of popular insurrections in traditional societies? For the mid-level cadres, it was often the "half-educated" who rallied to the movement. Among the troops, it was the peasants who enlisted. The party's role (a cadre was at the same time a priest, a teacher, and a sergeant) was to inculcate devotion to the cause, develop responsibility, enhance group cohesion, and introduce a Western sense of time—essential for military operations—along with respect for equipment and efficiency. This patient training was often difficult in traditional societies. In fact, the "new man" for the revolutionaries was not the builder of the economy of peace but a combatant. He was a positive role model who, through his example, would gain the support of the masses faced with the oppressor.

Revolutionary guerrilla movements were based on permanent learning: for mid-level cadres, for the men and women of the troops, and for the population. Every revolutionary guerrilla movement could be identified immediately by the style of its militants. The discipline of the Vietnamese and the Eritreans (of the Popular Front for the Liberation of Eritrea) had much in common. Palestinians (Fatah) and Afghans showed much less discipline and were not as efficient (lack of cohesion).

The necessity of harsh and prolonged struggles compelled the party to be strong, disciplined, and unbending, in a word, to be militarized. A Marxist-Leninist party was an admirable war machine powered by clandestinity, organization, and control. Its rigid organizational structure permitted the party to survive militarily and, after victory, its organization often became the basis of a bureaucratic state.

Although in the course of the struggle Marxist-Leninist parties often formed temporary alliances with other dissident forces, their long-term goal was to rule. As a matter of fact, given its organization, cohesion, discipline, rigid adherence to the doctrine, and strict internal controls, the party remained, after nationalism, superior to all other political movements in organizing revolutions. After the Marxist-Leninist party seized power, it would usually marginalize and then eliminate previously allied organizations during a transitional period.

Endurance was essential in guerrilla conflicts, because only over time would the party gain enough strength to win politically and militarily. The revolutionary guerrilla movement opposed a political power supported by an administration, the police, and the army. Only if the insurrection succeeded in gaining the active and passive support of the population could the insurrection prevail. Control of the population was essential because the revolutionary guerrilla movement was fighting a political war. In order to win, the guerrilla movement tried to create what has been called "parallel hierarchies" in the liberated regions that it controlled either militarily or clandestinely.

For instance, the guerrillas often created new elected administrations (village assemblies that elected their representatives) in order to organize the villages that they controlled. The movement would also create a self-defense militia among the youth in occupied villages, install dispensaries, and establish schools. In short, the revolutionary movement tried to substitute for the state and to show its legitimacy through good behavior and enhanced social services. The combatants' attitude was fundamental in recruiting the population and emphasized the contrast with the behavior of the brutal colonial army or with the usually corrupt and predatory local government. The behavior of the guerrilla movement toward the population was its business card.

In liberated regions, guerrillas were supported by a segment of the population who participated actively in the fight. The movement's links with this segment of the population needed to be permanent. This support could be lost because of a psychological mistake, an injustice, or lassitude. Thus, it was necessary to constantly explain, persuade, and indoctrinate the population. Force was used only as a last resort. A major obstacle was often the desire for security in the population, which the army often exploited at the beginning of the insurrection when the connection between the guerrillas and the population was still fragile. Support could also wane if the war dragged on, degrading conditions in rural areas.

When the guerrilla movement managed to control an area, "a liberated region," the guerrillas became the guarantors of law and order. Their propaganda emphasized the difference between the justice and social services provided by the movement and the corruption, oppression, and inefficiency of the state.

On the military level, the goal of the guerrilla movement was to disperse its armed forces as much as possible. Extending the struggle to the cities (sabotage, selective terrorism) and the countryside forced the adversary to divide its troops and mobilize new soldiers in a debilitating psychological climate.

At the beginning of the operations, guerrillas always had the initiative. Their choice of the terrain was important for the first operations. The most important factor was the population itself, and this is why successful insurrections could sometimes be organized in lowland areas seemingly under state control, such as the Yugoslav Voivodina or the delta of the Red River in Vietnam. However, it would be absurd to disregard geographical isolation: mountains, jungles, forests, marshes, and groves often provided important shelter for guerrillas.

The size of the country was important. Effective guerrilla movements, such as Amílcar Cabral's, could be more easily organized in a small country like Guinea-Bissau (13,948 square miles). On the other hand, a vast country with a small population sometimes proved more difficult for the state to control. However, if the country was vast with a sizable population, it was advantageous for the guerrillas to spread to multiple regions. Small zones are generally easily controlled by government forces, unless the terrain is particularly favorable to guerrillas. As for demography, mobilizing large rural populations proved easier when liberation movements were fighting foreign powers. In the cities, colonial control and repression were generally more effective.

The most important aspect of the liberation movements, besides the support of the population, was the early creation of bases where the guerrillas could enjoy relative security. These bases were vital, except in cases where the movement could find sanctuary in a neighboring country. A foreign sanctuary was extremely helpful logistically, and to do without one required exceptional ingenuity (Sri Lanka). Bad weather (the rainy season or winter) was often advantageous to guerrillas. Obviously, monsoon rains presented logistic difficulties, but, more important, they hindered government troop movements and aviation. Finally, the terrain was another important factor to be exploited. Morale, as well as determination, was critical. The outcomes of guerrilla conflicts often remained uncertain, and a determined state with an ability to adapt often prevailed.

A good communications and transportation system complicated the guerrillas' task. Therefore, governments often focused on building roads and communication links. Thus, a limited road system, as in present-day Afghanistan, was a considerable advantage for insurrections. However, the fundamental military factor remained the state's counterinsurgency efforts.

MILITARY AND MATERIAL FACTORS

Initially, finding arms was not usually a problem for a guerrilla movement, whose needs were limited at the start, because it had few troops: a small quantity of guns, hand grenades, and mines were usually enough. The first surprise attacks often allowed the guerrillas to capture additional arms from the enemy. This was often easy at the beginning of an insurrection and at the end when the army fled or was in disarray. After the first guerrilla bases were established, it was often possible to expand geographically by sending political cadres to favorable zones. In the first phase, it proved advisable to operate far from the adversary's centers of power, targeting zones where communications were poor. At the beginning, it was important to instill confidence from early successes won through surprise and initiative. Generally, the first operations were not followed by pursuit and the guerrillas had time to withdraw in good order.

Selective terrorism, which played only a minor role in rural guerrilla actions, had several important functions in urban regions: eliminating the adversary's officials, sabotage, and gaining media recognition. In the countryside, terrorism allowed the guerrillas to disrupt the administration's structure and to gain popularity, particularly if government agents were corrupt and unpopular. However, violence needed to be used judiciously, because it could be counterproductive. It could trigger an insurrection, but it could also frighten and discourage partisans. This was true for both the guerrillas and the state. Excessive repression could provoke deep and long-lasting resentment. Sometimes, in countries where different groups coexisted, seemingly indiscriminate and cruel terrorist acts were used to divide different ethnic and religious groups.

A second, more prolonged phase usually followed the political introduction of the movement and the beginning of military operations. It included the extension of military operations and the creation of liberated zones. During this phase, it was important to be lenient to prisoners, because brutality would encourage resistance.

The strength of the regular army generally decreased in proportion to the increased power of the revolutionary forces. When the balance of power became favorable, the revolutionary movement would choose when and where to strike the decisive blow, the blow that would break the resolve of the adversary. Very few revolutionary guerrillas have reached a phase of warfare where conventional frontal attacks preceded final victory. The primary exceptions are China, Vietnam, Cuba, Cambodia, and Nicaragua.

Purely military victories were extremely rare in the context of national liberation movements fighting a colonial or industrial power: Dien Bien Phu in Vietnam is the only example. Historically, violence was used to force negotiations in the colonial homeland after international and domestic opinion became opposed to the war. These negotiations were always the result of a protracted struggle by the liberation movement.

They were the product of the psychological and political crises transplanted into the colonial homeland itself. They also happened—and it should not be forgotten—because the challenge was not seen as important enough in the homeland. For example, the Vietnam War was impossible for the United States to win decisively on the battlefield because of the restrictions that it had imposed on itself (e.g., on escalation). The United States lost the Vietnam War when it lost the support of public opinion: to the electorate, it did not appear to be worth the cost. The peace movement, which increased in influence after the shock of the Tet offensive, was very influential. War was perceived as unjust and U.S. objectives were found unconvincing. The impact of the publication of the *Pentagon Papers* (1971) was also very important. The costs of the war were high in terms of money and casualties. It was also unpopular because it became a protracted stalemate. In spite of the propaganda stressing the domino theory of Communist expansion in Southeast Asia, the U.S. Congress itself was not convinced that critical U.S. interests were in play. In contrast, the Viet Cong and North Vietnamese never wavered. It proved impossible for the United States to create a legitimate government in Saigon that had both the will and the popular support needed to continue the war.

Elsewhere, guerrilla victories against colonial powers were far from universal. The British defeated the (Chinese) Communist underground in Malaysia (1948–57) by regrouping populations and by promising independence to the traditional Malay Muslim ruling class. The British also crushed the Mau-Mau movement in Kenya (1952–56), one of the few traditionalist guerrilla movements, along with that in Afghanistan (1978–89).

Revolutionary guerrilla movements in independent countries faced a very different problem: there is no possibility of negotiation. Military victory was imperative, otherwise, the guerrilla movement was eliminated or condemned to marginal survival. In the Philippines, the Hukbalahap insurgency, which started during the Japanese occupation and faded at the end of the 1950s, was defeated for three reasons: independence was granted by the United States as early as 1945; the Huks remained limited to the island of Luzon; and government action under President Ramón Magsasay, with U.S. support, looked promising, creating a decrease in the support to the movement.

In independent countries, two major factors were in play. First, the strength of the state was paramount. In this context, strength does not mean necessarily brutal repression by police forces, but rather the determination of the state and the support it receives from the people. The brutality of the Somoza regime's repression in Nicaragua was legendary. However, over time, the corruption, mismanagement, and despotism of the regime had left Somoza with only the support of his praetorian guard.

There have been few examples of victorious revolutionary guerrillas in independent countries: the Communist insurrection in Greece (1946–49) was defeated because its popular support was decreasing and its strategy of frontal attack was flawed. Moreover, its logistics were impacted by the split between Tito and Stalin (1948), which cut off supplies through Yugoslavia. In contrast, the government forces gradually improved with the help of the United States.

We shall not discuss here the Cuban model of the *foco*, which attempted to enlist populations without political preparation. Its many failures in Latin America during the 1960s are well known. The success of the Cuban revolution itself did not reflect the strategy of the *foco*, but three other factors. First, it won early support from a significant part of the urban population as an anti-Batista insurrection, not a Marxist-Leninist revolution. Initially, Castro opposed Batista's tyranny in the name of "bread and liberty," in the name of "a humanist revolution" with populist connotations. Second, the social isolation of the Batista regime and its lack of determination to fight also played important roles. In fact, the state was weak. Third, the United States remained benevolently neutral. Over a period of twenty-five years, armed insurrections in Latin America succeeded in only two countries, Cuba and Nicaragua, and the success of the latter was temporary.

In Africa, Eritrea was close to winning in 1978 before the USSR gave Ethiopia arms for a counteroffensive. Eritrea only succeeded in its long struggle for independence because the collapse of the Soviet system put an end to the aid that it provided to the regime of Colonel Mengistu.

In the Middle East, neither of the two Kurdish insurrections (Iraq, 1961–75; Iran, 1979–84) succeeded, notwithstanding real popular support for them among the Kurdish population. These insurrections were struggles by minorities in undemocratic, independent countries. Within the context of the United Nations, the only struggles that received widespread popular support were those directed against colonial states. The right of the people to self-determination was limited to the right of colonized populations to liberate themselves, except in the special cases of Eritrea and Western Sahara.

Minorities were usually crushed with the blessing of the state. The isolation of the guerrilla movements was a significant factor except when rivalries between states encourage one to attempt to weaken another by helping a rebel minority. This ethnic strategy was used by Iran and Iraq, which formed alliances with and against the Kurds for two decades. When East Pakistan became Bangladesh, it was primarily because the Indian Army supported the Bangladeshi uprising in order to weaken Pakistan.

Guerrilla movements are complex phenomena, and generalizing about them is difficult, but there are nonetheless rules and conditions that determine their success or failure. For example, Afghan resistance began in 1978 in opposition to a Marxist-Leninist regime that had little support in the countryside, with its popularity largely limited to Kabul. In 1979, the insurrection became general, and after Soviet intervention (Christmas 1979), the struggle against the foreign occupier combined with the rejection of the Kabul regime. More than six movements competed for the support of the regional populations. They included three "fundamentalist" movements and three "traditionalist" ones. As a result, although the insurrection had the support of a large segment of the population, it lacked a unified strategy and had limited tactical integration. The guerrilla war remained disorganized, except in the Panshir Valley, where the insurrection was led by a gifted political and military commander, Ahmad Shah Massoud, who, with local leaders, introduced revolutionary guerrilla tactics.

The Afghan resistance benefitted from the Pakistani sanctuary that allowed for the transportation of armaments and ammunitions, as well as doctors and medicines needed for field hospitals. With Pakistani help, Afghan resistance spread in spite of Soviet resistance. Afghan refugees increased in number. The USSR, which had not anticipated such strong opposition, had only 120,000 troops in a country the size of France, with much more difficult terrain. The Soviet occupiers, who controlled only Kabul, the other large cities, and the main communication routes, tried to stabilize the regime with the help of the secret police (the KHAD). However, besides occasional counterattacks, there were few major offensives against the rebels between 1980 and 1984, and an even less aggressive strategy was used after Mikhail Gorbachev came to power in 1985. In spite of its superior firepower, the Soviet army of draftees was relatively immobile and not very efficient (paratroopers excepted). Crucially, Soviet forces failed to attack the lines of communication that enabled the rebels to easily cross the Pakistani border.

The USSR was prepared for a conventional war, not a guerrilla conflict, and Afghanistan played the same role for Gorbachev as Algeria did for Charles de Gaulle. The Soviet withdrawal was wrongly considered as a military victory for the Afghan resistance. With the exception of Massoud's Tadjik fighters, the resistance remained disorganized and of limited efficiency. Despite the fact that the Afghan resistance faced an unpopular and isolated Communist regime, it would take almost three years after the Soviet withdrawal for it to take Kabul (1992).

CHAPTER 18

From Total War to Asymmetrical Conflict

On the eve of World War I, with theoreticians such as Alfred Thayer Mahan, Charles Ardant du Picq, Jean Colin, and Friedrich von Bernhardi, strategic thinking had developed considerably. But reality can trump theories. None of the theoreticians foresaw the immobilization of the trenches and slaughter that characterized the 1914–18 conflict. To my knowledge, Charles de Gaulle provided the most accurate description of the surprise of the soldiers and their officers when, in August 1914, they encountered the devastating effects of firepower at the beginning of World War I:

> As soon as he arrives, the recruit is absorbed by multiple preparations. Enlisted, dressed, armed, equipped, inspected, he is caught up in mundane tasks. On departure day, he finds his place, next to his comrades who will be with him in combat, under the gaze of his superiors, who will lead him into battle. He maintains the required silence, the prescribed lining up, and the compulsory standing at attention. Drill practice in handling arms strengthens the troops in the recognition of their collective power. Everything is ready. Now is the hour. Final orders. And the soldier, sustained by the rich discipline of military order, marches on firmly to his destiny. The first shock is immensely surprising. Strategically, the scope of the enemy circling maneuver and the use of his reserve units immediately upsets our plans. Tactically, the revelation of the consequences of firepower invalidates all of our preexisting strategies. Morally, the armor of our illusions is smashed in the twinkling of an eye.
>
> This surprise affects the whole army, which, between August 10th and 23rd moves from perfect confidence to paroxysms of fear. Some elements,

cavalry, some guard detachments had already seen fire. But it was only epi-sodic. Suddenly, in a single push, from the High Rhine to the Sambre, 1,200,000 Frenchmen enter into battle.

From that moment on, the initial battle plans of the High Command had to change radically. We had thought at first to seize the initiative by moving four of our five armies from west to east, but had to hastily send three armies to the north. The decisive battle, which was to have taken place in Lorraine, would occur in Belgium. And yet we had excluded the Belgian Army from the Unified Command. Seventy-four French divisions of cavalry and infantry moved ahead the same day. All had the same mission, whether in the Lorraine plateau, the Meuse countryside, the Ardennes forest, or the Charleroi plain: advance and drive back the enemy wherever he is met.

The large unit has formed into a column. At first, the troops believed that it was a maneuver, similar to many others with the same order of the rank and file, the same showy display, and same hard marches with sun, dust, and the heavy weight of the backpack. Suddenly, a feeling of crisis arises with the rumbling of the cannon. To the physical pain of the effort is added the insistent worry of the approaching unknown. But very quickly, goodwill and a certain curiosity take over. The meeting with the enemy is brutal. For the latter, who had strategically begun the offensive before we did, adopts a defensive tactic. He had first gone astray. Our "point" strikes his "fork." The French vanguard unexpectedly encounters a line of fire, from the enemy already dug in, which means that they are decimated and immobilized. Whereas the division general was expecting to get the necessary information to plan the attack, he sees, instead, his column decapitated. Should he want to disengage, he could not but with difficulty behind a disrupted cover which is calling for help. Anyway, he does not even think about it. The enemy is here and must be confronted. The command to attack, given at once, and carried at a gallop, arrives when the troops have already begun the fight.

The infantry has left the road. It advances toward an unknown drama, scattered in the fields in a line of small columns. The advance no longer plays out on a fictional shooting range. Silently, with a lump in their throats, looking at their officers who force themselves to smile, the men move forward, anxious but resolute. Suddenly at the top of a hill, at a crossroads at the end of the woods, the first shells arrive. They often are only shrapnel, detonated far away and exploding high in the sky, that are only moderately efficient. This reassures the inexperienced combatants. But soon the shooting gets more precise. The ground is blasted with bullets. The first bodies collapse to the utter disbelief of the fellow combatants. Then comes the heavy artillery shelling. The hissing and shattering projectiles give an impression of a cataclysm. Although the losses are rarely in proportion to the subjective effect, this is not immediately realized. At this time, many troops who are confronting this barrage feel traumatized and find their morale crushed. The shaken infantrymen, gone astray from the direction of the advance, and mixed with others, approach the zone where they will have to fight. As prescribed, the commanding officers precede their troops, with detachments patrolling ahead, and everybody tries to locate the enemy. But nothing appears on the empty battlefield. How is it possible, in these conditions to fix objectives, to combine a maneuver? Let's march on, we'll see!

Bullets hiss now, first rare and almost hesitating, then in clusters, multiplied over each exposed group of soldiers. They are less brutal than shells, less frightening, because they injure or kill silently. Orders and training propel the troops forward. And they run with a thumping heart in the harvested fields of the end of August, their hand grasping a rifle which they decline to use, their hips scratched by the rifle butt.

Suddenly the enemy fire becomes precise, concentrated. Second by second, the bullets rain down accompanied by the thunder of shells. Those who survive dive for cover, stunned, among the screaming wounded and humble corpses. Officers who simulate calm are killed in their tracks with their bayonets fixed and the bugles sounding the charge. Nothing works despite isolated feats of supreme heroism. In the twinkling of an eye, it appears that all the virtues of the world cannot prevail against firepower.

While the infantry was rushing to assault, the artillery was taking its positions. No matter how diligent and well-prepared, the artillery still had to look for emplacements for its pieces of armament, for its observatories, and for its communication links. What was there to shoot at anyway, when the enemy was revealed only through the indistinct flashes of well-hidden cannons? Of course, if the infantrymen could locate the resistance that they met, the artillery would intervene efficiently. But how could those men, in a hellish situation, three kilometers away from the artillery batteries, provide good information? Often, the artillery has not even finished preparing to fire when the attack has already been lost.

Our cannons' blasts will only serve as a belated retaliation to the fait accompli. From the improvised post where he has settled, the commander in chief of the large unit realizes the failure of the front ranks. He still has his reserve, which he intended to use in the "final attack." But the sudden halt to the troops' advance does not provide any indication of what maneuver would be suitable. Most of the time, the available troops will be used to "feed the attack." Perhaps, thanks to "mass multiplied by speed," the troops will regain their élan?

While combat was occurring in the front lines, the reserve troops, more or less sheltered, fell prey to violent emotions. The casualties that they sustained, without being able to hit back, the dramatic stories of those who came back from the front line, the sight of the flow of wounded, bloody soldiers, all troubled the reserve troops, and the more so as they remained inactive. When the order to march is given, anxiety has already become acute. The troops advance to the field of death, their morale already shattered. In this state, they cannot resist the storm of fire. They stop, disperse on the rough terrain, mixed up with the front ranks that had the mission to lead. It even happens that, when an unexpected accident occurs in these highly tense units, it causes a nervous breakdown that shatters the will. Panic erupts in the ranks. It is only a brief lapse, rapidly controlled, but proves that sending more troops into fire from an unscathed enemy would only multiply the dead.

Soon, exhaustion is such that there is nothing else to do but bring to the rear the troops that can do nothing on the ground. From one end of the line to the other, harried or not by the enemy, our troops retreat sadly. Later on, reports, historical accounts, and military journals will seek to impose an appearance of logic on these confused events. But the actors, in the heat of the moment, have only one thought: It's absurd!*

Europe was never more powerful than in the nineteenth century. Europeans, who constituted 17 percent of the world population in 1800, saw their populations increase to 25 percent of the world total by 1900, notwithstanding that tens of millions had emigrated to the New World. The population of the Americas was only one hundred and seventy million in 1900, about half of that in the United States and Canada. The United States accounted for 30 percent of the world's industrial output, but Europe produced twice as much. The globalization of the world economy accelerated rapidly. Europe was the cradle of scientific and technical innovation (physics, chemistry, automobiles, radio), led by a few advanced countries (Germany, France, Great Britain, Italy), whereas the United States specialized in mass production. On the eve of the Great War, Europeans had explored the entire surface of the globe, including the Arctic and Antarctic. European dominance had never been as systematic or as global. Great Britain and France had colonized much of the world. Russia had conquered the steppes from the Don to the Pacific and had become the largest country in the world.

In the 1990s, Samuel Huntington introduced the phrase "clash of civilizations" to describe the post–Cold War world.† However, a clash of civilizations occurred in the nineteenth century with the brutal expansion of European imperialism. Another clash provoked the Mongols' conquests, and one of the greatest clashes of civilizations took place when fewer than two thousand Spaniards took Tenochtitlán and overthrew the great Aztec Empire (1519–21). That conquest was the consequence of European innovations and was a victory of a conceptually and materially more advanced society, which possessed better armament and superior discipline, cohesion, and organization. The Spaniards

---

* Charles de Gaulle, *Le Fil de l'épée* (Paris: Plon, 1932). See id., *The Edge of the Sword*, trans. Gerard Hopkins (New York: Criterion Books, 1960), for an alternative translation.
† Samuel P. Huntington, *The Clash of Civilizations and the Remaking of World Order* (New York: Simon & Schuster, 1996).

also had a much more radical conception of war.* The Mexican conquest was thus an asymmetrical war.

However, colonial military conquests rarely succeeded in achieving permanent pacification. Rebellions erupted again and again, and were often subdued only with difficulty. Pacification was soon followed by another rebellion. The "Belle Époque" of the well-to-do in Europe was a time of confrontation in the colonies. In the period 1900–1914, there were more than twenty sizable military campaigns in sub-Saharan Africa in addition to the Anglo-Boer War, the Italian conquest of Libya, and the conquest of Morocco.

The deadly combination of tanks and aircraft in World War II restored military mobility, lacking in World War I. The war in Asia further modified the map of the world. World War II ruined Europe, both the winners of the war as well as the losers. Europe would no longer be the political epicenter of the world.

AMERICAN STRATEGY

In 1945, the world lay in ruins, but the United States remained prosperous, with more than 40 percent of the world's industrial production and a monopoly on nuclear weapons. The Soviet Union had made the largest contribution to the victory of the Allied forces in Europe, but the human toll of the war in Russia had been considerable. The Eastern Front was critical in World War II: it was where the fate of Europe was decided. In the Pacific, Japan lost the war on December 7, 1941, at Pearl Harbor. Japan could not compete industrially with the United States, despite the courage of its troops. American naval superiority would play a decisive role. The emergence of nuclear power was a qualitative mutation (Hiroshima and Nagasaki, 1945). Soon, the USSR had developed its own nuclear bomb (1949), and, starting with the Korean War (1950–53), "total war" was no longer possible. Besides the Soviet-American arms race, this led to conflicts of a different kind: indirect strategies, crises (Berlin, 1948; Cuba, 1962), and proxy wars fought through allies. In this situation, guerrilla revolutionary wars played an essential role in wresting power from European colonial governments (1945–62).

During the Cold War, the American strategy of containment consisted mainly in defending the peripheral countries in Eurasia from the

---

* See Hugh Thomas, *Conquest: Montezuma, Cortés, and the Fall of Old Mexico* (New York: Simon & Schuster, 1993).

continental power of the USSR. The USSR had to be contained. Mutually assured destruction, based on the acknowledgment of the second strike capability of the adversary after a preemptive strike, maintained a tense global peace. After Soviet ballistic missiles became capable of striking the American homeland, President Reagan's "Star Wars" initiative proposed building a missile defense shield around the United States, restoring its insular tradition. This introduced a new challenge in the arms race.

The strategic choices of the United States were largely a reflection of its particular strategic culture. Henry Kissinger drew American attention to the foreign concept of a balance of power, which had been the consistent focus of European strategy. Previous American victories in the nineteenth century, from 1845 until 1945, had always been absolute.

After World War II, the Americans became the sole guarantors of European security. Washington undertook to defend the "free world" on its own. In the following years, different strategic doctrines revolving around nuclear power were developed by civilian theoreticians such as Bernard Brodie, Henry Kissinger, Thomas C. Schelling, and Albert Wohlstetter. Their strategies contributed to nuclear-age stability, but the United States's attitude remained unchanged. Americans prefer high-intensity wars with rapid results to limited and prolonged conflicts, and often rely on technical solutions. This attitude was made possible because of the U.S. military's superior logistics, technology, and equipment in comparison with those of its adversaries.

The insularity and the vastness of the United States help to explain Americans' relative lack of interest in other countries and cultures. The increasing superiority of the United States, unrivaled since the collapse of the Soviet Union, has encouraged hubris.

WAR IN A UNIPOLAR WORLD?

The containment of the Soviet Union during the Cold War was followed by its disintegration and the reconfigured borders of the Russian Federation that replaced it. In the following decade, the Russian Federation faced a difficult economic and financial situation. During the Yugoslav crisis, the wealthy European Union showed its military impotence by twice requiring help from the United States to end European conflicts in Bosnia (1993) and Kosovo (1999). In the aftermath of September 11, 2001, the American capacity for leading risk-free air wars against the adversary was amply illustrated in Afghanistan and Iraq. By contrast, the occupations of Iraq and Afghanistan were ill-prepared and complicated by political miscalculations. The occupation stretched American power to its limits. Now, the new Shia regime in Iraq itself does not seem to be able to put an end to the simmering Sunni insurrection. As for terrorism, it is a minor military phenomenon whose impact is mostly psychological, and though it is an important and costly nuisance, it cannot overthrow a democratic state or alter the world status quo.

Whatever the morality of armed conflicts, history has been shaped by war, which both creates and destroys. War has exhausted societies and sometimes annihilated them, but it is also war that has engendered the changes that are necessary for innovation and renewal.

CHAPTER 19

Conclusion

All societies are to some extent self-centered and provincial, with varying understanding of other cultures and traditions. This still remains true in an era of commercial globalization: international trade has increased much more than mutual cultural understanding.

Until the end of the nineteenth century, the United States remained focused on its continental expansion and global free trade. Americans, protected by two oceans, followed the advice of George Washington's farewell address and kept out of European conflicts. This spared Americans from the balance-of-power concerns that so preoccupied European nations. American exceptionalism further limited the lessons that the United States might have learned from European conflicts. What did Americans, who were creating an entirely new history, forged in uniqueness and destined to enlighten the world, have to learn from ancient Europe? In any case, foreign geostrategic concerns were of little interest to the businessmen and lawyers who dominated U.S. politics.

At the same time, the Americans opposed European meddling in the Western Hemisphere (e.g., the French in Mexico under Napoleon III) as articulated by President James Monroe (Monroe Doctrine, 1823). Although the Americans were anti-colonialists in much of the world, they behaved like imperialists in the Americas and became an imperial republic following the Spanish-American War in 1898.

Until World War I, America's relations with Europe were concerned primarily with free trade and immigration: tens of millions of Europeans migrated to America and helped to settle and develop the country. Despite its role as a belligerent in World War I and the hopes of President Woodrow Wilson, the United States, the world's greatest industrial power, refrained from active participation in international diplomacy. However, with Europe prostrate after World War II, America became the primary bulwark of democracy and provided support for anti-Communist regimes, regardless of their credentials.

The world of yesterday was relatively simple. As George Kennan noted, it was essential to contain Communist ideology and to stop Stalinist expansionism. Containment and dissuasion became the fundamental principles of Cold War conflicts around the world. To a great extent, the struggle against Communism was ideological. What was the use of understanding Russian history and tradition? China was largely ignored. It took twelve years after the Sino-Soviet breakup for Nixon and Kissinger to apply more subtle geopolitical strategies to the containment of the USSR.

During the Cold War, the USSR was the adversary, and any real or potential Soviet allies were considered enemies. The world was divided into Manichean camps, good and evil, which discouraged more nuanced geostrategic analyses. For example, the war in Vietnam was undertaken based on a flawed analysis: China proved not to be the Vietnamese ally that Washington had imagined. While the domino theory was relevant to the former French colonies in Indochina, it proved not to apply to Southeast Asia as a whole. Over time, notwithstanding Kissinger and Brzezinski, many American decision makers continued to apply ahistorical analyses to Cold War conflicts, while largely ignoring the advice of regional specialists such as Bernard Fall (on Vietnam).

Forty years later, the lessons learned from the failure in Vietnam were largely forgotten by the politicians who directed the Iraqi war of choice (Dick Cheney, Donald Rumsfeld, Paul Wolfowitz, Paul Bremer, etc.). In contrast, General David Petraeus, who had long studied the strategic implications of the Vietnam War, was able to develop a more successful counterinsurgency strategy in Iraq.

After the fall of Communist Europe (1989–91), geostrategy became more complicated and nuanced. Globalization and the economic rise of the developing countries required a deeper understanding of the historical and cultural roots of the existing global balance of power. President George W. Bush's global "war on terror" largely ignored the cultural and historic complexity of the challenge.

For the United States, September 11, 2001, was traumatic: fortress America had been brutally violated. In response, the neoconservatives and their allies gained traction. They proposed to remodel the Greater Middle East in accord with American principles. However, after the initial success of the Iraqi intervention and the fall of Baghdad, this strategy proved a fiasco. Prolonged and uncontrolled urban looting occurred after the occupation forces foolishly marginalized Iraqi Sunnis at all levels of society. The neoconservatives underestimated the importance of the insurrection. At the beginning, it was led by the remnants of the Baathist state and therefore had arms, money, technical capacity, and Sunni support. The American forces were insufficient in number and otherwise ill-prepared to undertake necessary pacification and reconstruction efforts, due in part to overoptimistic intelligence reports that suggested that the Iraqis would massively rally to the occupiers. Counterinsurgency efforts led to the scandal of torture and sexual humiliation at Abu Ghraib (2004). As some of the would-be liberators were accused of torture, Vice President Cheney's response was to declare later that practices such as waterboarding were not torture.

Paradoxically, the American intervention in Iraq transferred power to the Shiites, the longtime allies of neighboring Iran, which had been designated by President G.W. Bush as part of the "axis of evil." America's policies also strengthened Iraqi Sunni support for Al Qaida, which was only temporarily held in check by Petraeus's surge (2007). In the meantime, conditions in Afghanistan (occupied in 2001) continued to deteriorate, largely owing to the American focus on Iraq. Thus, Afghanistan suffered collateral damage from the Iraq war as the Afghan insurgency grew and developed sanctuaries in Pakistan with the support of Pakistani Inter-Services Intelligence (ISI).

America's distant wars proved to be long, costly, and without victory. They were asymmetrical on two levels. On a technological level, they pitted the world's most technologically advanced army against an ill-equipped ragtag opposition. On the ideological level, they pitted Western armies that were preoccupied with minimizing casualties against enemy forces who accepted or sought martyrdom in jihad.

The failure of the Vietnam War, with 58,000 American deaths, was the beginning of increased sensitivity to battle casualties in public opinion. In the era of classic wars (1792–1945), the goal, according to Clausewitz, was the physical annihilation of enemy forces on the battlefield. However, since the Tet offensive in Vietnam and the publication of the *Pentagon Papers,* the battle for public opinion has become as central to military success as victory on the battlefield. Public opinion was critical in determining the outcome of the wars in Iraq and Afghanistan.

A new sensitivity to military casualties became evident when President Ronald Reagan ordered the retreat of allied forces from Beirut in 1983 following suicide attacks that killed 241 U.S. marines and 58 French paratroopers. The paradoxical slogan of the so-called Revolution in Military Affairs (RMA) was a war with "zero deaths." Indeed, the allied coalition lost only a few hundred men in the 1991 Gulf War against Saddam Hussein, which was also the first war in history where the victors did not report enemy casualties. Revealing the imbalance of casualties (1,000 to one, or perhaps more) would have shocked Western public opinion. In 1993, the retreat of American forces from Somalia after the loss of eighteen marines confirmed the opposition of the public to casualties in faraway conflicts.

Nevertheless, the 1990s were a triumphant decade for American power.* For fifteen years, U.S. dominance exceeded that of any other power in history: America was a state without rivals, one that could defeat any potential coalition of adversaries. The U.S. stock market was booming. At the end of the Cold War, Russia was in a crisis and its sphere of influence shrank from the boundaries of the USSR to the frontiers of Russia (Ukraine, Georgia, etc.). As the ruble collapsed, American neoconservatives proclaimed the Project for the New American Century (1997).

In the following year, there were two Islamist attacks against American interests (in Nairobi and Dar es Salaam), following previous attacks in Saudi Arabia (1995–96) that had killed twenty-four American soldiers. The Islamist attacks refocused American interest on Afghanistan, which Washington had neglected following the Soviet retreat (1989) and the fall of the USSR (1991).

However, the most critical year for understanding the current geostrategic situation is neither 1991, with the fall of the USSR, nor 2001, with September 11, but rather 1979, when the following events happened:

---

* Among the three most celebrated books to be published after the fall of the Soviet Union are Francis Fukuyama's *The End of History and the Last Man* (New York: Free Press, 1992); Samuel P. Huntington's *The Clash of Civilizations and the Remaking of World Order* (New York: Simon & Schuster, 1996); and Zbigniew Brzezinski's *The Grand Chessboard: American Primacy and Its Geostrategic Imperatives* (New York: Basic Books, 1997). The latter offers the most sophisticated analysis of the new strategic conditions and describes how the United States should respond. Along with Brzezinski's *Strategic Vision* (2011), it remains a guide to the preservation of U.S. preeminence following the financial crisis of 2008.

- Deng Xiaoping visited the United States and began the economic reforms that would transform China into the world's second-largest economy over the following three decades.
- Ayatollah Khomeini took power in Iran and began a policy of exporting militant, anti-American Islam throughout the Muslim world. Iran's Shiite version of Islam threatened Saudi Arabia, which had begun to provide support to militant Sunni Islam from sub-Saharan Africa to South Asia after the first oil crisis (1973). The regional conflict between Iran and Saudi Arabia is currently being played out in Syria.
- A second oil crisis occurred, after which America, Europe, and Japan have lived beyond their means, with growing debt.
- Confident after their successes in Angola (1976) and Ethiopia (1977), the USSR sent a conscript army into Afghanistan to preserve the Afghan Communist regime. Soviet intervention gave rise to a Sunni jihad supported by Saudi Arabia, Pakistan, and the United States. Two decades later the United States would experience the unanticipated consequences.

The year 2008 saw another fundamental change in contemporary history: a financial and economic crisis from which the developed world, particularly southern Europe, has yet to emerge. It also saw the emergence of China as the world's second-largest economy, ahead of Japan. Other emerging powers also experienced rapid economic growth: India and Turkey reemerged to recover their eighteenth-century status as major regional powers. This transformation signals the end of *absolute* world domination by Europe and the United States, which had lasted since the end of the eighteenth century. The rule of the G7 nations (Canada, France, Germany, Italy, Japan, the United Kingdom, and the United States) was coming to an end, owing in part to a forty-year fall in birthrates in the developed world.

The last asymmetrical war is now winding down in Afghanistan, following the large-scale deployment there of Western forces. For the foreseeable future, irregular wars will largely be fought with proxy armies (e.g., the occupation by U.S.-supported Ethiopian troops of parts of Somalia). Nevertheless, the success of proxy wars depends on a sound knowledge of cultural history and can lead to unanticipated regional consequences. Was it wise for Washington to send Christian troops from Ethiopia, Somalia's traditional enemy, into Mogadishu? This intervention is akin to sending Russian troops to crush a Polish insurrection.

Future conflicts will also depend increasingly on robot warfare, such as the drones used in Yemen since 2002 and in Pakistan since 2004. The use of drones will likely increase, given their efficacy. The war against terrorism will continue indefinitely, because no negotiated settlement is likely to be sought by Islamic jihadists until repeated failures discourage them. Finally, the role of elite strike forces will increase, given their success in operations such as the elimination of Osama Bin Laden and the effective French Special Forces response to Al Qaida insurgents in sparsely populated regions in Mali.

The United States has recently refocused its geopolitical strategy on the Asia-Pacific region and will remain geostrategically preeminent for the foreseeable future. Nevertheless, the world is gradually becoming more multipolar, and regional powers such as China may attempt to modify the long-standing status quo.

Current geostrategic crises remain concentrated in the Middle East. In particular, Iran desires to restore its traditional influence over the region and seems able to develop nuclear capacities. The Syrian civil war, which pits insurgent Sunnis (local and international, the most radical being helped by Saudi Arabia and Qatar, among others) against the ruling Alawite Shiites, has profound regional implications for the long-term balance of power between Saudi Arabia and Iran. It has repercussions in Lebanon (Hezbollah) and may even threaten Shia dominance in Iraq. Russia has regained its international diplomatic and military stature in the Middle East thanks to the Syrian conflict. After Iraq, Afghanistan, and Libya, the involvement of the United States in the Middle East has been discreet. Diplomacy now seems to prevail with Iran, although the outcome remains uncertain. In the meantime, the Syrian conflict has been a boon to Al Qaida and Islamist insurgents. The most probable outcome is a continuation of the armed struggle.

For decades, progress in the Arab world has been hamstrung because of the dominance of hidebound dictatorships and the conservative influence of diverse fundamentalist groups, while Muslim Turkey, despite having no oil or gas, has been able to generate economic growth. China and India, with different regimes, have both been able to become important powers, showing that economic growth and education have changed the lives of hundreds of millions of people in those countries, as in other emerging or in reemerging countries, such as Brazil, South

Korea, and Indonesia. In contrast, Arab oil resources have made prosperity possible for a happy few.

Dominance in the world of tomorrow will largely depend on the economic and educational dynamism of different regions and countries. Nevertheless, successful strategies will continue to depend on the understanding of the cultural and historical traditions of other societies.*

---

* Two important works have appeared since the French-language publication of my book (2005), Edward Luttwak's *The Grand Strategy of the Byzantine Empire* (Cambridge, MA: Belknap Press of Harvard University Press, 2009), and Francis Fukuyama's *The Origins of Political Order: From Prehuman Times to the French Revolution* (New York: Farrar, Straus & Giroux, 2011).

Select Bibliography

Abrahamian, Ervand. *A Modern History of Iran.* New York: Cambridge University Press, 2008.

Amitai-Preiss, Reuven. *Mamluks and Mongols: The Mamluk-Īlkhānid War, 1260–1281.* 1995. Cambridge: Cambridge University Press, 2010.

Ammianus Marcellinus. *The Later Roman Empire (A.D. 354–378).* New York: Penguin Books, 1986.

Ayalon, David. *The Mamlūk Military Society.* London: Variorum Reprints, 1979.

Barfield, Thomas J. *The Perilous Frontier: Nomadic Empires and China.* Cambridge, MA: Blackwell, 1989.

Bartol'd, Vasilij Vladimirovič [W. Barthold]. *Histoire des Turcs d'Asie centrale.* Paris: A. Maisonneuve, 1945.

Blin, Arnaud. *Tamerlan.* Paris: Perrin, 2007.

Browning, Robert. *Byzantium and Bulgaria: A Comparative Study across the Early Medieval Frontier.* Berkeley: University of California Press, 1975.

Cahen, Claude. *Introduction à l'histoire du monde musulman médiéval.* Paris: J. Maisonneuve, 1982.

Central Asiatic Journal. Wiesbaden, 1956–.

The Cambridge History of China. Vols. 7, 8, and 9. Cambridge: Cambridge University Press, 1978.

The Cambridge History of Inner Asia. Cambridge: Cambridge University Press, 1987.

The Cambridge History of Iran. Vols. 5 and 6. Cambridge: Cambridge University Press, 1968.

The Cambridge History of Islam. 2 vols. Cambridge: Cambridge University Press, 1970.

Collins, L.J.D. "The Military Organization and Tactics of the Crimean Tartars during the Sixteenth and Seventeenth Centuries." In *War, Technology and Society in the Middle East,* ed. V.J. Parry and M.E. Yapp. New York: Oxford University Press, 1975.

Comnena, Anna. *The Alexiad.* London: Penguin Books, 1982.

Documents sur l'histoire des Mongols à l'époque des Ming. Translated and edited by Louis Hambis. Paris: Presses universitaires de France, 1969.

Dreyer, Edward L. *Early Ming China.* Stanford: Stanford University Press, 1982.

Dreyer, Edward L., et al., *Chinese Ways in Warfare.* Edited by Frank A. Kierman Jr. and John K. Fairbank. Cambridge, MA: Harvard University Press, 1974.

The Encyclopaedia of Islam. 2nd ed. Edited by P.J. Bearman et al. 12 vols. Leiden: E.J. Brill, 1960–2005.

Fauber, L.H. *Narses: Hammer of the Goths.* New York: St. Martin's Press, 1990.

Fromkin, David. *A Peace to End All Peace: Creating the Modern Middle East, 1914–1922.* New York: Holt, 2001.

Giovanni da Pian del Carpine [Johannes de Plano Carpini (1182?–1252)]. *Histoire des Mongols.* Translated and annotated by Dom Jean Becquet and Louis Hambis. Paris: A. Maisonneuve, 1965.

———. *Kunde von den Mongolen, 1245–1247.* Translated and edited by Felicitas Schmieder. Sigmaringen, Germany: J. Thorbecke, 1997.

———. *The Story of the Mongols Whom We Call the Tartars = Historia Mongalorum quos nos Tartaros appellamus: Friar Giovanni di Plano Carpini's Account of His Embassy to the Court of the Mongol Khan.* Boston: Branden, 1996.

Glubb, John Bagot. *Soldiers of Fortune: The Story of the Mamlukes.* New York: Stein & Day, 1973.

Grousset, René. *Conqueror of the World.* London: Oliver & Boyd, 1967.

———. *L'Empire des steppes.* Paris: Payot, 1939.

Haldon, J.F. "Some Aspects of Byzantine Military Technology from the Sixth to the Tenth Centuries." *Byzantine and Modern Greek Studies* 1, no. 1 (1975): 11–47.

History of Civilizations of Central Asia. Edited by A.H. Dani and V.M. Masson. 6 vols. Paris: UNESCO, 1992–2005.

Hodgson, Marshall G.S. *The Venture of Islam: Conscience and History in a World Civilization.* 3 vols. Chicago: University of Chicago Press, 1974.

———. *Rethinking World History: Essays on Europe, Islam and World History.* New York: Cambridge University Press, 1993.

Hourani, Albert. *A History of the Arab Peoples.* Cambridge, MA: Belknap Press of Harvard University Press, 1991.

Howard, Michael. *War in European History.* New York: Oxford University Press, 1976.

Howarth, Patrick. *Attila, King of the Huns: The Man and the Myth.* New York: Carroll & Graf, 2001.

Inalçik, Halil. *The Ottoman Empire: The Classical Age, 1300–1600.* Translated by Norman Itzkowitz and Colin Imber. London: Weidenfeld & Nicolson, 1973.

Inalçik, Halil, and Donald Quataert, eds. *An Economic and Social History of the Ottoman Empire, 1300–1914.* New York: Cambridge University Press, 1994.

Irwin, Robert. *The Middle East in the Middle Ages: The Early Mamluk Sultanate, 1250–1382.* Carbondale: Southern Illinois University Press, 1986.

Joveynī, ʿAlā al-Din ʿAtā Malek [1226–83]. *Genghis Khan: The History of the World-Conqueror.* Translated by J.A. Boyle. 1958. Manchester: Manchester University Press, 1997.

Keegan, John. *A History of Warfare.* New York: Knopf, 1993.

Kwanten, Luc. *Imperial Nomads: A History of Central Asia, 500–1500.* Philadelphia: University of Pennsylvania Press, 1979.

Lattimore, Owen. *Studies in Frontier History: Collected Papers, 1928–1958.* Oxford: Oxford University Press, 1962.

Lewis, Bernard. *The Emergence of Modern Turkey.* 2nd ed. London: Royal Institute of International Affairs, 1968.

Manz, Beatrice Forbes. *The Rise and Rule of Tamerlane.* Cambridge: Cambridge University Press, 1989.

Marshall, Christopher. *Warfare in the Latin East, 1192–1291.* Cambridge: Cambridge University Press, 1991.

Maurice, emperor of the East. *Strategikon: A Handbook of Byzantine Military Strategy.* Translated by G.T. Dennis. Philadelphia: University of Pennsylvania Press, 1984.

Morgan, David. *The Mongols.* Oxford: Blackwell, 1986.

Muir, William. *The Mameluke or Slave Dynasty of Egypt, 1260–1517.* London: Smith, Elder, 1896. Piscataway, NJ: Gorgias Press, 2007.

"Novgorodian Chronicle." In *Medieval Russia's Epics, Chronicles, and Tales,* trans. Serge A. Zenkovsky. New York: Dutton, 1963.

Oman, Charles. *A History of the Art of War in the Middle Ages.* 1898. 2 vols. New York: Greenhill, 1959.

Procopius. Translated by H.B. Dewing. Loeb Classical Library. Cambridge, MA: Harvard University Press, 1914–40.

Ratchnevsky, Paul. *Genghis Khan: His Life and Legacy.* Translated by T.N. Haining. Oxford: Blackwell, 1991.

Reischauer, Edwin O., John King Fairbank, and Albert M. Craig. *A History of East Asian Civilisation.* 2 vols. Boston: Houghton Mifflin, 1960–65.

Ross, John. *The Manchus; or, The Reigning Dynasty of China: Their Rise and Progress.* London: Paisley & Parlane, 1880.

Rossabi, Morris. *Khubilai Khan: His Life and Times.* Berkeley: University of California Press, 1988.

Roux, Jean-Paul. *Babur: Histoire des grands Moghols.* Paris: Fayard, 1986.

Rubrouck, Guillaume de. *Voyage dans l'empire mongol.* Edited and translated by Claude-Claire Kappler and René Kappler. Paris: Imprimerie nationale, 1985. Translated by Peter Jackson as *The Mission of Friar William of Rubruck: His Journey to the Court of the Great Khan Möngke, 1253–1255* (London: Hakluyt Society, 1990).

Smail, R.C. *Crusading Warfare, 1097–1193.* 1956. 2nd ed. Cambridge: Cambridge University Press, 1996.

Smith, V.A. *The Oxford History of India.* 4th ed. Edited by Percival Spear. Oxford: Clarendon Press, 1981.

Thompson, E.A. *A History of Attila and the Huns.* Oxford: Blackwell, 1996.

Vernadsky, George. *The Mongols and Russia.* New Haven, CT: Yale University Press, 1953.

Watt, W. Montgomery. *Islamic Political Thought.* Edinburgh: Edinburgh University Press, 1968.

Index

The letter m *following a page number denotes a map. The letter* t *following a page number denotes a table.*